Journal of Prisoners

on Prisons

... allowing our experiences and analysis to be added to the forum that will constitute public opinion could help halt the disastrous trend toward building more fortresses of fear which will become in the 21ˢᵗ century this generation's monuments to failure.

Jo-Ann Mayhew (1988)

Volume 26
Number 1&2
2017

JOURNAL OF PRISONERS ON PRISONS

EDITORIAL STAFF:

Editor-in-Chief:	Bob Gaucher	Prisoners' Struggles Editor:	Vicki Chartrand	
Associate Editors:	Susan Nagelsen	Book Review Editor:	Jeffrey Monaghan	
	Charles Huckelbury	Editorial Assistants:	Barbara Brown	Jarrod Shook
Managing Editors:	Justin Piché		Paula Hirshman	Carla K. Stewart
	Kevin Walby			
Issue Editors:	Jarrod Shook, Bridget McInnis, Justin Piché and Kevin Walby			

The *Journal of Prisoners on Prisons* publishes two volumes a year. Its purpose is to encourage research on a wide range of issues related to crime, justice, and punishment by prisoners and former prisoners. Donations to the *JPP* are welcomed.

SUBMISSIONS:
Current and former prisoners are encouraged to submit original papers, collaborative essays, discussions transcribed from tape, book reviews, and photo or graphic essays that have not been published elsewhere. The *Journal* does not usually publish fiction or poetry. The *Journal* will publish articles in either French or English. Articles should be no longer than 20 pages typed and double-spaced or legibly handwritten. Electronic submissions are gratefully received. Writers may elect to write anonymously or under a pseudonym. For references cited in an article, the writer should attempt to provide the necessary bibliographic information. Refer to the references cited in this issue for examples. Submissions are reviewed by members of the Editorial Board. Selected articles are corrected for composition and returned to the authors for their approval before publication. Papers not selected are returned with editor's comments. Revised papers may be resubmitted. Please submit bibliographical and contact information, to be published alongside articles unless otherwise indicated.

SUBCRIPTIONS, SUBMISSIONS AND ALL OTHER CORRESPONDENCE:
Journal of Prisoners on Prisons
c/o Justin Piché, Associate Professor
Department of Criminology, University of Ottawa
Ottawa, Ontario, Canada K1N 6N5

e-mail: jpp@uottawa.ca
website: www.jpp.org

SUBCRIPTION RATES FOR 2015:	**One Year**	**Two Years**	**Three Years**
Prisoners	$15.00	$28.00	$40.00
Individuals	$30.00	$56.00	$80.00
Prison Libraries & Schools, Libraries & Institutions	$60.00	$110.00	$150.00

Subscriptions by mail are payable in Canadian or American dollars. In Canada, 5% HST must be added to all orders. We encourage subscription purchases online at http://www.press.uottawa.ca/JPP_subscription

INDIVIDUAL COPIES AND BACK ISSUES:
Each regular issue is $15 and each double-issue is $25 (Canadian dollars) + shipping costs. In Canada, 5% HST must be added to all orders. Back issues can be purchased from the University of Ottawa Press at www.press.uottawa. ca/subject/criminology. If interested in obtaining issues that are out of print, please contact the JPP directly. Further information regarding course orders and distribution can be obtained from the University of Toronto Press at:

University of Toronto Press Inc.
5201 Dufferin Street
Toronto, Ontario, Canada M3H 5T8

phone: 1-800-565-9523
fax: 1-800-221-9985
e-mail: utpbooks@utpress.utoronto.ca
website: www.utpress.utoronto.ca/utp_D1/home.htm

Co-published by the University of Ottawa Press and the *Journal of Prisoners on Prisons*.

Printed and Bound in Canada

ISSN 0838-164X
ISBN 978-0-7766-2597-3 (print)
ISBN 978-0-7766-2598-0 (PDF)

IN THIS ISSUE

DISPATCHES FROM THE QUEBEC REGION
Port Cartier Institution

Établissement de Cowansville

DISPATCHES FROM THE ONTARIO REGION
Bath Institution

Beaver Creek Institution (minimum)

DISPATCHES FROM THE PRAIRIE REGION
Stony Mountain Institution

Saskatchewan Penitentiary

Riverbend Institution

Drumheller Institution

DISPATCHES FROM THE PACIFIC REGION

Mission Institution

Mountain Institution

Kent Institution

RESPONSE

More Stormy Weather or Sunny Ways?
A Forecast for Change by Prisoners of the Canadian Carceral State

APPENDIX

Call for input and/or submissions

PRISONERS' STRUGGLES

Prisoners' Legal Services on Segregation

Call for Artwork – 50th Anniversary /
Oeuvres d'art recherchées – 50e anniversaire

COVER ART

"Maple Leaf" (front cover)

"If You Build It..." (back cover)

INTRODUCTION FROM
THE CO-MANAGING EDITORS

Prisoners of Penal Intensification and Sunny Ways[1]
Justin Piché and Kevin Walby

In recent decades, Canada has been heralded for its restrained approach to penality amid the wave of penal intensification that took hold in the United States and other western democracies (e.g. Meyer and O'Malley, 2005; Doob and Webster, 2006). However, denunciation, deterrence and incapacitation became increasingly privileged carceral logics under successive minority (2006-2008, 2008-2011) and majority (2011-2015) Conservative federal governments. Then Prime Minister Stephen Harper and his team framed the consensus that existed for several decades across party lines backing rehabilitation and community integration of the criminalized as symptoms of a broken justice system in need of an overhaul (Webster and Doob, 2015).

Although the Conservative punishment agenda – comprised of a series of sentencing, penitentiary administration and (dis)integration measures (Piché, 2015; also see Shook and McInnis, this issue) – have yet to translate into a boom in Canada's rate of incarceration, in our work with the *Journal of Prisoners on Prisons* (JPP) we have published writings by Canadian prisoners that illustrate the profound impact that these regressive reforms have had on the lives of federal prisoners (see Collins, 2008; Anonymous, 2009; Acoby, 2011; Glaremin, 2011; "Petey", 2011; Convict, 2013; Shook, 2013; Abbotsbury, 2014; Shook, 2014; Vivar, 2014; Fry, 2015; Shook, 2015a; Shook, 2015b; Shook, 2015c; Fayter, 2016; Villebrun, 2016).

Following the 2015 federal election, which resulted in a majority Liberal government led by Prime Minister Justin Trudeau who promised "sunny ways", there were signals that abandoning the most egregious punishment measures introduced during Prime Minister Harper's near decade in power might happen. Among them was the mandate given to Minister of Justice and Attorney General of Canada Jody Wilson-Raybould upon her appointment, which included the following instruction:

> ...conduct a review of the changes in our criminal justice system and sentencing reforms over the past decade with a mandate to assess the changes, ensure that we are increasing the safety of our communities, getting value for money, addressing gaps and ensuring that current provisions are aligned with the objectives of the criminal justice system.

Outcomes of this process should include increased use of restorative justice processes and other initiatives to reduce the rate of incarceration amongst Indigenous Canadians...

With a penal system review underway, we felt it was important to ensure that federal prisoners were able to contribute their insights into the material impacts of legislative and policy changes introduced by the Conservatives and what reforms they envisage as necessary to enhance living conditions behind penitentiary walls in ways that contribute to safety beyond them. During the winter 2017 semester, a section of *SCS 4150: Directed Research in Social Sciences* was created at the University of Ottawa where students were tasked with initiating and producing a *JPP Dialogue* comprised of submissions from Prisoner Committees and individuals held within Canada's federal penitentiaries operated and managed by the Correctional Service Canada (CSC). Jarrod Shook, a former federal prisoner, current parolee and undergraduate student at the University of Ottawa, along with Bridget McInnis, who was in the last semester of her undergraduate degree (Social Work major and Criminology minor) and was set to begin law school in fall 2017, registered for the course. As part of their course work, Jarrod and Bridget wrote a letter to prisoners in every Canadian federal institution and security level soliciting submissions to the *JPP* (see *Appendix*). In keeping with the journal's mandate, our hope was that this project would illuminate realities of incarceration and offer paths for change 'from below' (Piché *et al.*, 2014).

This project almost never got off the ground. On 22 March 2017, the professor for the course (Justin Piché) was contacted by staff from CSC's National Headquarters via email. A CSC official noted that "one of our regional offices forwarded to us a letter that you had sent to the chairpersons of inmate committees (dated 1 March 2017) requesting their input and observations about how corrections has changed over the years". Also included in the email was a request "to arrange a time sometime soon to discuss your project so that I can have a clearer idea of what is involved".

Sensing that our efforts to facilitate prisoner writing on penality in Canada were at risk of being shut down, a meeting was initiated with CSC staff in Ottawa to ensure that those held in federal penitentiaries could have the opportunity to express themselves in writing, as is allowed in section 2(b) of the *Canadian Charter of Rights and Freedoms*. Entering the 23 March 2017 meeting, Justin expected resistance to the project from CSC, which is known for being an opaque, secretive organization (see, for example, Culhane, 1991; Martel, 2004; Yeager, 2008; Piché, 2011). Discussions focused on whether or not the project was a traditional academic research endeavour involving data collection through quantitative and qualitative instruments, which needed to go through CSC's research protocol. After all parties at the meeting concluded that prisoners writing about their own experiences did not fall within these parameters and that prisoners had the right to free expression, it was agreed that the letters, which had been intercepted by institutional authorities and held in the mailing rooms of some federal penitentiaries, could be received by their intended recipients.

For us, this decision signals that something has changed as a result of the 2015 federal election. By allowing the project to go forward, CSC showed its willingness to hold a mirror up to itself and be subject to scrutiny, to be transparent and to be held accountable in a public forum. While we cannot demonstrate the motivations underlying this decision, it is no secret that many inside CSC's ranks were troubled by much of what the Conservative punishment agenda entailed (see, for example, Comack *et al.*, 2015; Clark, 2017). Thus, catalysts for progressive change such as this project are perhaps welcome. This is a good sign with respect to the health of our democratic institutions, however imperfect they may be under a first-past-the-post federal electoral system with increasing power centralized within the Prime Minister's Office (Marland, 2017).

Once the letters made their way inside Canada's penitentiaries, what followed was a steady stream of thoughtful written submissions from Prisoner Committee representatives and other federal prisoners across Canada. Our expectations were exceeded to the point that we decided to dedicate an entire double-issue of the journal to this *Dialogue*. While many of the pieces depart from the narrative and socio-political articles that normally appear in the journal, they offer a snapshot of the main issues Canadian federal prisoners face today. As noted in the *Response* (Shook and McInnis, this issue), there are several recurring themes cutting across the hundreds of pages we received.

As we started to review the submissions and get a sense of just how dire things have become inside CSC institutions, we were faced with having to decide if prisoners should have their names published alongside their contributions, knowing that formally exercising the *Charter* protected right to free expression behind bars can lead to informal retribution in many forms, from being physically harmed by prison staff to having negative comments attached to one's 'correctional' assessments that influence things such as parole decisions (see Piché *et al.*, 2014, pp. 456-457). Letters were subsequently sent out to potential contributors seeking their input on this matter as they are best positioned to decide what risks they are willing to take from where they stand. As such, many contributions have been anonymized, while others have not. It is our hope that by getting these works out in the open that CSC staff and officials read these contributions and see that prisoners are working in good faith to try to improve living and working conditions behind bars.

Within these pages there is a lot to take in. There is so much that needs to change so long as carceral spaces exist in the world. But there is hope. This issue is a testament of where we are now and what we could become if we take the words of the criminalized and punished seriously. As these contributions show, there are concrete actions that can be taken today to improve life and work inside Canada's penitentiaries. This is a call to respect human dignity to the degree that is possible within the walls of federal institutions. It is incumbent upon parliamentarians and the Government of Canada to act now to diminish the violence of incarceration not just for the sake of prisoners, but their families and Canadians more broadly.

ENDNOTES

[1] We thank Brendan Roziere, Joanne DeCosse and Bilguundari Enkhtugs for their assistance in copy-editing this volume.

REFERENCES

Abbotsbury, Chester (2014) "What's In a Name? Depersonalization at the Hands of the State", *Journal of Prisoners on Prisons*, 23(2): 23-31.

Acoby, Renée (2011) "On Segregation", *Journal of Prisoners on Prisons*, 20(1): 89-93.

Anonymous (2009) "Dear Sanity", *Journal of Prisoners on Prisons*, 18(1&2): 71.

Clark, Robert (2017) *Down Inside: Thirty Years in Canada's Prison Service*, New Brunswick: Goose Lane.

Collins, Peter (2008) "Education in Prison or the Applied Art of 'Correctional Deconstructive Learning'", *Journal of Prisoners on Prisons*, 17(1): 71-90.

Comack, Elizabeth, Cara Fabre and Shanise Burgher (2015) *The Impact of the Harper Government's "Tough on Crime" Strategy: Hearing From Frontline Workers*, Winnipeg: Canadian Centre for Policy Alternatives.

Convict, Joe (2013) "Conservative Strategies for Dismantling Independent Oversight and Advocacy", *Journal of Prisoners on Prisons*, 22(1): 64-67.

Culhane, Claire (1991) *No Longer Barred from Prison: Social Injustice in Canada*, Montreal: Black Rose Books.

Doob, Anthony N. and Cheryl M. Webster (2006) "Countering Punitiveness: Understanding Stability in Canada's Rate of Imprisonment", *Law & Society Review*, 40(2): 325-368.

Fayter, Rachel (2016) "Social Justice Praxis within the Walls to Bridges Program: Pedagogy of Oppressed Federally Sentenced Women", *Journal of Prisoners on Prisons*, 25(2): 56-71.

Fry, J. John (2015) "Pardon Me!", *Journal of Prisoners on Prisons*, 24(1): 24-28.

Glaremin, T.A. (2011) "A New Direction for Federally Sentenced Women, Foiled Once Again", *Journal of Prisoners on Prisons*, 20(1): 84-88.

Marland, Alex (2017) "Strategic Management of Media Relations: Communications Centralization and Spin in the Government of Canada", *Canadian Public Policy*, 43(1): 36-49.

Martel, Joane (2004) "Policing Criminological Knowledge: The Hazards of Qualitative Research on Women in Prison", *Theoretical Criminology*, 8(2): 157-189.

Meyer, Jeffrey and Pat O'Malley (2005) "Missing the Punitive Turn? Canadian Criminal Justice, 'Balance' and Penal Modernism", in John Pratt, David Brown, Simon Hallsworth and Wayne Morrison (eds.), *The New Punitiveness: Trends, Theories, Perspectives*, Portland: Willan Publising, pp. 201-207.

"Petey" (2011) "Reflections on My First 'Free' Prisoners' Justice Day", *Journal of Prisoners on Prisons*, 20(1): 98-101.

Piché, Justin (2015) "Playing the 'Treasury Card' to Contest Prison Expansion: Lessons from a Public Criminology Campaign", *Social Justice*, 41(3): 145-167.

Piché, Justin (2011) "'Going Public': Accessing Information, Contesting Information Blockades", *Canadian Journal of Law and Society*, 26(3): 635-643.

Piché, Justin, Bob Gaucher and Kevin Walby (2014) "Facilitating Prisoner Ethnography: An Alternative Approach to 'Doing Prison Research Differently'", *Qualitative Inquiry*, 20(4): 449-460.

Shook, Jarrod (2015a) "Collins Bay Institution: A Cluster F*#k", *Journal of Prisoners on Prisons*, 24(1): 49-51.

Shook, Jarrod (2015b) "Incentive to Scrutinize", *Journal of Prisoners on Prisons*, 24(1): 52-54.

Shook, Jarrod (2015c) "Undelivered Mail?", *Journal of Prisoners on Prisons*, 24(2): 75-78.

Shook, Jarrod (2014) "Business as Usual", *Journal of Prisoners on Prisons*, 23(2): 10-22.

Shook, Jarrod (2013) "Debunking Double Bunking in the Correctional Service of Canada: A Critical Qualitative Account", *Journal of Prisoners on Prisons*, 22(1): 64-67.

Villebrun, Vincent Charles (2016) "If a Red Horse is Red, Is a Blue Horse Blue?", *Journal of Prisoners on Prisons*, 25(2): 47-55.

Vivar, Jose (2014) "The Truth About Provincial Prisons", *Journal of Prisoners on Prisons*, 23(2): 6-9.

Webster, Cheryl Marie and Anthony N. Doob (2015) "American Punitiveness 'Canadian Style': Cultural Values and Canadian Punishment Policy", *Punishment and Society*, 17(3): 299-321.

Yeager, Matthew (2008) "Getting the Usual Treatment: Research Censorship and the Dangerous Offender", *Contemporary Justice Review*, 11(4): 413-425.

DIALOGUE ON
CANADA'S FEDERAL PENITENTIARY SYSTEM
AND THE NEED FOR PENAL REFORM

Dispatches from Federally Sentenced Women

The Impact of the Conservative Punishment Agenda on Federally Sentenced Women and Priorities for Social Change
Rachel Fayter and Sherry Payne

INTRODUCTION

Life in a federal penitentiary is extremely challenging and tedious. We are removed from our friends, families and communities, and placed into a restrictive, oppressive environment. One of the primary purposes of prison is to rehabilitate and assist in our eventual reintegration into the community. However, once the Conservative government came into power under Prime Minister Stephen Harper, the focus of criminal justice laws, policies, and practices from 2006 to 2015 primarily became punishment. The following essay consists of a collection of observations and experiences from women incarcerated at Grand Valley Institution (GVI) in Kitchener, Ontario. The focus is on current policies and practices of Correctional Service Canada (CSC) that directly affect incarcerated women and our loved ones.

We identify ten key priorities for change based on our own observations, experiences, and through several meetings and discussions with fellow prisoners at GVI. These priorities are organized according to the following themes: justice, employment issues, programs and education, food and nutrition, visits and correspondence, reintegration and parole, media and communications, the focus on punishment, health and dental care, and mental health care. Within many of these categories are various sub-themes, which go into greater detail. Each section provides an overview of our experiences and observations. We then highlight some of the negative impacts on women at GVI because of these punitive policies and practices. Since so many negative impacts overlap, we return to these intersections towards the end of the paper. Finally, we suggest some recommendations in terms of priorities for change.

PRIORITIES FOR CHANGE

Justice
The lack of justice is the largest category and the number one priority for change. Justice is absent behind these walls, which is evidenced from the lack of dignity and privacy afforded to us, our defective internal grievance system,

the overuse of segregation, involuntary transfers based on allegations, and institutional charges.

Lack of Dignity and Privacy

Guards are extremely loud when completing their rounds through the living units, which is especially disruptive at night when prisoners are sleeping, where they also shine lights in our eyes. They also repeatedly wake up prisoners while we are napping during the day. It is rare that a guard treats us with respect or dignity. They demean us, lie, make accusations and assumptions, tease us, restrict our choices, belittle us, swear and call us names. For example, guards have made fun of what clothing women wear, our make-up, our weight and how much junk food we purchase at canteen.

The guards conduct searches of each unit at least once a month and can search once a week or more if the institution deems it necessary. Guards read and seize our personal journals, notes, address books, and schoolwork during searches. They throw our belongings around our living spaces and destroy personal property without any repercussions. It is possible to file a claim for broken possessions. However, the warden approves or denies claims within the institution. Thus, they are often denied. After a search, it can take hours to clean our living unit.

Defective Internal Grievance System

When a woman puts forth a complaint, it goes to the correctional manager. A first level grievance is sent to the Warden or Assistant Warden. At this point, the warden can either grant your grievance or deny it. Often, first level grievances are denied for unclear reasons. Only a second level (highest level) grievance goes to National or the Commissioner of CSC. The entire process is internal, as CSC staff make all decisions on whether the grievance is approved. Therefore, no one is watching the watchers or holding CSC accountable. This process allows CSC to abuse their power. Many women feel powerless and fearful of fighting for their rights. They distrust the system and experience significant amounts of stress.

We believe an external independent group[1] should be created to deal with prisoners' grievances. Allowing CSC to 'investigate' itself is an inherent injustice and lacks transparency. Additionally, prisoners' grievances should be handled fairly and efficiently, within three months of being filed, not three years, as is often the case.

Overuse of Segregation
CSC regularly places prisoners in segregation for over 15 days, including those who are living with or experiencing mental health issues. Despite the deaths of two young women in segregation at Grand Valley Institution in less than a decade (Ashley Smith in 2007 and Terri Baker in 2016), management continues to place women with histories of mental health issues and self-harming behaviours in segregation. Both writers have spent time in segregation at GVI, and one author was in the segregation unit for 32 days just 3 months after Ms. Baker's death, for a minor, non-violent offence. Anytime a woman self-harms, no matter the severity, she is placed in segregation. The conditions in the segregation unit are deplorable. Being placed in segregation results in a deteriorating attitude, feelings of isolation, alienation, loss of identity, increased mental health issues, and feeling oppressed and disconnected from the community.

Involuntary Transfers and Allegations
We denounce the transfer of prisoners based on unproven allegations. Security intelligence files are created based on 'reliable sources' consisting of information from other prisoners given to CSC staff in secrecy. We are never allowed to know who or what was said exactly or able to confront our accuser in a transparent process. Other prisoners provide information, often false, for personal gain and favour from staff. This information can impact our security rating and parole hearings, restrict our access to visits with family and friends, limit community access, and eliminate our employment positions. If our security levels are increased we can be transferred from the minimum unit to the medium compound or from medium to the secure unit. Once a prisoner is transferred, it can take months or even years to return to a lower level setting. This requires women to start all over again, resulting in a loss of community and having to rebuild relationships. Women feel powerless, hopeless and anxious in such circumstances.

Institutional Charges
According to CSC policy, each time a prisoner is perceived to disobey an institutional rule, the guard should attempt to informally resolve the situation

first. It was formerly a principle of the *Corrections and Conditional Release Act* (CCRA) that in the event of disciplinary action in such matters, that the 'least restrictive' action should be utilized. With the passage of *The Safe Streets and Communities Act,* the "least restrictive measures" principle was removed from the *CCRA*, and replaced with what the OCI described in his 2014/2015 report as "more ambiguous language", such as "proportionate and necessary measures"[2] (OCI, 2015). Despite these correctional 'principles', guards virtually never attempt to informally resolve an issue at GVI before dispensing a charge.

In minor court, a Correctional Manager (CM) rather than an outside adjudicator facilitates the process. The CM will universally find us guilty regardless of facts. This charge will follow the women through their entire sentence and be mentioned in all of their paperwork under institutional adjustment and behaviour. These areas are the domains that are looked at for your security rating scale, which makes you a minimum-, medium- or maximum-security prisoner. Your scale can restrict you from earning a transfer to minimum-security. Additionally, this charge could potentially pose a concern to the police and halfway house when transitioning into the community post-release.

Employment Issues
The most salient employment issues within prison today include a lack of job opportunities and wage cuts. Employment is an integral aspect of prisoners' correctional plans and central to our future success in the community after our time inside comes to an end.

Lack of Job Opportunities in Prison
Our security classification restricts our ability to apply for certain jobs. Women in maximum-security can only hold one job. At the minimum-security unit (MSU) there are no full-time jobs. However, women in minimum-security can apply for temporary absence work release programs to access employment in the community. These jobs are often limited due to lack of placements and difficulty to maintain them. If there are any issues within the prison, such as a lockdown, we are not able to leave the prison for work.

The "position of trust" clause restricts many women from finding, keeping and maintaining a job. Virtually every job, except for a few cleaning jobs depending on their location (for example, in the gym, bathroom or hallway) are all positions of trust. We lose our job if we get a major charge. Certain jobs, including canteen operator, can be lost with a minor charge, which includes innocuous activities like passing food or borrowing clothing.

The new Drug Strategy, which emanates out of the *Roadmap to Strengthening Public Safety* (Sampson et al., 2007) can prevent us from working for three months at a time or up to six months or more.[3] Women can easily lose their job if they receive an institutional charge or are placed in segregation without being charged, even when the charge or the situation is completely unrelated to their employment. The lack of job opportunities in prison means we have little opportunity for skill development and limited financial resources to keep in contact with our family or prepare for our eventual release.

Wage Cuts and "Double Dipping" Taxes

The Government of Canada convened a parliamentary committee in 1981 to determine what prisoners' wages should be based on the minimum-wage at the time, while also taking into account the cost of room and board. They determined our daily wage for full-time work should be $5.80 per day. The maximum daily wage rose some years later to $6.90 per day. Then, in November 2013, the federal government implemented a policy to take an additional 30%[4] off our wages for "food and Accommodation" (22%), as well as the administration of the "inmate telephone system" (8%) essentially causing us to pay this fee twice. At full-time pay we only take home $29 every two weeks. Our wages have not been reviewed in over three decades, despite the increased cost of living. Women use this money for hygiene, snacks and contact with family (e.g. phone calls and letters).

We should have access to real wages, not pennies. CORCAN (Corrections Canada Industries) is an entity within CSC whose mission is to provide meaningful employment and skills. It once provided additional opportunities in the form of incentive pay[5] that allowed long-term prisoners to keep their families together and short-term prisoners to save money for release. All bonuses and incentives were cut in 2013. Our pay rate should be equal to the provincial minimum wage.

Programs and Education

Concerning programs and education, for the federally sentenced women we spoke to the central issues pertain to the mother-child program and unnecessary bureaucratic control over volunteer-led programs. Additionally, there is a lack of access to computers and the library, and limited access to trades and post-secondary education programs.

Mother-Child Program

The mother-child program was one of the many programs that was substantially overhauled during the Conservative government's reign from 2006-2015. In its previous iteration, the program enabled women to live with their young children, ages five and under in a cottage designated as the mother-child unit located on the general compound. Due to its location, there were no delays for a pregnant woman between the time she gave birth and when she was able to live with her child. A prisoner who was pregnant would work with a social worker and her case-management team at GVI in order to live in the mother-child unit, and following the birth of her child would be able to return to the unit with her newborn.

This program was shut down for years and has only recently been reinstated at the minimum-security unit (MSU) approximately one year ago in spring 2016. The current mother-child program is only a shadow of what it once was.[6] There is one mother-child floor at the MSU, which is an apartment-style complex. There is only space for four women and their children to participate in the program at any one time. There are many bureaucratic constraints and extraneous processes so it can take eight to twelve months or even longer for a woman's child to be able to move in. Aside from the required paperwork, a woman also has to earn her minimum-security rating and finish all necessary programming prior to moving to the MSU. This results in her not seeing her child outside of visits for twelve months or more. The visiting room is not a conducive location for a mother to bond with her child. Aside from the guards, search dogs and overall institutional atmosphere, women have been denied the opportunity to hold their baby, breastfeed and change diapers. The guards often make allegations that prevent women from participating in the mother-child program. For example, below is a recent story from a young woman who was pregnant and gave birth while incarcerated at GVI. She has been striving to participate in the mother-child program and move to the MSU since she learned she was pregnant.

Kendall's Story[7]

When Kendall gave birth to her son this year, two female guards, who were present at all times, escorted her to the hospital. The child's father, Kendall's boyfriend, was not allowed to be present in the room while she was in labour. Once her child was born, he was immediately brought to the Natal Intensive Care Unit (NICU) due to breathing difficulties. Kendall was not initially allowed down to the NICU to see her son because the guards were unclear whether she had to be accompanied by a social worker or not. Kendall was forced to wait until the following day when a hospital staff member was able to contact the CSC social worker so that Kendall could spend time with her newborn son.

This was clearly devastating for Kendall, who wanted nothing more than to hold and establish a bond with her newborn child. Kendall has been a model prisoner since arriving at Grand Valley in 2016. She has completed all required programming, attends school, is employed within the institution and works closely with her case management teams. Her goal is to earn her minimum- security rating so she can move to the MSU and live with her son. Kendall is serving a three-year sentence. After almost one year she should not only be deemed a minimum-security prisoner, but she should also be eligible for day-parole, if not full-parole. The Children's Aid Society (CAS) is supportive of Kendall having her son live with her at GVI, but the institution keeps making allegations that she is engaged in illicit activities, without having any evidence to substantiate their claims. The prison has intercepted her phone calls for two months, conducted random urinalyses (all of which came back negative), and requested a strip search (which she consented to) in order to determine whether she has received any new tattoos while incarcerated. Each of these situations have resulted in delaying Kendall's security-level review, causing a lengthier wait for her to spend time bonding with her son at this critical point in his life.

Being disconnected from one's children can negatively influence a mother's relationship with her child indefinitely. Women separated from their children feel isolated and alone, which leads to feelings of anxiety, frustration, anger, and low self-esteem. We recommend the full reinstatement of the mother-child program as it was prior to the Conservative government coming into power, for women in the medium- and minimum-security level areas of the prison.

Bureaucratic Control over Volunteer Lead Programs

The institution practices unnecessary bureaucratic control over positive education and social programs. Since the Walls-to-Bridges (W2B) program began in 2011, the prison is increasingly using their power to control the initiative. Students now have to submit papers to institutional teachers prior to submitting them to the outside professor. The inside teacher and outside professor must now report to the prison if anything in a student's paper can be deemed "too radical". Teaching assistants, who are hired by professors from an outside university, can be fired by the institution after receiving an institutional charge.

Volunteers from the community lead other programs such as Celebrate Recovery, Alternatives to Violence, and Stride, often having to jump through various bureaucratic hoops in order to enter the prison, bring snacks or supplies, and take us on temporary absences. These volunteers have been attending the prison for years and are generally well-known by CSC staff, yet are sometimes treated with suspicion and disrespect. Staff have threatened to cancel full-day programs that occurred over countless times simply because a few prisoners had to use the washroom during the 'lockdown' time.

As soon as an activity is legitimized as a program (i.e. a formally structured activity approved by institution), it has the potential to be shut down by management. At GVI, we had an active music program that was available to women during the afternoons when we had no other work or required programming scheduled. The music program had been operating informally for one year with the approval and support of a Social Program Officer (SPO). The music program involved an instrument-lending program, vocal lessons, song-writing workshops and lessons for various instruments (e.g. guitar, keyboard, bass guitar and drums). Within one month of the SPO staff retiring, who had supported the program, middle management shut us down. Apparently, certain guards do not like the fact that women are able to attend this program during the day.

Lack of Access to Computers and Library

It is extremely difficult for women to access computers. Teachers and other CSC staff control access to the rooms that contain computers and often will not allow us to enter the room. Access to personal computers in our living units should be reinstated. The library is only open Tuesday, Wednesday and Thursday. Women can only access the library from 10:00am to 10:30am and 2:00pm to 2:30pm, as well as during their living unit day and hour. Sometimes the library is closed on these days if the librarian is absent. The library should get more up-to-date educational books, and be open during evenings and weekends. It is extremely difficult for women to study and do our schoolwork. This leads to feelings of frustration, anger, hopelessness and powerlessness.

Lack of Access to Trades, Training and Post-Secondary Education

Over the past twenty years, CSC has cut off our access to almost all trades programs and eliminated access to post-secondary education in the community. Women at GVI are currently working on an amendment to the *CCRA* for an education release, which is similar to a work release. GVI has extremely outdated computer hardware without any access to the internet. Not having the internet available for educational purposes inhibits our ability to access many high-school and post-secondary courses since print-based courses are no longer available.

We should have access to post-secondary education so that we can pursue academic degrees while incarcerated. We should have access to education about technology. Progressive changes to technology in the community leave us struggling to function upon our release. We should have access to the internet that is monitored and restricted. Many software programs are available to facilitate this process. The high school program is mostly self-directed independent adult learning, but students must sit in classroom to "prove" they are working, even if they are diligent and hardworking, while other students are disruptive. Students with lack of education, learning disabilities or mental health diagnoses are held to a lower standard and given their high-school credits without doing much work, while at the same time not provided with a tutor or support to understand the concepts being taught. For example, a woman in grade 11 English cannot write a grammatically correct paragraph without a spelling error and is being assigned books such as *The Little Engine That Could*. Students can receive a suspension from school for 90 days for simply falling behind or missing days.

We recommend the reinstatement of all social programs closed during the Conservative reign, including Lifeline, Prison Farm programs and life skills programming. There should be a reduction in wait times for access to programming. The elimination of access to education and social programs should no longer be used as a punishment. The high school program should be evaluated, improved and updated. Prisoners with high school degrees should be hired to work as tutors in the secondary school program. Many women would benefit significantly from the individual support.

Food and Nutrition
Food and nutrition affects our overall health and wellbeing. National regulations and the high cost of food make it difficult to eat healthy. A lack of training for food safety and knowledge concerning how to prepare healthy meals are other common issues that women in prison face.

National Regulations and High Cost of Food
In the medium- and minimum-security areas of the prison, we cook our own food and receive $35.21 each per week to purchase our groceries. This amount has decreased within the past two years from $35.35 and the overall budget of approximately $35/week has not increased in the past 20 years since GVI opened, despite inflation and rising food prices. Produce, dairy and meat are expensive, while processed, unhealthy items are cheaper and more affordable to eat.

CSC National Headquarters has recently regulated our menu in order to make it consistent with other institutions across Canada. Healthy menu items were removed and replaced with canned goods and processed, unhealthy food. For example, the maximum-security unit at GVI previously received 1% milk and now they get powdered milk every day.

By standardizing what we eat for every penitentiary across the country, we have less variety and choice, resulting in less cultural expression from each region of the country and cultural groups within each region. Many women enjoy cooking and baking, which is a positive, pro-social activity. Restricting our choices makes us feel worthless and inferior. The unhealthy food negatively affects our physical health.

Lack of Training for Food Safety and Preparing Healthy Meals
Some women have never cooked before. They do not know how to prepare a meal, create a meal plan or budget. Within the living units, several serious fires have occurred causing thousands of dollars in damage. At least five fires have occurred in the past four years due to inexperience and lack of knowledge or awareness of how to cook with oil or handle a grease fire. This lack of training and knowledge is not only unsanitary, but can also lead to the spread of infectious disease, bacteria and pathogens.

Visits and Correspondence

The most common issues within the area of visits and correspondence include the disrespectful and suspicious treatment of our family and friends, the loss of visits as a punishment, a reduced number of family socials each year, as well as the loss of the annual Pow-Wow. Additionally, there are problems with our mail and phone systems.

Disrespectful, Suspicious Treatment of our Family and Friends

Ion scanner machines are designed to be able to detect trace amounts of particles, such as drugs, on clothes, money, jewellery, keys and other personal items. CSC has placed these devices in the lobbies and mailrooms of penitentiaries in an attempt to reduce the flow of drugs into the institution. False positives or very faint amounts can prevent visitor access. These devices are extremely sensitive and can pick up trace amounts of particles in the air. Once a visitor tests positive for a substance, the guards conduct a 'risk-assessment' to determine whether the visitor can enter the institution. Often, visits are suspended for a set period of time or indefinitely. Sometimes visits are closed (i.e. in a secure 'box' where the prisoner and visitor are separated by glass). Even if the visitor is allowed into the prison, the incident is noted on the prisoner's file and follows us throughout our sentence. Visits can also be suspended or closed due to allegations from 'reliable sources' or prisoner informants with no substantial evidence. Additionally, without notice, guards suddenly cancel visits or deny family members from seeing prisoners, even when they have travelled for hours from out of town. Guards and search dogs are intimidating to our visitors. The guards in the visiting area tell our visitors where they can sit. Additionally, guards intervene if visitors stretch or visitors and prisoners sit too close, hold hands, hug, or touch for more than three seconds.

Loss of Visits as a Punishment

Family Day or socials are an opportunity for women to visit with family and friends for up to six hours in an informal atmosphere with music, food, games, and entertainment. Socials occur much less frequently than in the past. For several years now, there have only been two socials per year at GVI. Prisoners without family attending are no longer permitted to participate in the event, despite paying fees to their respective prisoner welfare committees all year to fund the event. Prisoners charged with a minor or major offence within the institution, within three months of the event are not able to attend. One of the authors was notified just 12 hours prior to the start of the event that she was unable to attend, without any charges being laid. This causes significant inconvenience to our families who have taken time off work or drive long distances and stay at a local hotel to visit. The volume and rate of charges drastically increase months before Family Day. Because of these sanctions, less and less people have been attending each year.

We recommend the reinstatement of regular Family Day socials, at least six per year. We believe that every prisoner should be able to attend family day regardless of whether she has guests attending. We build relationships with one another and with each other's social networks, and the socials are an opportunity to strengthen those ties. We should not be banned from attending a social simply because we have received an institutional charge within three months of the event.

Annual Pow-Wow
Only identified Indigenous prisoners can invite guests to the annual Pow-Wow. As of this date, the annual Pow-Wow has been cancelled without reason and without any communication to prisoners.

Correspondence
As one of our only means of accessing the outside world, regular postage mail is extremely important to us and can brighten a prisoner's day. According to CSC policy, we are entitled to our mail every business day. CSC is supposed to deliver prisoners' mail in the same manner that Canada Post does. However, we receive our mail infrequently as it is treated like a privilege. Some days we do not receive our mail at all and it can take weeks to receive local correspondence.

Phone System in Disrepair
There is one phone in the segregation unit. Over a one-month period the phone was broken five afternoons. In recent months, three living units experienced a period in which their phone was unavailable for days or even weeks. After every power outage, the telephone in several living units goes down for a period of time until it is fixed by Technical Support. The phone card uploads only occur once a month and the money has to be in your

account one week prior. If a woman arrives at GVI around the date of the upload, the money has to be in their account and they have to wait an entire month to make any calls. These women are unable to contact their family and let them know how they are doing, and unable to arrange to have their boxes of personal belongings sent, which must arrive within 30 days of intake. Women are not able to contact any family or support persons who reside overseas. For example, a woman was unable to add a phone number in Europe to speak with her children and another woman was unable to call her mother overseas.

For long-distance calls, the rate is $0.11 per minute. For local calls, the rate is $0.56 per hour. The phone system is very sensitive and calls are often disconnected due to a "three-way call alert", which can be triggered by background noise or a portable phone. Maintaining strong family ties and connections to our community through visits, correspondence, and phone calls are vital to the rehabilitation and reintegration process that CSC claims it supports. However, the damage caused by this flawed system is counter-productive. Furthermore, our family and friends are being punished by being disconnected from us and having to contribute to the costs of maintaining what little connection we have. They too are doing time even though we are the ones behind bars.

The negative impacts of having these issues with our visits, correspondence and phone system are numerous. Contact and relationship building with family and friends are vital to community reintegration. Without these outside connections, we feel isolated, lonely, disconnected, hopeless, powerless, frustrated, anxious, angry and unsupported. We recommend that CSC fix the phone system so the phone does not cut-off anymore. In addition, when our calls are cut-off, we should be reimbursed for the cost.

Reintegration and Parole
CSC, as per the *CCRA*, is mandated to assist with the rehabilitation of prisoners and our reintegration into the community. CSC is currently not fulfilling its reintegration mandate. Parolees are sent back to prison frequently for issues that could be handled and managed in the community. While prisoners are still serving their sentences, it is difficult to connect people to supports in the community.

More community groups should be allowed into the institution as volunteers to make connections, as well as build relationships that help us to reintegrate back into society. This would assist with a healthier transition for individuals leaving the institution and making connections to the community.

Community Access for Women Serving a Life Sentence
Women serving life sentences must go before the Parole Board of Canada (PBC) when asking for any Escorted Temporary Absences (ETAs), Unescorted Temporary Absences (UTAs) and work releases. The current system makes it tedious and time consuming for women serving life sentences to work on their reintegration. We recommend that the warden regain the ability to grant permission for ETAs and UTAs, along with work release as opposed to the PBC.

Challenges on Parole
Upon release, women are expected to work while on parole. However, many places will not hire someone serving a federal sentence. Additionally, the PBC can place further stipulations restricting us from working anywhere that serves alcohol or involves financial transactions, such as retail establishments, restaurants, fast food, and call-centres.

Women on parole are required to attend programming once a week for two hours for about a minimum of twelve weeks. Additional programming or treatment may be recommended. We are also required to meet with our parole officer. This makes working during the day extremely difficult. There is little to no support at all for employment once released. Additionally, many women do not have any personal identification. Furthermore, there is limited assistance with transportation and housing. If women reside in a halfway house and work, we are required to pay rent, which makes saving up to move to our own apartment difficult.

Women are not able to collect government assistance (e.g. Ontario Works, Ontario Disability Support Program, etc.) at most halfway houses in Ontario. Therefore, a woman with a disability cannot receive her cheque even though a doctor has said she is unable to work. One of the main reasons women cite for reoffending is due to financial difficulties and being unable to secure employment.

There are not enough halfway houses for women in Ontario. Women are waiting weeks or even months to get a bed in southern Ontario, in cities such as Hamilton and Toronto. Currently, there are only seven halfway houses for women located in London, Hamilton, Toronto, Brampton, Barrie, Kingston and Ottawa. Many women are forced to live hours from their community when released on day-parole, especially those from northern Ontario. We are often forced to waive our full parole, which would allow us to go home, in favour of day-parole in a halfway house. Women should be able to return to their homes and families via parole after serving a third of their sentence, as outlined in the *CCRA*.[8]

Due to the many issues with reintegration and parole outlined above, women often feel unprepared, anxious, unsupported, and ultimately unable to function independently in the community. Women can also experience a lack of self-esteem, lack of confidence, lack of skills and be distrustful of the system.

We recommend alternatives to imprisonment for parole violations when the law is not broken. For example, a non-association clause requires parolees to assess people they just meet within the first 15 minutes to determine whether that person has a criminal record, an active police file or is engaged in any illegal activities. This can be an awkward or even dangerous conversation. The PBC should cease imposing this clause. Women have also been sent back to prison on a parole violation for being a few minutes late to an appointment. This is unjust.

Media and Communications
Prisoners are discriminated against in the media. News articles and television shows focus on high profile cases and violent offences. Negative media attention increases unfounded fears. With a constant focus on the sensational, we face discrimination upon release into the community, especially with regards to employment. We recommend that rehabilitation and successful reintegration stories be celebrated in the media to demonstrate the hard work and dedication of prisoners and our families. Having an open-minded, understanding community is necessary to reduce harm, decrease recidivism and encourage successful reintegration. Community advisory councils, made up of volunteers that visit women inside the prison, can play an educative role in their local communities, so that we are seen as an integral and valuable member of the community once released. They can act as allies and advocates to break down stereotypes and prejudice.

Recently, the media has requested to speak with individuals regarding the death of a prisoner while she was in segregation. Terri Baker died in July 2016. As we mentioned above this was the second death of a young woman in segregation at GVI. The first death was Ashley Smith in October 2007.

Both women lived with mental health issues. The prison did not approve any media requests for these matters. The media has also attempted many times to access prisoners to hear our stories (e.g. *The Fifth Estate*), but the administration and the staff blocked access. We have found creative means to get our stories out to the public, but if we are discovered, we are penalized. Media should be given access into all areas of the prison to speak with prisoners as a means of fostering government accountability.

Focus on Punishment
The federal penitentiary system has become increasingly focused on punishment as opposed to rehabilitation. This can be seen in prisoners' common mistreatment by guards, the restriction of our pro-social activities and the deployment of a drug-strategy used to punish, rather than offer treatment or support.

Mistreatment by Guards
The entire system from the top down practices paternalistic control over incarcerated women. We are treated like children who are unable to make independent choices. The policies and practices are designed to restrict and control, rather than rehabilitate and reintegrate. The focus of the institution is on punishment and security. Staff are generally insensitive. Guards mistreat us through verbal comments, a lack of understanding and compassion, and ignorant remarks. The LGBTQ community at GVI feel they are not accepted as individuals and especially not as a community. Gay relationships are prohibited and are not accepted by the guards. An individual's partner is often mentioned in paperwork. Women in relationships have not been supported for parole due to their relationship and their partner of choice. Same-sex couples are also not permitted to have Private Family Visits together.

Restricting Pro-Social Activities
There is no lounge or common area outside of our living units that women can use for social activities, aside from the gymnasium. When the weather does not allow for outdoor gathering, women are forced to use the gym as a multipurpose room for eating, playing cards, doing crafts, playing music, playing sports and working out. The gym should be strictly for athletics. Guards restrict women from using the classrooms for social activities. We are not able to visit each other's living units without risking a major charge.

We recommend the creation of a lounge for women to socialize, play cards, share a meal or simply just have a conversation with another as human beings. We also believe that visiting between living units should be allowed each evening and every weekend so friends can watch television, listen to music, cook and eat together, and build relationships.

Drug Strategy

When the drug strategy is deployed, it has serious consequences, many of which impose restrictions that have nothing to do with drug use. The drug strategy can be implemented if a woman fails to provide a urinalysis within a two-hour period of it being requested, tests positive from a urinalysis, improperly stores her medication (i.e. has a prescribed medication out of the blister pack), is found with a sewing needle, is found with over-the-counter medicine that is not prescribed (e.g. Tylenol) or is the subject of allegations. CSC claims that the drug strategy assists women, helping them to avoid using substances and to keep drugs out of the prison, but neither of these objectives are met. Instead, the strategy is a punitive instrument comprised of many sanctions.

Some punishments of drug strategy include pay deductions, moving living units, losing one's employment, and being unable to be a part of socials or activities in the prison. An individual is unable to work for the entire duration of their drug strategy term, which is usually 90 days, but the duration can be extended for up to six months or more, for whatever reason CSC deems necessary. An individual on the drug strategy is also not able to attend the Walls-to-Bridges education program or be the teaching assistant as it is a job within the institution. While on the drug strategy, an individual can be denied visits and is unable to have any Private Family Visits. Being placed on the drug strategy causes us to feel a loss of identity, because everything positive is taken from us. We also feel targeted, controlled, helpless, powerless, frustrated, labeled, stereotyped and isolated. Addiction should be recognized as a mental health issue requiring treatment, as opposed to a behavioural issue that requires punishment.

Health and Dental Care

There is a lack of accessibility to proper medical services inside the prison. Many people wait years for a diagnosis, and then even longer for any necessary surgery. It can take weeks or months to see a doctor or dentist, even for antibiotics or a common cold or flu. The dentist at GVI specializes in extracting teeth and prefers pulling a tooth to providing a filling. There are no teeth cleaning or preventative care appointments available. CSC blocks most standards of care and prohibits many necessary medications from being prescribed. For example, simple non-narcotic nerve medications and standard muscle relaxers are not available, even on a direct observation provision from nurses. Instead, doctors prescribe various psychotropic and mood stabilizing medications instead of pain relievers. Holistic care is difficult, if not impossible to access. There is no access to a chiropractor or massage therapist, even if women are willing to pay for it themselves. It is challenging to get items such as wrist or knee braces.

Not having proper access to health care is dehumanizing and causes us to feel worthless and inferior, as if nobody cares. Preventable health conditions occur and current health problems worsen. This can lead to chronic pain, physical exhaustion, and depression or anxiety. Lack of access to proper dental care can lead to bleeding or inflamed gums, cavities, and teeth being pulled out. Preventative health services should be made more accessible. Female prisoners should have the same access to preventative health care, such as breast cancer screening and annual pap tests, as women in the community. CSC should honour prescriptions written for us by doctors outside the facility. Teeth cleanings and regular dental check-ups should be available for people.

Mental Health Care
Many women are over-medicated with psychiatric drugs. Psychology only allows twelve sessions even if someone is in severe distress (e.g. has self-harmed or recently been released from serving more than fifteen days in segregation or maximum-security). The focus of CSC Psychology is on women with serious diagnosed mental health issues (e.g. schizophrenia, bipolar, borderline personality disorder). Counselling sessions are supposed to be confidential, unless we are a risk to ourselves or others, or are jeopardizing the security of the institution. However, since psychologists are employed CSC staff, women do not feel comfortable sharing their feelings and struggles based on the fear that what they say will end up in their paperwork. Their case management team could be notified of anything they say, which would affect security ratings, temporary absences and parole. If a woman expresses that she may hurt herself she is quickly placed in

segregation, stripped of her clothing, placed in a canvas "baby-doll dress" and strapped to a table until the institution believes she is able to keep herself safe. GVI does not have the capacity to care for women with severe mental health issues. The lack of appropriate mental health care leads to verbal and physical altercations in living units, women feeling misunderstood, exacerbated mental health issues, distrust, self-harm, and even death. We recommend that CSC return to hiring external social workers on contract to work with women in distress and those living with mental health issues, rather than CSC-employed psychologists.

CONCLUSION

Throughout this essay, we identified ten priorities for change based on our own experiences of incarceration. These key themes include: justice, employment issues, programs and education, food and nutrition, visits and correspondence, reintegration and parole, media and communications, a focus on punishment, health and dental care, and mental health care. Within each category, we elaborated on the problems we have observed and/or experienced, discussed the impacts these issues have on incarcerated women, and suggested some recommendations for change.

There are numerous impacts of the previous Conservative government's punitive agenda, which shaped criminal justice laws, policies and practices. This in turn resulted in many negative impacts on federally sentenced women. The most common issues that affect us due to the punitive prison environment include low self-esteem, stress, anxiety, fear, feeling disconnected from one's community, a sense of hopelessness, helplessness, worthlessness, isolation, alienation, frustration, oppression, inferiority, loneliness, distrust, feeling dehumanized, intimidated, and unable to function independently in the community. These negative impacts affect women emotionally, psychologically, physically, socially and spiritually.

Our overall recommendation is that CSC revisit and implement the recommendations outlined in *Creating Choices: The Report of the Task Force on Federally Sentenced Women* from 1990. This document was built on principles of empowerment, meaningful and responsible choices, respect and dignity, and a supportive environment. The six federal regional facilities for women across Canada were intended to be created, developed, and built on the principles and recommendations in the Creating Choices document. While their implementation was imperfect, the vision has been sidelined since 2006, when the Conservatives were elected to form a minority government. *Creating Choices* is a comprehensive study, which covers the issues we discussed in this paper.

ENDNOTES

[1] It should be recognized that the Office of the Correctional Investigator (OCI) is mandated to provide independent oversight of CSC. However, the CSC internal grievance process is self-regulated. Unlike the OCI whose powers extend only as far as making recommendations to CSC, the authority of those who respond to grievances is final. At the first level of the grievance process the authority is granted to the warden or manager in charge of the department being grieved and at the second level the authority is CSC's Commissioner.

[2] Interestingly, the Liberal government's latest act to amend the *CCRA* includes the following: "The Bill proposes to reinstate the CCRA guiding principle "least restrictive measures" in Part I of the Act. For consistency, the guiding principle of "least restrictive determination" would be reinstated to deal with conditional release in Part II of the Act" (Canada, 2017).

[3] According to Commissioners Directive 730 *Offender Program Assignments and Inmate Payments*, in effect 2016-08-22, paragraph 38: "The inmate's program/work supervisor will complete an assessment of the inmate's participation in the program assignment using the Inmate Performance Evaluation form (CSC/SCC 1138) at least once every six months, and any time the program assignment ends" (Correctional Service Canada, 2017a).

[4] As stated in Commissioners Directive 860 *Offenders Money*, section 6: "Inmates at pay level D to pay level A, as defined in CD 730 – Inmate Program Assignment and Payments, will normally contribute 22% of their CSC payment toward the cost of food and accommodation" and paragraph 16: "Inmates at pay level D to pay level A, as well as at the two allowance levels, as defined in CD 730 – Inmate Program Assignment and Payments, will normally contribute 8% of their CSC payment toward the cost of the administration of the inmate telephone system" (Correctional Service Canada, 2017b).

[5] According to a *Toronto Star* op-ed: "Prisoners who work for the profitable CORCAN program, producing products and services for government and private sector contracts in the areas of manufacturing, construction, textiles and other services such as laundry, earn an additional hourly "incentive" pay that is approximately $1.25 to $2.50 per hour on top of the flat daily rate" (Devellis, 2012).

[6] According to Commissioners Directive 768 *Institutional Mother Child Program* in effect 2016-04-18 (Correctional Service Canada, 2017c) substantial changes to that directive were made which restricted access to the program, specifically the following: "The eligibility criteria, documentation requirements and procedures for the residential program have been modified as it relates to inmate participants, babysitters and inmates residing in a housing unit where children reside on a full-

Journal of Prisoners on Prisons, Volume 26(1&2), 2017

time or part-time basis and "The child's upper age limit for the part-time residential program in the living units has been lowered (from 12 to 6 years of age)" (Correctional Service Canada, 2017d).

7 Kendall is a pseudonym used to protect the anonymity of the woman who shared her story with us.

8 Unless otherwise directed by the judge or in the case of those serving a life sentence, an individual is eligible to apply for parole at the 1/3 mark of the sentence. This is outlined in Commissioners Directive 712-1 *Pre-Release Decision Making* in effect 2017-01-23 (Correctional Service Canada, 2017e).

REFERENCES

Correctional Service Canada (2017a) *Commissioners Directive 730 Offender Program Assignments and Inmate Payments*, Ottawa. Retrieved from http://www.csc-scc. gc.ca/acts-and-regulations/730-cd-eng.shtml

Correctional Service Canada (2017b) *Commissioners Directive 860 Offenders Money*, Ottawa. Retrieved from http://www.csc-scc.gc.ca/lois-et-reglements/860-cd-eng. shtml

Correctional Service Canada (2017c) *Commissioners Directive 768 Institutional Mother Child Program*, Ottawa. Retrieved from http://www.csc-scc.gc.ca/politiques-et-lois/768-cd-eng.shtml

Correctional Service Canada (2017d) *Policy Bulletin 531*, Ottawa. Retrieved from http:// www.csc-scc.gc.ca/politiques-et-lois/531-pb-eng.shtml

Correctional Service Canada (2017e) *Commissioners Directive 712-1 Pre-Release Decision Making*, Ottawa. Retrieved from http://www.csc-scc.gc.ca/politiques-et-lois/712-1-cd-eng.shtml

Correctional Service Canada (1990) *Creating Choices: The Report of the Task Force on Federally Sentenced Women*, Ottawa.

Devellis, Leah (2012) "Plan to cut inmates' pay will accomplish nothing", *Toronto Star* – May 14. Retrieved from https://www.thestar.com/opinion/editorialopinion/2012/05/14/ plan_to_cut_inmates_pay_will_accomplish_nothing.html

Office of the Correctional Investigator (2015) *Annual Report of the Office of the Correctional Investigator 2014-2015*, Ottawa.

Public Safety Canada (2017, June 19) An Act to amend the Corrections and Conditional Release Act (CCRA) and the Abolition of Early Parole Act (AEPA). Retrieved from https://www.canada.ca/en/public-safety-canada/news/2017/06/ an_act_to_amend_thecorrectionsandconditionalreleaseactccraandthe. html?=undefined&wbdisable=true

Sampson, Robert, Serge Glascon, Ian Glen, Clarence Louis, and Sharon Rosenfeldt (2007) *A Roadmap to Strengthening Public Safety*, Ottawa: Minister of Public Works and Government Services.

À l'établissement pour femmes de Joliette nous avons vécu plusieurs changements sous l'ère Harper. L'ensemble des prisonniers ont perdu des privilèges importants qui facilitaient pourtant une réinsertion sociale optimale.

Voici une liste exhaustive de ce que nous avons perdu :

1. Le droit à la semi-liberté, accordée automatiquement au sixième de la sentence, pour une première infraction n'ayant aucune codification de violence et / ou d'autres restrictions.

2. Des placements extérieurs qui favorisaient la responsabilisation du prisonnier faisant en sorte de redonner à la communauté sous forme de bénévolat dans les centres d'hébergement ou tout autre organisme à but non-lucratif.

3. Beaucoup de permissions de sortie avec ou sans escorte. Ces sorties sont cruciales pour la réinsertion sociale. Elles favorisent le resserrement des liens familiaux, ainsi qu'avec la collectivité.

4. Le droit de fréquenter les institutions scolaires : CEGEP et université extérieurs à l'établissement de détention. Le résultat est que le manque de scolarisation diminue grandement les chances de placement communautaire pour les prisonniers.

5. Les prisonniers âgés n'ont plus le droit de recevoir la pension de vieillesse du gouvernement. Le résultat est qu'elles n'ont aucun revenu pour subsister à l'intérieur des murs et doivent travailler au-delà de 65 ans.

6. 30% de nos salaires ont été amputés, malgré l'augmentation du prix de tous les produits d'usage. De plus, les salaires des prisonniers n'ont pas été indexés depuis les années 80. Avec notre salaire net, nous devons acheter notre cantine (nos produits essentiels de base et d'hygiène), les articles du catalogue, les cartes d'appel (au coût de 0.57$ pour un appel local ou 0.11$ par minute pour un appel à l'extérieur de Joliette), les articles pour les loisirs et également contribuer à la caisse du Comité des détenus.

7. Plusieurs des produits que nous retrouvions sur notre liste d'épicerie que l'on pouvait se procurer avec l'allocation de 35.00$ par semaine ne sont désormais accessibles que par notre cantine.

8. Nous sommes maintenant contraintes d'acheter nos vêtements et autres produits de remplacement dans le catalogue carcéral seulement. Le fournisseur vend des vêtements de piètre qualité au prix des grandes chaines de magasin. L'achat par catalogue est tout à fait inaccessible entre autres en raison des prix imposés et du délai de réception de la marchandise (environ trois mois). Notre pouvoir d'achat est très limité par le fait que plusieurs femmes ne peuvent pas travailler, ne reçoivent pas d'argent de l'extérieur et que le système de paye pour prisonniers n'a pas été indexé à l'inflation depuis les années 1980. Notamment pour les femmes qui gagnent ou perdent du poids et aussi que les longues sentences, il est pratiquement impossible d'arriver à économiser assez pour renouveler ou remplacer les articles de vêtement ou de base. Il en résulte assurément une grande perte d'estime de soi ce qui crée un cercle vicieux auquel nous sommes soumises.

9. Le délai pour l'obtention d'une suspension du casier judiciaire (demande de pardon) est passé de 5 à 10 ans après l'expiration de la peine, soit le double, pour plusieurs infractions. Pour une personne seule, il est très difficile – voire même presque impossible – avec un casier judiciaire de combler ses besoins de base comme l'obtention d'un logement, de crédit et même l'assurance.

10. Les sentences vie ont perdu le droit à une révision judiciaire après 15 ans.

11. Les programmes de mise en liberté graduelle et structurée qui sont immanquablement la première étape de la réinsertion sociale dans la collectivité, sont devenus plus difficilement accessibles durant les mandats du gouvernement Harper.

12. Avec toutes les coupures budgétaires effectuées depuis 2006, nous devons dorénavant défrayer les coûts de la caisse du Comité des détenues, ainsi que les coûts de remplacement et d'entretien de l'ameublement qui constitue selon nous la base de notre maintien d'un milieu décent :
    - Congélateur
    - Télévision
    - Machine à coudre
    - Table pique-nic

- Ameublement extérieur des unités pour les visites familiales privées
13. Également, l'approvisionnement de plus en plus difficile de fruits et légumes frais, ainsi que les nombreuses coupures de plusieurs items sur notre liste d'épicerie nous ont forcées à restreindre drastiquement notre alimentation.

Il est essentiel que le gouvernement fédéral et le Service correctionnel du Canada renverse les changements notés ci-dessus afin d'améliorer les conditions de vie des prisonniers et les résultats d'incarcération qui en découlent pour la société.

Grand Valley Institution for Women
Anonymous Prisoner 1

Honourable Prime Minister Trudeau needs to bring back Accelerated Parole Review, which was eliminated by the previous federal government. This is a very important law and policy that must be in place to allow certain first-time federal prisoners to re-enter society at one-sixth of their sentences so that they can avoid the damage of incarceration, which undermines community safety.

The harsh punishments and mandatory minimum sentences also need to be changed, with sentencing based on an individual's offences, as well as a close examination of the conditions that contributed to their acts where relevant, including childhood abuse and suffering. These individuals need love, self-care and inner healing.

Grand Valley Institution for Women
Josephine Pelletier

It is my hope that Prime Minister Justin Trudeau will follow through with his "promise" to Indigenous people across Canada, which includes seeing through an inquiry into missing and murdered Indigenous women. I have personally been a walking target on the streets and in every jail that I have been in. Therefore, I know first-hand how discrimination and violence affect people like me, as an Indigenous person, a woman, a mother, a citizen, a daughter, a prisoner, a sister, a friend. The list goes on. In 2006, I was made an example of as "a young woman". I was 21, naïve, with an ego bigger than the men that I grew up with. I was facing a dangerous offender application while I was on remand for 4.5 years at Pinegrove in Saskatchewan. I was on segregation status for 18 months and what they call "red-card" status.

In Pinegrove Correctional Centre, all my experiences over many years almost left me for dead in a lonely, cold, isolated cell feeling suicidal and hopeless. These past three years have been a wake-up call to my spirit. My sister and father passed away three months prior to one another. They were my only support throughout my life. I believe that I died inside when I was denied the opportunity to attend, not only their funerals, but those of all of my relatives. Not once have I been granted an escort to attend any of my family's burials. Yes, it killed me inside, but as a spiritual woman, the belief I have is that they are all around me. This has helped me spiritually, but has also left me painfully grieving to hear their voices, see their faces. Despite this, I am determined to make it in this life, to carry on their legacy.

Once in the federal penitentiary system, I experienced numerous changes as part of the Harper government's "punishment agenda". The negative changes I have been subject to occurred as much of Correctional Service Canada's budget was diverted to expanding its capacity to confine prisoners and cut thereafter include:

1. Malnutrition for maximum-security prisoners because our food is all processed and we are given powdered milk with no calcium.
2. There is little to no health care and mental health nurses in a maximum-security setting.
3. There is limited access to programming because of a lack of facilitators.
4. The further pay deductions impacts our communication with society because with the little pay we get every two weeks we have

to make choices between things like purchasing hygiene items or using the money to call family or get stamps to correspond to help time go by. I usually put money on my phone card to call my son and the remainder goes towards my hygiene.

5.   There are no life skills training for maximum-security prisoners, impacting my rehabilitation and reintegration into society as a Canadian citizen.

6.   Elders rarely enter the maximum-security settings, which undermines our efforts to connect to our culture and spirituality.

Many aspects of the previous government's punishment agenda were unconstitutional, pushing prisoners to make a decision between life and death. I chose a life sentence in a lonely isolated cell. What I would like to see moving forward is that Mr. Trudeau follow through on his promise to Indigenous people to seek out and do something about the root cause of this problematic factor that is killing my people every-day in and outside of prisons. We are not supported or believed in by this discriminating judicial system and the Government of Canada more broadly. I believe that I will always remain a walking target, because I am a talking target behind these walls. I will not stop! I have written numerous letters without receiving any responses, no real action, not being respected.

POST-SCRIPT

With a lot of things going on, contributing to this collection was a priority to me because Harper's government had really made my life a living hell. Indigenous women continue to be overrepresented in federal penitentiaries today, a deplorable issue that seems to be dismissed or ignored. I am so tired and afraid that CSC is going to kill me and my death is going to be ruled off as a natural cause from a heart attack or a suicide. I am afraid to tell anyone how I feel in this place because they are not here to help me, they are here to do their job. Five days ago, I told the staff and my Parole Officer that I wanted to kill myself. I received an institutional charge for disrespecting him because he heard me say something else. The system is simply not setup to help people.

S erving a life sentence, I have been fortunate to have the privilege of gaining many skills and teachings here at Fraser Valley Institution (FVI) due to my willingness and open-minded, forward thinking. I was held in a remand centre for nearly two years before I got sentenced. I then sat in max here at FVI for two years on the Lifer two-year rule before coming out to medium population. Up to that point, there was only dialectical behavioural therapy[1] and school available in the max, which were both certificate programs. I had two pipe ceremonies in the two years I was in max. I was fortunate to come into this institution culturally strong, and forwarded my teaching and our way of life to others. I had anxiety and headaches due to lack of socializing when I came out in the medium population. With the help of other ladies here I was able to overcome this.

The ladies that remain in max now feel they are not having their spiritual needs met by the Elder that is in the position to assist them. We have had changes in elders since I have been here. The Inmate Committee still receives complaints on the lack of services available from the Elder (e.g. not being available when a crisis approaches, no clear communication, stating there would be a sweat or pipe ceremony and not following through, not giving the max ladies a schedule to follow, no access to drumming or singing, making appointments and not showing up, no follow-ups, lack of respect and communication, causing the ladies to become spiritually isolated). There are ladies that are culturally strong, we make our way back to the max to do drumming and singing, as well as teach them songs and aspects of our own rooted teachings. We believe this is the turning point to become grounded and the assistance of the Elder, who is under-resourced, is detrimental.

Our population is fast becoming increasingly Indigenous, the majority of whom are culturally weak. It is hard to witness. Many ladies lack social skills. We have also noticed language barriers, which is a form of disability in mainstream approaches. This leaves the unfortunate ones in the dark and misunderstood.

We have had many complaints on the lack of awareness for the ladies regarding the mental health needs that the majority of the population have to deal with. We have also noticed the lack of approach towards dementia and elderly care. We have a number of older ladies and they are not respected in that manner.

There is peer support training that was put in effect after the Ashley Smith recommendations. This is a half-day paid position. More trades training should be available that would benefit the ladies if pursued. This would assist them to become productive members of society.

The population was not too sure on how to approach submissions for this collection that is to be submitted to parliament, as this is the very first connection we have made with our government. There have been numerous incidents that have occurred and some of the ladies are somewhat hesitant to share. Although we had the privilege to share our stories and our experiences with Kim Pate, prior to her becoming a Senator, and the Canadian Association of Elizabeth Fry Societies, there remains a lot that needs to be done to improve things at FVI, which have started to change since Justin Trudeau was elected our Prime Minister.

The max has changed how they allow the ladies to integrate into medium population. They used to have levels from 1 to 4. Now it is levels from 1-3. We are now seeing more ladies going on ETAs (escorted temporary absences) and day parole today than before. Section 84 which allows Indigenous prisoners to be held in community facilities[2] is being brought forward and explained to us.[3] This was not the case in the past. We are now hearing of more work releases and limited day parole granted for treatment purposes in the community.

In the minimum that houses twenty ladies, we have heard a lot of complaints about the lack of work resources. We had ladies come back into medium population from minimum to work in the kennels and the kitchen commissary. We continuously hear of how boring it is over there in the minimum.

We are now finding our own voices and are grateful to have been heard. We become strong as we come together in solidarity.

ENDNOTES

[1]   Please see Blanchette, K., J. Flight, P. Verbrugge, R. Gobeil and K. Taylor (2011) *Dialectical Behaviour Therapy within a Women's Structured Living Environment* (R-241), Ottawa: Correctional Service Canada.

[2]   The *Corrections and Conditional Release Act* (CCRA) which states in section 84, "If an inmate expresses an interest in being released into an aboriginal community, the Service shall, with the inmate's consent, give the aboriginal community (an) adequate notice of the inmate's parole review or their statutory release date, as the

case may be; and (b) an opportunity to propose a plan for the inmate's release and integration into that community".

[3] It should be noted that According to the most recent Departmental Performance Report for the Correctional Service of Canada, CSC (2016) self-reported that "The percentage of Aboriginal offenders with CCRA section 84 release plans did not meet the expected result".

REFERENCES

Corrections and Conditional Release Act (S.C. 1992, c.20) Retrieved from http://laws-lois.justice.gc.ca/eng/acts/C-44.6/section-84.html

Correctional Service Canada (2016) Departmental Performance Report, Ottawa: Minister of Public Safety and Emergency Preparedness. Retrieved from http://www.csc-scc.gc.ca/005/007/092/005007-4500-2015-2016-eng.pdf

Fraser Valley Institution for Women
Stephanie Deschene

My name is Stephanie Deschene. I am a 26-year-old, third-time Indigenous federal prisoner currently serving time in Fraser Valley Institution for Women (FVI). I was incarcerated in September 2016 for property related crimes, at which time I was approximately 20 weeks pregnant.

During my time in a remand centre in Prince George I made the decision to transfer down to the Lower Mainland in hopes that I could be a part of the Mother-Child Program at Alouette Correctional Center for Women (ACCW). The morning I departed for ACCW (at 28 weeks pregnant), I was made to wear both leg-shackles, as well as hand-cuffs. When I gently protested, I was subsequently called very rude and derogatory names, and told to shut up.

When I arrived at ACCW I was met by an official in upper manager who proceeded to ask me questions related to an incident that happened, at that time, eight years ago where I had been involved in a staff assault and was unlawfully at large. She asked me questions like "why would you even bother coming here, don't you know we will just make this an uphill battle for you?" and "are you forgetting what happened last time you were here?" Now, I understand the seriousness of what happened and I did take full responsibility. I was sentenced to more time for those charges and now, many years later, they were still trying to punish me further by denying me the opportunity to be with my child after he was born.

Three days after I arrived at ACCW, I put in an application for the Mother-Child Program (MCP) in medium-security. Two days after I submitted the application, I had a programs staff bring it back to me telling me "why bother? It is just going to be denied". I submitted it anyways and had my application "disappear". I felt so alone, and frustrated. I could not understand why I would not be allowed this chance.

Due to my lack of forward progress in ACCW, I decided to plead out early in hopes that I could go to a federal penitentiary where I would be more likely to keep my son once he was born. I arrived at FVI at 34 weeks pregnant with a five-year sentence. I was shocked, but not surprised, that FVI decided to place me in maximum-security as well. I was placed in maximum-security for reasons such as having an *allegation* for assault in October 2015 and being in an abusive relationship, of which my baby's father was the aggressor.

The institution and my case management team could have made an executive decision to allow me an opportunity to be in medium-security with a behaviour contract based on positive behaviour and obvious dedication to

40

changing my life for the better in hopes of not being separated from my child once he was born. There are options offered to women here that go in and out of segregation (e.g. for fights, drug involvement, suicidal behaviours, etc.) that would have been appropriate given my circumstance and would have mitigated any alleged risks my case management team identified. Yet I was not offered any such options.

Prior to my son's birth, I asked to have my friend send me a couple things for my son for when he left the hospital and was told by the institution that I was *not allowed* because I was quote "not in the Mother Child Program (MCP)". It is the understanding and direction of the Correctional Investigator that *I am* in fact in the MCP, just not the *residential* portion and should be treated as such. To this day, I have still not started working with the MCP co-ordinator.

I went into labour on 13 January 2017. The day after the birth of my son the staff received direction that I was to be shackled and cuffed. How was I supposed to breastfeed, hold, and cuddle my son safely? Their lack of compassion baffles me.

I was informed by my social worker and the institution that once my son was born I would be able to pump breast milk and send it out to him. However, the day after I returned from the hospital I was pulled into a meeting with my Institutional Parole Officer (IPO) and informed that, in fact, I would *not* be allowed to provide breast milk for my son due to the possibility of "contamination", along with the fact that the ministry would want weekly periodic urinalysis (due to past involvement back in 2012, in the institutional drug subculture), which CSC would not provide me with. It is my understanding that women in the MCP could be provided such testing when required, yet FVI was and *is* still treating me as if I am not a part of the program.

Due to the lack of knowledge and co-ordination between both the institution and the Ministry of Children and Family Development on how to deal with mothers who are incarcerated in maximum-security, I have seen my son only *three* times since he was born two and a half months ago. It is a very good thing that I had supportive women living on my unit during this time, because if I become depressed there is no actual psychological help for women to access unless they are suicidal, due to lack of funding. Women who are trying to work past trauma and create healthy outlets are told they will be put on a waitlist. Should we not be *preventing* suicidal thoughts and actions not *treating* them once they happen?

I had to request my six-week post-partum medical check-up. The good news is that I am supported by my social worker to have my son here once I get to medium-security and apply for the residential portion of the MCP. At the time of writing, my security review had been in the works for two weeks. Yet due to ridiculously long-time allowances to complete such reports (i.e. 30 days), I must wait. Every day spent not having that report finished is another day I am away from my son, and another day that I lose to bond with him.

During this federal sentence, I have not received any bad logs, warnings or charges. I am involved with many pro-social activities in the institution, yet they treat me as if I still do not deserve to be in medium with my son. Keeping my child with me is not only the best thing for me and my son's relationship, but it is best for my family and my community as having him here with me means it is less likely that my son will end up in the system like so many other children of Indigenous prisoners. Not only would there be less chance that I re-offend post release, but there would be less chance that my cycle of drug abuse and crime will repeat itself in the next generation.

It has been my understanding that incarcerated pregnant women ought to be in a safe and supportive environment where they feel encouraged to be a good parent. The sad fact is that I do not feel as if I was supported or encouraged in my parenting role very much at all. I was not offered any of the basic courtesies that mothers in medium or minimum are afforded. I believe that CSC should ensure all its staff are familiarized and well-informed regarding all aspects of the MCP, as it is such a vital program to women prisoners. Pregnant women and women intending to have custody of their children should be managed according to the least restrictive measures as it relates to *relevant* safety and security concerns of the institution. In the case that another pregnant woman be made to stay in maximum-security I believe it is imperative that CSC staff be trained on how to respectfully deal with pregnant and post-partum women prisoners in *all* situations and security levels, not simply medium- and minimum-security women.

It is important that programs staff, upper management, and the identified MCP co-ordinator be trained on the non-residential portions of the program that, in fact, apply to women such as myself (i.e. non-residential portions of the MCP that provide different means to maintain the mother-child bond during incarceration such as the use of ETA or UTA for family contact/parental responsibilities, private family visits, recording of stories, pumping and storing of breast milk, etc.). *All* women should be given equal opportunity to be with and maintain healthy bonds between themselves and their children.

There are a number of significant issues that prisoners face that should be changed. I have included the most significant to me.

The *grievance procedure* is too lengthy and is one-sided in terms of who holds the power to extend times to reply. Prisoners usually get only about twenty days to submit or reply within the grievance process. The institution can extend as much and as often as it wants. Obviously, this is an exceedingly unfair manner in which to conduct conflict resolution. The party with the most power has the most lenient of timelines. This is why grievances can take as long as two years to complete! Further, I am always within the system at every step of the grievance process when it should be someone independent from the institution deciding these matters.

Private Family Visits should not depend on participation in programming when the program content demands that if you do not admit to the crime for which you have been convicted you cannot complete the program. Moreover, you are given a bad report and suspended from the program. This results in a very bad report being put on your file. If you are attempting to appeal your conviction, this takes away the ability to complete a program. It puts a prisoner in an impossible catch-22 situation.

The *wages* are far below minimum community standards. What is even more unfair is that because I would not admit my guilt, my wages were dropped to E pay from C pay[1] because I could not participate in programs since I am appealing and cannot be forced to admit guilt.

Medical and dental are urgent issues. I have waited for fifteen months to get a crown for my two front teeth that I broke while eating a meal. The other tooth is loose now. The only offer from the dentist was extractions and false-teeth. The alternative was to pay for it myself at a cost of $6,000.00 a tooth. I need four root canals as well. Further, in the rear of my mouth again only extractions were offered. Paying for it myself was the only option. As my pay was reduced to E pay, the lowest (about $2.50 per day), it will be difficult to afford this.

The *removal of my old age pension* was unwarranted. I believe it is against the *Charter of Rights and Freedoms* to take it away. Also, I still pay taxes.[2]

Since my income from outside sources is *less than a livable income*, I should be getting the $50.00 refund three times a year for HST for purchases that are taxable within the penitentiary. This includes vitamins, personal items and so on. We pay to have such amenities as cable, phone use and the institution welfare fund.

We need to repeal all the detrimental laws, policies and practices CSC initiated while Prime Minister Stephen Harper and his successive governments were in power. These laws have made prisoners lives unbearable and do not contribute to our rehabilitation. I hope that the current federal government will look over these urgent issues and address them in a manner that assists us in changing the system quickly for the benefit of all Canadians.

ENDNOTES

[1] According to CD 730 *Offender Program Assignments and Inmate Payments*: "Inmate payments or allowances will normally be awarded based on the following daily rates (see Annex B): payment level A ($6.90), payment level B ($6.35), payment level C ($5.80), payment level D ($5.25), allowance ($2.50), basic allowance ($1.00). Moreover, Pay reviews and decisions to increase or decrease an inmate's pay level should be based on the following as defined in Annex B: (a) attendance and punctuality (b) *performance in meeting the expectations of the program assignment, including interpersonal relationships, attitude, behaviour, effort, motivation, productivity and responsibility* (c) involvement in his/her Correctional Plan, including level of accountability, motivation and engagement, pursuant to CD 710-1 - Progress Against the Correctional Plan (d) overall institutional behaviour, including conviction(s) for disciplinary offences, positive or refused urinalysis, etc. (e) affiliation with a security threat group pursuant to CD 568-3 - Identification and Management of Security Threat Groups (f) placement in a specialized unit (Special Handling Unit, segregation for disciplinary reasons, etc.) (g) duration of time inmate has been at his/her current pay level" (Correctional Service Canada, 2017).

[2] It should be noted that prisoners do not pay a traditional government tax on the income that they receive for the work that they carry out in institutions. However, when they make purchases at canteen or through the institutional purchasing program, they pay taxes on purchases and are also subject to a 22% "food and accommodation" tax and 8% charge to cover the costs of "administration" for the "inmate telephone system".

REFERENCES

Correctional Service Canada (2017) *Commissioners Directive 730 Offender Program Assignments and Inmate Payments*, Ottawa. Retrieved from http://www.csc-scc. gc.ca/acts-and-regulations/730-cd-eng.shtml

With many changes over the last decade, I have come to notice the following:

- The staff are more distant and not as encouraging;
- We have on paper, but really do not have in practice, a case management "team" to discuss where we are, what is expected and where we are going;
- We have lost our town hall meetings, which were our chance to interact with and ask questions to the warden;
- We have lost our voice and are warned that filing a grievance can have repercussions;
- We have lost triplicate request form,[1] which we once used for our protection;
- We have lost everything positive for Lifers (e.g. meetings in the community on Friday nights, links with folks who would come in to assist us with any information we needed information on, support groups, monthly meetings for Lifers, and access to newsletters like *Out of Bounds* magazine or *Cell Count*);
- We have lost recognition and ability to engage in fundraising to support different committees;
- We have lost the incentive to work and work for higher pay;
- We have lost access to regular and proper dental care, to see a psychologist, and to be able to work full-time;
- We have lost the ability to shop from a retailer and purchase magazine subscriptions;
- Work release is rare now due to (un)availability of staff;
- ETAs (escorted temporary absences) are being cut back; and
- We have lost funding for programs, recreation opportunities and staff to help with positive hobbies, a full-time librarian, and updated software on the computers.

As a Lifer doing a long sentence it is not so much the sentence that is troubling, but rather the negative, lonely and hopeless environment with day-to-day inconsistent treatment from the staff. I have personally found doing my first eight years in EIFW – Edmonton Institution for Women – often thought to be one of the worst facilities for incarcerated women in

Canada, to be the most encouraging and positive, and it taught me to stand up for myself in a positive and constructive way. I was meek, timid, shy, and scared to speak-up when I first came to prison because of the life I had led and thanks to the staff in Edmonton, they taught me how to use my voice, be assertive and stand up for myself. The staff taught me that my ideas and thoughts did matter, encouraged me to speak up for what I wanted and also that I was in charge of the path I took. Back then, I was able to meet with a psychologist regularly for my mental health and see a psychiatrist every three months to ensure my medications were helping. I was also seen regularly by a dentist and a doctor, while being encouraged to socialize through group activities such as card games held in the gym, scavenger hunts or simple hobby crafts that were held every Sunday to help us find a positive way to pass our time. There were also socials that the whole institution would partake in, bringing us all together where we could bring in our approved family and friends to show how we have grown and are working in concert. Staff would come through the houses for their regular walks, but take the time and talk with us, and ask how we were doing. They would share with us something they experienced or try to help if we had a dilemma, treating us like we are human, never looking down on us. I knew who most staff were and their position and if I had a question, I was able to ask that staff member directly. If they were unable to talk at that time, which rarely happened, I must say, they would come back in a bit, but either way you got an answer to your question rather fast and no question was regarded as less important. They also held monthly meetings in the board room to talk with a representative from each house to bring questions forward, address any issues girls were having and bring forward the problems staff were having. I speak highly of EIFW because it was an institution that strived to do its best, willing to help us to become a better individual, with staff that cared.

In 2011, I came out here to FVI – Fraser Valley Institution – where everything I had come to know, was no longer accepted. I was no longer allowed to talk with staff members as I had done in Edmonton or ask questions as I had for years. I was referred to fill out a request and it will be looked at, when they had time. I am left to feel conflicted about what I learned in Edmonton, which made me feel empowered and strong. In contrast, my whole life has prepared me for what prison has become because I am once again made to feel I have no voice, no choice and that I do not matter. I am no longer able to see a psychologist because I am told "I am not a high need", even though I told them I felt I need to see one because I was struggling day-to-day. I also asked and put in a request to see a psychiatrist regarding the medications I was on, but was told once again "I was not in need and the doctor would not help me". I have to say though, the doctor – when I have seen her – has done her best to help me and I do appreciate all she has done, especially given that mental health issues are on top of all the other issues she monitors.

In the last six years, my mental health has taken a turn for the worst, where I have had many breakdowns with the feeling of hopelessness. I struggle to continue most days, suffering in silence due to the cut backs and the fact that there is no one to help me. I have come to learn I also suffer from PTSD, I have developed a tremor, but nothing more will be done other than to prescribe me another medication. I have also developed a degenerating neck C3 to C7. I am given a pill to deal with the day-to-day pain, rather than a proper pillow, which I think would be more helpful than a pill. Before prison, I was in great health and took care of myself, but how are we to take care of ourselves when we are not given the opportunities or resources? I have had a tooth ache for the last three months and I am told, once again, that I will have to wait due to the lack of funding. I have become a burden on society with my many ailments that continue to grow and get worse over time. Before coming to prison, I was a productive member of society, and I believed in the justice system and that people were treated with dignity and rehabilitated.

Since being incarcerated for many years now, I have yet to see how prisons have moved forward in helping people and giving them a fair opportunity to improve their lives, to become a better individual when getting back out into society. I get that we have a punitive system and we still resort to the old ways of "what happens here, stays here", but we need to move past that thinking. People, who have the mentality of "lock them up and throw away the key" are doing society no favours, because how are we to get out and lead a better, more productive life without skills and training? I had worked for many years before coming to prison and have now become unemployable due to my lack of skills being away from the rest of society.

I used to feel good (i.e. in EIFW) when working to give back to society and felt like I was contributing in some way, for as they say, "idle hands do the devil's work". Unfortunately, I am told they do not do that out here in FVI, due to cut backs and that they are unable to pay people. I am lost and fail to understand how even something as simple as giving back to our communities has to be taken away from us due to "cut backs" from the previous government that still persist today. We must remember that prisoners are not making a great deal to begin with and pay back thirty percent of what little is made, thanks again to the previous government. We have not had a raise in wages for decades. Yet, I know myself like many others live off what we make in here, contributing to my struggles for phone money to stay in contact with what family I have left, while trying to save money for when I get out. The prison has become a place for us to just be housed, cut-off from society to complete our core programs until our time comes when we get out.

Now we are told that the Trudeau government wants to make improvements in the federal penitentiary system and wants to make a difference. So far, the two-year rule for Lifers in max is no longer mandatory, while the use of segregation is declining. As a Lifer who has seen the loss of many things over the years, I feel the importance of a positive, encouraging and strong rehabilitation system would be more effective than what we have now. Is prison not meant to not just punish us for our crime, but to give us the opportunity to live a better and healthier life upon release? I am also hoping to see the new government put something in place for the women's minimum. The only difference between medium and minimum right now is a fence. The minimums are segregated to a building, with nowhere to go and nothing to do, where I fail to see anything positive, all due to the loss of funding from the government for the women's prisons. I will hope the minimum prisoners will be treated fairly, rewarded for good behaviour and encouraged to be part of the community they will be entering. I truly hope that the Trudeau government is serious about change, but that change cannot come soon enough in a system so broken.

ENDNOTES

[1] Triplicate request form refers to "inmate requests", which had an original copy with two color coded carbon copies, one yellow and one pink. The original would get placed on the file, the yellow would be used for circulation and the pink form could be kept by the prisoner so that they had a record of having submitted a request that is to be returned within 14 days.

TOUGH ON CRIME?

The Harper government's "tough on crime" campaign negatively affected many basic aspects of incarceration. Suddenly, earned pay levels were dropped because a prisoner would not "confess" to a crime, even if appealing it and therefore the prisoner would be deemed "not accountable". There were also severe cut backs to health and dental care. Even important, minor privileges were removed like the ordering out for food, paid for by the prisoners themselves and the use of the barbeque every weekend was reduced to once a month. There are no longer any full-time librarians to help with the needed legal research, obtaining books or even the stocking of new, necessary books, and the librarian's hours were reduced to the equivalent of one day a week. Instead of being able to order necessary supplies from the community so that the variety and the prices were much better, prisoners can only order from a national catalogue that has a very limited stock and does not meet their needs. The prices are also exorbitant. Fundraising has become so restrictive with rules that do not allow viewing before buying or discretion as to what sells best (e.g. ice cream, blizzards, alarm clocks etc.). Furthermore, all food items being brought in must be pre-packaged and store bought. These are just some of the salient points. Below, I have itemized the main issues and offered a solution where possible.

Fundraisers
The fundraisers have changed so dramatically that it is virtually impossible to make a profit. The restrictions from National Headquarters (NHQ) do not make any sense, but we must adhere to them or not run the fundraiser. Items that bring in the most money, like ice cream, are not allowed to be included. This restricts the ability to make any profit. All of the fundraising items must be sold before announcing the next. This limits profits again. Pre-packaged food is all that is allowed at any social or fundraiser. This means that we do not have the fresh, home cooked food that will allow us to turn a profit for charity. There is a strict rule that there is to be "no food out" at the socials and the fundraisers. A lot of food is thrown out, instead of being sold and taken to a house. This is an outrageous waste and a huge loss of income. There has been such a reduction in fundraising monies that FVI can no longer send out money to worthy charities. The solution is to

give the discretion back to the Prisoner Committee about fundraising and about socials. Food should be allowed out of the socials or fundraisers so that profit is made and there is no wasting of expensive food.

"Accountability"

Programs officers and facilitators have now become the new judge and jury for those convicted. Prisoners have been told that they must "confess" to a crime or they cannot complete a program as they are not being "accountable". Yet, another concern has arisen regarding programs. Recently, a prisoner was granted the right to take the program without having to confess to the crime. The discriminatory application of Commissioners Directive 730 *Offender Program Assignment and Payments*,[1] section 35 has to be changed (CD 730 is linked to CD 710-1 *Progress Against the Correctional Plan*,[2] Annex C where "accountability" amounts to a confession of the crime). There have been no changes to these CDs. Many prisoners had their pay reduced when CD 730 and CD 710-1 required this "accountability". There needs to be a uniform application of these CDs. One prisoner cannot be required to confess and the next one does not. Obviously, prisoners would prefer not to have accountability linked to a confession or crime cycle. However, if it is to be linked to this, then everyone must be required to adhere to this standard. Exceptions cannot be made for one or two people. Further, the pay level should not be linked to the "accountability". Many prisoners worked hard to raise their pay levels, only to have them reduced because they would not confess. This is patently unfair.

Dental Care

Standard dental care should be returned. Prisoners used to get cleanings once a year, fillings as needed and other dental care. Now prisoners do not get cleanings, fillings without mercury, crowns or periodontal care. Prisoners have only substandard dentists come in who are only allowed to work about 4 hours every six weeks. Lifers will be toothless soon. Basic dental care should be a given. After that, long-term prisoners may elect to pay into dental plans. This should be an option to cover most of the dental expenses.

Prisoner Pay

There used to be incentive wages of about $20.00 a day for some construction jobs. Now we are paid well below minimum wage for every job (approximately 41 cents an hour after deductions and hours worked). How can any of the prisoners afford basic dental care and supplements (especially for the aging population)? Prisoners must pay community prices, but are not paid community minimum wage. The solution is simply to raise the pay to a minimum level so that prisoners can take care of themselves and some of their family members. It should be noted there has not been a pay increase since the 1980s.

Libraries

In the past, there has been a full-time librarian who helped obtain legal texts and other needed books. However, now the librarian is limited to essentially one day a week. This does not allow her to help any prisoner with access to legal materials. The library does not house the necessary texts and case law so that appellate work can be done. With the severe cuts in legal aid, this raises the specter of justice denied. No one can do the legal work required or hire someone if there are no funds to do so. The solution is to pay for the necessary legal texts and case law access and the practice guides so that justice can prevail even after conviction. Having a full-time librarian is a necessary aid as well.

Computers

Prisoners were allowed their own computer in their rooms. This is no longer permitted. It is important to do legal work at every hour that a prisoner can and with the necessary privacy to keep the privilege intact. The necessary safeguards on computers are inexpensive and easy to place on the computer.

Purchasing

Prisoners used to be allowed to order from a variety of stores in the community. Pricing was affordable and the necessary items available. Prisoners must now order from the national prisoner catalogue, which is understocked and overpriced. The prisoner's needs cannot be met on this basis. Some prisoners need supplements that will save their eyesight, for example, and cannot get these needed items. In the past, prisoners could get hair dyes and other hair supplies. Some institutions still allow this, but not Fraser Valley Institution for Women (FVI). At FVI, prisoners must pay a hair dresser to do the coloring and cuts. The prices are exorbitant. There is enough depression and lack of self-esteem in just dealing with the daily issues at FVI. Prisoners should be able to purchase their own coloring supplies and apply it themselves.

Accommodation
Prisoners' room and board costs now cut into our minuscule pay that was setup to take those costs into consideration. We are also charged for telephone administration. This is a huge loss of money that has detrimental impacts on our lives.

Disciplinary Measures
The charging process has become harsher. In the past, informal resolutions were tried first. However, now prisoners are usually being charged without first a verbal warning, then a written one and finally the charge. The process should revert to the informal resolution process with a charge being at the end of the line, not at the beginning as it is in most instances.

Food
The per diem for the grocery food is still at $36.05 after approximately 34 years, while the cost of food has risen substantially. The per diem should be raised to about $50.00 per week. More healthy food should also be returned to the grocery list (e.g. like mixed nuts, popcorn for snacks, almond milk without the corn syrup, etc).

Medical Privacy
Medical privilege was something that seems to previously have been safe guarded. It is not now. CD 566 *Security* Escorts,[3] states that guards are not to be in the operating room or in the medical office when someone is discussing her health issue with the doctor (only sight of the prisoner is required so that medical privilege remains intact). Yet, the head of FVI claims that doctors will not meet without the guards in the room. This has not been the experience of prisoners at FVI. Doctors have even asked for the privacy to maintain medical privilege and the guards have erroneously replied that they cannot leave the room. To honour the CD's intention of maintaining medical privilege, the guards must stay outside the room during consultations and leave the operating room once the prisoner is anaesthetized. Only doctors who agree to this can be hired so FVI's own rules are not violated.

Prisoner Relations

It seems that prisoners in the past were allowed to share their clothes and food. Prisoners face charges if they do that now. They should be allowed to give each other clothing, food or any allowed item without fearing charges. Many prisoners do not have money or family to help them buy clothes, canteen or health and hygiene products. The institution says it does not want this because of possible bullying. The obvious solution is to have the prisoners wishing to share, sign a form in front of an admissions and discharge staff member to make sure it is consensual. The way it presently is, the institution is the bully, and prisoners are not allowed to act humanely with each other.

Material and Entertainment

Previously, an organization named LINC, was allowed to provide televisions to those who could not afford them. Under the Harper government, this charitable and needed act was not allowed. Prisoners must now purchase a television that is about $200.00 or more. A television is a means to stay connected to the world in such an isolated place as prison. Few want to risk being harmed by sitting out in the common areas. Further, a room is a place to get away from everything. A television in one's own room is absolutely necessary to maintain mental health and stay connected in some sense to the outside world.

CONCLUSION

It is obvious from the items discussed above that the Harper government's "tough on crime" changes created substantial hardship for those in prison. In everyday life, it is the small, continuous deprivations that increasingly take away any sense of life being fair or worthwhile. Deprivations do not create better citizens. They do not "rehabilitate". As in the community, where fair play, kindness and human decency create stronger alliances with doing the "right thing", so it is in prison. The highlighted changes that fail to do anything but increase the likelihood of recidivism must be revoked and more humane measures must be put in their place. Everyone, including society in general, will benefit greatly.

ENDNOTES

[1] Please see: Correctional Service Canada (2017a) *Commissioners Directive 730 Offender Program Assignments and Inmate Payments*, Ottawa. Retrieved from http://www.csc-scc.gc.ca/acts-and-regulations/730-cd-eng.shtml

[2] Please see: Correctional Service Canada (2017b) *Commissioners Directive 710-1 Progress Against the Correctional Plan*, Ottawa. Retrieved from http://www.csc-scc.gc.ca/lois-et-reglements/710-1-cd-eng.shtml

[3] Please see: Correctional Service Canada (2017c) *Commissioners Directive 566-6 Security Escorts*, Ottawa. Retrieved from http://www.csc-scc.gc.ca/lois-et-reglements/566-6-cd-eng.shtml

Dispatches from the Atlantic Region

Dorchester Institution
Daryl Haug

My recent attempt at attaining sufficient access to amenities for the research and processing of legal proceedings have been thwarted. Without sufficient access to a computer, computer programs, photocopying, legal research material, and the like I cannot defend my rights as a human being. I have also lost all arguments and opportunities to seek legal redress due to lack of access.

This has been an issue in all institutions I have been detained in over the past thirteen years. I did purchase a personal computer in 2015 so I could have it in my cell to do my legal work. This has been refused and I am forced to use Correctional Service Canada (CSC) supplied computers, which I can only access for a few hours a week. My legal arguments lack precision due to this continual denial of access to proper legal amenities and I am at my wit's end as CSC refuses to grant me such sufficient access to these required amenities.

If Canada wishes to be a beacon for human rights, it must provide its citizens who are subject to state power the tools needed to defend themselves against abuses. This injustice can be remedied by allowing access to the following:

1. Personal computers in cells;
2. Case law and research;
3. A photocopier with reasonable printing rates;
4. Computer programs for educational purposes; and
5. Electronic transmission of legal aid materials to courts and lawyers.

I would also like to see the following addressed:
1. Allowing the local purchasing of goods through local shops, not via a catalogue that contains items available for ludicrous prices;
2. A viable and transparent means for those deemed to be "dangerous offenders" to work their way towards their rehabilitation and eventual safe re-entry into society;
3. To eliminate and replace the current prisoner grievance process so that CSC no longer polices itself; and
4. Change the Correctional Investigator system in a way that holds CSC to account and results in recommendations being adopted for the betterment of prisoners and public safety.

I take full responsibility for my offences and truly have an abundant amount of empathy for my victims. I was not emotionally well during those times and I am sincerely sorry for having harmed others. In time, I would like to receive a pardon from the Parole Board of Canada (PBC), so that I may truly have a chance to succeed as a pro-social, former prisoner thereafter.

There were many negative changes to the justice and prison system under successive federal governments led by Prime Minister Stephen Harper. This analysis is based on my personal experiences and from witnessing the dramatic changes. I will be as accurate as I can be, drawing on statistics from the Office of the Correctional Investigator of Canada's 2015-2016 Annual Report where possible to corroborate what I have observed at Dorchester Penitentiary in recent years. I will elaborate on six subjects to generate awareness about problems that exist at the level of the courts and in Canada's penitentiaries. A central problem connecting the two is systemic racism, which I will elaborate upon below.

THE RIPPLING EFFECT

Our Courts and Conditional Release
It is essential for the criminalized passing through our courts that the composition of the latter reflect the populations they serve. Currently, we have what an article in the *Globe and Mail* calls a "Judiciary of Whiteness" (Tutton, 2016). Minorities entering the Justice System would like to witness an increase of ethnic judges on the benches in our courts, which would decrease the bias experienced when before Caucasian judges, who neither can relate to their struggles, nor understand the social pressures of their culture within their communities. In most cases an ethnic judge can relate to a minority to some degree, as I am most certain that this judge has suffered from racial bias, under the same or similar circumstances, no matter their social status, or where he/she comes from in their community. This is not to say that everyone who a minority comes in contact with is prejudiced thereafter. However, there must be safeguards against discrimination, particularly when someone's freedom is at stake.

As a number of Indigenous and African Canadians are entering the justice system it is crucial that they have the same opportunity to be equal before the law so that they are being properly sentenced and are given the chance to reintegrate in a timely fashion. Currently, Black prisoners are being warehoused in Canadian federal penitentiaries in the Atlantic Region, where they often are not given the same conditional release opportunities as their white counterparts.[1] The end result is that minorities serve more lengthy periods of incarceration. This experience of discrimination, whether when entering or exiting the penal system, is discouraging and needs to be changed.

Central to the gating of minority and other prisoners is the fact that parole officers within the penitentiaries often do not have our casework information ready in time for parole hearings or are non-supportive of a release. We are also blindsided by sudden changes to our case management team, notably changes in our institutional parole officer who needs to get up to speed on our files. Whether stalling tactics or not, such changes often keep a prisoner incarcerated until their Statutory Release date, which happened more frequently during the years of the Harper government.

PBC will only see a prisoner if their casework information has been completed by their parole officer in a timely fashion. Prisoners are often asked to sign a waiver postponing their parole release hearing by another two months or more to accommodate processing delays. One could even have successfully completed their rehabilitation programs, remain idle in prison without an engaged parole officer for years, while not having access to any psychological counselling to help avoid becoming institutionalized and losing hope about the lack of support they are receiving towards earning a rational release. Many minority prisoners are warehoused in our Canadian penitentiaries.

Accountability / Rehabilitation
When I entered the federal penitentiary system I was an emotional train wreck, suffering from severe depression and uncontrollable anxiety due to traumatic events in my life. Mental abuse, physical abuse and sexual abuse, coupled with the trauma I experienced while trying to save a two-year-old's life decades ago. I developed PTSD and sleep insomnia from these tragic events, and then eventually I naively began to self-medicate through the use of crack-cocaine. In my thirties, I ended-up in prison for the first time after committing a violent robbery. If it were not for participating in a rehabilitation program, I would not have changed.

Having willingly participated in a rehabilitation program realizing that I had some problems, I learned a lot about my emotional problems and my mental state of mind during the commissions of my offences. I have learned a lot more about my condition than if I would have had I not participated in this rehabilitation process. I wanted to know what led me to commit my offences through programming. Some of it was in regard to developing an expensive addiction to crack-cocaine back then, while trying to deal with my unresolved depression, my anxiety, and the negative thoughts of feeling worthless from sexual abuse. I had no clue how to manage my condition until I participated in the rehabilitation program that I successfully completed. I had brief counselling through a penitentiary psychiatrist regarding my trauma and began treatment. Presently, I am pleased to say that I am now on the medications that manage me pro-actively and pro-socially. Rehabilitation, when encouraged by the institution, can help one's thinking, ability to cope with feelings, and manage their life in a positive direction without the addiction. Rehabilitation is truly beneficial.

A prisoner must take responsibility for their offence and realize that they do have problems that need to be addressed. Then and only then, the prisoner is opened to change and seeks the assistance that they need. However, they must want this change through the rehabilitation process. If a prisoner does not participate in the program that is set in their penitentiary correctional plan, six out of ten will more than likely reoffend once released.[2] Rehabilitation programming is essential! However, if the prisoner is in denial or perhaps does not care that they have committed an offence causing harm against their victims, there is no hope for rehabilitation. Their reasoning for committing an offence is much stronger and this will eventually be their demise. This being said, this type of prisoner is a continual threat to themselves and the safety of the public in general.

There are several reasons that can contribute to the commission of an offence, including social pressure, an addiction, poverty and/or emotional instability. However, rehabilitation promotes self-awareness and provides prisoners with enough material to significantly change their lifestyle. This being said, rehabilitation only benefits prisoners who participate in their set programs with an open-mind, and they must acknowledge that they need assistance to change their lifestyle. There is enough information in these rehabilitation programs to significantly change a person's lifestyle if a prisoner takes their program seriously and really wants a change in their life. The program material is designed around contributing factors that encouraged the prisoner to commit their offence such as an addiction to a substance like cocaine, alcohol or opiates.

Rehabilitation, however, is only a fraction of what is needed for a positive pro-social recovery. Also central is the promotion of mental health, which requires access to psychological counselling and/or through a psychiatrist's evaluation to discover what works to manage their condition with the correct counselling and/or dosage of medications. Without this, a prisoner living with mental health issues will try something else to bury their inner pain and/or emotional instability, often through returning to addictive behaviours that lead them to come into conflict with the law.

Cultural Advisory / Human Rights
Having spoken to a number of Indigenous and Black prisoners, minorities should be entitled to have an Ethno-Cultural Advisory Committee to address human rights issues and abuses of authority in our Canadian penitentiaries owing to discrimination. This committee should comprise of an independent official that is culturally connected to the communities of minority prisoners, serving as a complaint liaison to mediate between prisoners and CSC. This would perhaps go a long way in addressing the warehousing of racialized prisoners in this region.

An Ethno-Cultural Advisory Committee should be implemented into government policy. Prisoners want to work with an independent official who is willing to intervene at a regional level to provide assistance to deal with human rights violations. Many of us do not have regular meetings with parole officers and other members of our case management teams. This must change, as disengagement causes more chaos than good.

Perhaps there is no funding for such a committee or perhaps no one actually cares in government, as the majority of prisoners are not seen as being relevant to most in Canadian society. This may be why we are warehoused in our prisons and going nowhere. One can observe that there is bias, due to lack of engagement and a non-supportive release system.

There is more than an unacceptable amount of bias against minorities by CSC employees. More training involving cultural diversity for CSC employees is needed. This being said, the general demeaning and dehumanizing of prisoners and their character is insensitive and cruel, which seeps into relations behind the walls. This creates bitterness, as well as a sense of worthlessness to the individual receiving this kind of treatment.

As it stands, there are cultural needs and traditions that are not being observed in our penitentiaries as there appear to be no officials in higher positions of authority realizing the importance for a minority to stay connected to one's culture and customs. Indigenous and African-Canadian prisoners need a cultural liaison[3] to represent these ongoing human rights abuses.

Grievances and Conflicts of Interest

Federally sentenced prisoners do have a grievance process to lodge complaints and seek resolution. However, the unresolved problem with this process is that you have a conflict of interest whereby CSC staff members investigate their colleague's demeanour and actions. Our complaints often go unanswered during the period where resolution would matter. Sending a second grievance to be addressed regionally or nationally thereafter is also no guarantee that action will follow.

Bias / Profiling

Discrimination towards minorities has been going on for far too long in our penitentiary system. Minorities routinely to realize that white prisoners tend to be processed more quickly. The obscured racism we face works its way through our paperwork and casework information, where an exaggerated and problematic picture follows us throughout our time in the system. Judgement is passed down on as our file shuffles through the hands of parole officers, that often change multiple times during our warehousing. This is reflected in the rates of incarceration for Indigenous and African-Canadian prisoners documented in the Correctional Investigator's 2015-2016 Annual Report.[4] Time-and-time again white prisoners are being released before a minority is even seen by the PBC.

This process and the treatment we experience causes more harm than good, as minorities are becoming institutionalized through the sheer length of their incarceration. This frustration leads to anger. Institutional parole officers have excessive powers when it comes to who is released from a prison environment and who stays there. This needs to immediately change. As I explain below, my Africadian (i.e. African-Canadian and French) background and features have resulted in discriminatory treatment while I have tried to safely exit prison.

Statutory Release

During a two-month period in 2015, I was released from prison on a residency clause to the Parrtown Community Correctional Centre in Saint

John, New Brunswick. However, I had no idea how strict a Community Correctional Centre environment was, as this was my first experience in such a facility. And I will admit that I was rather nervous for the most part being under a microscope by my community parole officer, who had a client who recently committed suicide on his caseload. This tragedy took place in my living unit prior to my arrival.

Within three weeks I began to experience that the staff members within this facility were not accepting me. With that I began to withdraw, developing a sarcastic demeanour with two of the officials within my case management team. I also had some minor complications transitioning from prison back into the community after arriving at this Community Correctional Centre, where I failed in my attempts to be sociable with a few of the staff members while trying to relax in this facility. After realizing this failure and apologizing, I knew that this was going to be more trying than I had anticipated, no matter if I was committed to pro-actively / pro-socially succeed in the Saint John community.

Realizing this, and not wanting to have any animosity directed towards me, I unsuccessfully attempted to have an intervention with my case management team, so that I would not be misunderstood moving forward. However, during this boardroom procedure members of my case management team disagreed amongst themselves regarding their responsibilities and regrettably resolved nothing. I tried to resolve any misunderstandings regarding my reintegration and was disappointed that this attempt at conflict resolution to correct any misconceptions did not bear fruit.

Alleged Risky Behaviour
In my second month in the community, I had an appointment with my community parole officer. Immediately after arriving in her office she had asked me about the bars I had attended and why I had not accurately disclosed these locations on my sign-out card. I had indicated that I had wrote "Uptown" on the sign-out card, as this is where the two bars are located. I even went as far as disclosing that I had danced with a couple of senior women while I was at the karaoke bars, which was a mistake. My honesty was used against me and framed as engaging in risky behaviour in a Community Program Performance Report. Having been deemed an increased risk and having been sarcastic with members of my case management team resulted in being labelled as having deteriorating behaviour. I was sent back to prison.

One of my release conditions is to report all sexual / non-sexual relationships, and/or friendships with women. As I was not engaged in a relationship with either women at the bars, nor had I befriended them, I thought there was nothing for me to disclose to my community parole officer at that time. I really did not think that having a three-minute dance with complete strangers could be characterized as risky behaviour.

When I did finally discuss the matter, my community parole officer did not ask me any questions pertaining to these women, after I had explained that there was no personal information exchanged between me and these women at the bars. No names were mentioned, no addresses were exchanged and no phone numbers were taken. Being in an intimate relationship with a woman was the furthest thing from my mind in this position. Yet my curfew was adjusted from 11:00pm back down to 6:00pm for not accurately disclosing the names of these Uptown bars on my sign-out card at the community correctional centre. I do take responsibility for this mistake.

Parole Suspended / Revoked
After having a minor disagreement with the facility psychologist about explaining or in her words "rationalizing" a recent offence, the two minor glitches trying to be sociable with staff members, and an assumption of being involved in risky behaviour, the Saint John Police were called to the Parrtown Community Correctional Centre with an arrest warrant for me. The revocation of my Statutory Release did not relate to a breach of my release conditions, another offence committed or even a failed urinalysis test.

Sadly, for me, I am once again being housed in a prison environment. At no point was I at risk of violating my conditions, nor was I at risk of committing any offences before my Warrant Expiry Date while in the Saint John community. Nor was I ever an unmanageable public safety threat against anyone in the community correctional centre, nor had I put myself at risk by intimately befriending any women. I firmly believe that I have endured more punishment than a person who has committed an extremely violent offence or has breached a release condition. I am now exceeding my parole eligibility by 43 months and there were no aggressive factors involved in my recent offence. There are no records of serious incidents committed by me in this penitentiary, nor is there any record of involuntary segregation in my case file information as I am a model prisoner. I have been rehabilitated through CSC. However, trying to convince my case management team is tough.

My fate is now in the hands of the PBC. For now, I remain in this negative prison environment where my parole officer has not prepared my casework information in due time, setting me back by another two or more months. Unfortunately, I am not receiving any credit for my efforts to remain pro-active and pro-social, nor the assistance that I want without the counselling and/or therapy in this prison. I can only access this kind of treatment through the community.

I cannot understand why I was not given any leniency or an opportunity to succeed like many other prisoners. I have fully co-operated in my reintegration and was doing my best to complete my sentence in the community. I was truly engaged in my Community Correctional Plan, and went beyond by completing a Community Maintenance Program through the Horizon Mental Health Clinic in Saint John. I had participated in some coping skills sessions, a six-week course, with a successful completion certificate.

I am left to conclude that my ethnic background seems to be my main impediment, as I have actively participated in my rehabilitation process and have followed my assigned Correctional Plan, inside and outside penitentiary walls. I have not failed any urinalysis in seven years. I did not threaten public safety, nor did I commit any recent offences, and I did not breach any of my conditions while I was briefly in this community. There is no valid reason why I should remain in this prison environment.

Facing obscured racism that came in the form of a negative Community Program Performance Report, I am drained. I will no longer discuss my recent offences that led to my current sentence, this way I am sure that no information will be misleading and be manipulated against me in a future program performance report, which is currently underway.

Mental Health / Treatment
There has been a recent study of the prevalence of psychotropic medications being offered to the incarcerated.[5] These medications are being prescribed to candy-coat the real issues of a prisoner's state of mind, rather than providing access to counselling and treatment. Keep in mind that the pharmaceutical manufacturing industry is a multi-billion-dollar industry annually.

These medications are more commonly prescribed to federal prisoners rather than any other person in our Canadian communities (i.e. 30.4%

vs. 8% of Canadians), and the most commonly prescribed medication category are anti-depressants. This being said, there are considerably more than incarcerated women (45.7%) than men (30.6%) being prescribed psychotropic medication prescriptions, rather than counselling / treatment thereafter. Would it not be less expensive and more effective in the long run to employ more psychologists and psychiatrists to assess these patients through rehabilitation / counselling as an alternative, before prescribing these medications to prisoners? Medication paves over unresolved issues that are buried deep within prisoners who live with mental health issues.

A previous assessment[6] of incoming male prisoners indicate the following prevalence rates of mood disorders (17.9%), alcohol or substance abuse disorder (50.6%), and anxiety disorders (30.5%). I mean earnestly, how can we get access to these stocks/shares for the medications that are being prescribed instead of counselling to address these conditions behind bars? Then there are the lifetime rates for borderline personality disorder (15.9%) and for anti-social personality disorder (45.1%). By any measure these ratings far exceed those found in our communities across Canada. The overmedication of federal prisoners must change, so that more resources can be dedicated to counselling.

Pay Levels / Finances
Prisoners I have spoken to are recommending that the Minister of Public Safety initiate a review of the prisoner payment and allowance system. At current levels, we cannot save enough to reintegrate back into society after prison. Ensuring that prisoners live in poverty upon their release is not a recipe for public safety.

Moreover, the introduction of a sole source supplier charging higher prices in our population canteens is inappropriate, unreasonable and unfair. It is important to highlight that the maximum amount that a federal prisoner can earn per day was set at $6.90 more than thirty years ago. Less than 9% of the entire population across Canada earns the maximum daily rate, while the largest proportion of the federal prisoner population across Canada earns a level C pay, which is $5.80 per day. This is before the 30% deduction, along with a 10% deduction for our Inmate Welfare Fund (IWF). On top of that, add another 5% deduction that our population has chosen to collectively lower the price of our canteen purchases. By the time all these deductions are added together, a typical prisoner employed full-time earns around 30 cents per hour. Those at a lower pay level who are unemployed, such as D level and E level, receive considerably less.

Despite inflation, there has not been a payment increase in 30 plus years, and Harper disengaged A level pay from the majority of the Canadian prisoners across the board with changes to CSC policy that now take into consideration the subjective notion of "accountability" when assessing pay levels. As this stands the majority of prisoners are now receiving C level pay, with two or three employment positions combined into one position (60% of the population). This has taken employment positions away from 40% of the prisoners in our prison populations who are unemployed on E level pay at $2.50 per day before deductions. Our decades old pay freeze and the loss of CORCAN incentive pay, coupled with the added Inmate Telephone Fund (ITF) deductions that prisoners are now paying into to cover the costs of administration, as well as the increased room and board deductions, makes it next to impossible to save money.

Since the Harper government instituted a series of prisoner "accountability" measures, federal prisoners now bear a greater proportion of the cost to keep themselves fed and cared for while in state captivity. These measures are short-sighted. Our pay must change to match the prices of our present inflation in our communities.

More importantly, a pay change must occur because without financial stability upon one's release there remains a significant barrier for prisoners to remain offence-free, especially after a long period of incarceration. Upon release, former prisoners need to get an apartment, groceries and other basic essentials. Without adequate pay while inside, the criminalized are placed in a position where they need to make fast cash to survive. For some, returning back to committing offences, for example selling street drugs, becomes the answer. When the Harper government implemented an additional 30% deduction for room and board without making the changes in this system's pay structure, it actually promoted the very activities it claimed it was fighting.

CONCLUSION

There are nearly 15,000 people incarcerated in our Canada's penitentiaries, the vast majority of which will one day be released, broken and financially broke. Our new Prime Minister, Public Safety Minister and Justice Minister must all come together, collaborating with researchers from coast-to-coast, to reform the penal system. In particular, they need to make changes to respect the human rights of all, including Indigenous and African-Canadians in prison. If we do not witness profound changes, safety in our communities is at risk.

ENDNOTES

[1] It should be noted that the Office of the Correctional Investigator (OCI) conducted a special study of diversity in corrections which indicated at paragraph 62: "According to Parole Board of Canada, statistics over the last 5 years (2007/08 to 2011/12) Black offenders have consistently been less likely than the general inmate population to be granted federal day or full parole" (OCI, 2013).

[2] According to the most recent statistics available from the Corrections and Conditional Release Statistical Overview in 2015/2016 63.1% of release prisoner completed their statutory release, 29.3% of violations were for technical breaches and 6.6% were for non-violent offences, while 0.9% of breaches were for violent offences resulting in revocation" (Public Safety Canada, 2017).

[3] While CSC does have an ethno-cultural advisory committee, with a dedicated National Headquarters (NHQ) position and Regional Headquarters (RHQ) positions of Regional Manager Ethno-Cultural Services, they do not, unlike for Indigenous prisoners, have a "cultural liaison" (National and Regional Ethnocultural Advisory Committees, no date).

[4] See Shook and McInnis (this issue).

[5] The prevalence of prescriptions of psychotropic medication was more common in Canadian federal offenders than in the general Canadian population (30.4% vs. about 8.0%). Please see: Farrell MacDonald, S., Keown, L.-A., Boudreau, H., Gobeil, R., & Wardrop, K. (2015). *Prevalence of psychotropic medication prescription among federal offenders* (Research Report R-373), Ottawa: Correctional Service Canada.

[6] According to the 2015 numbers, "mood disorders" (16.9%), "Alcohol and Substance Use Disorders" (49.6%), and "Anxiety Disorders" (29.5%). Please see: Beaudette, J. N., J. Power and L. A. Stewart (2015) *National Prevalence of Mental Disorders Among Incoming Federally-sentenced Men Offenders* (Research Report, R-357), Ottawa: Correctional Service Canada.

REFERENCES

Correctional Service Canada (no date) *National and Regional Ethnocultural Advisory Committee*, Ottawa. Retrieved from http://www.csc-scc.gc.ca/ethnocultural/002004-0002-eng.shtml

Farrell MacDonald, S., L.-A. Keown, H. Boudreau, R. Gobeil and K. Wardrop (2015) *Prevalence of Psychotropic Medication Prescription among Federal Offenders* (Research Report R-373), Ottawa: Correctional Service Canada. Retrieved from http://www.csc-scc.gc.ca/005/008/092/R373-eng.pdf

Office of the Correctional Investigator (2013) *A Case Study of Diversity in Corrections: The Black Inmate Experience in Federal Penitentiaries*, Ottawa. Retrieved from http://www.oci-bec.gc.ca/cnt/rpt/pdf/oth-aut/oth-aut20131126-eng.pdf

Public Safety Canada (2017) *Corrections and Conditional Release Statistical Overview: 2016 Annual Report*, Ottawa: Public Works and Government Services Canada.

Tutton, Michael (2016) "Advocates call for racial diversity as figures show 'judiciary of whiteness'", *Globe and Mail* – July 18. Retrieved from https://beta.theglobeandmail.com/news/national/advocates-call-for-racial-diversity-as-figures-show-judiciary-of-whiteness/article30959027/?ref=http://www.theglobeandmail.com&

I am grateful, along with a substantial portion of the prisoners of Dorchester Penitentiary (Medium Sector), for your journal's interest in prison issues. Having read the transcripts of the most recent Senate hearings concerning human rights in Canadian prisoners (1 February 2017 and 8 February), as well as having watched Correctional Service Canada (CSC) Commissioner Don Head giving testimony at other Senate committees, I feel compelled to contribute my knowledge concerning the institutional experience through whatever means necessary.

Initially, I am impressed the Senate Committee included Ms. Alia Pierini and Mr. Lawrence DaSilva as hearing witnesses. I find it incredible how, even after release, former prisoners maintain the communicative idiosyncrasies of prison. Reading the transcripts, it is like hearing the talk of the men around me right now. This, I submit, is indisputable evidence there is no complete release from prison – its scars are often subtle and permanent. While I am thankful for their testimony, I am concerned there may be an omission developed from limited prisoner testimony and I am encouraged the Senate Committee is planning on visiting various institutions across Canada. There are many types of prisoners – Indigenous, Black, women, short-timers and Lifers – and other sub-groups of prisoners within and beyond these categories. There does exist particular commonalities between all types of prisoners too. However, experiences vary greatly.

One of the prisoners mentioned in the Senate hearing witness statements was Matthew Hines. We called him "Chubbs". He was a brother, a cousin, a friend and a neighbour to many of us who still reside here in Dorchester (Medium) Penitentiary. Matthew had had his parole suspended when he was murdered. He was living with mental health concerns, which were not well-addressed in his years of incarceration, translating into breakdown during his release. No real gradual reintegration back into society occurred with Chubbs. He was sent back to prison, as a suspended parolee with only months left on his sentence. Matthew Hines was, in the opinion of many prisoners (including myself), murdered by CSC, which is an offence punishable by job termination or a good talking to. We heard the sounds he made as he was beaten outside our cells door. We listened to the pleas. We watched our brother taken to the hole for the last time where he was callously put to death. We watched the blood being cleaned up long before any investigation was launched. We listened to the talking points given to the media regarding this incident for a year while his own family was fed lies.

With regard to Matthew Hines' story, the testimony of Jason Godin of the Union of Canadian Correctional Officers (UCCO) was troubling to me, most particularly as Senator Ataullahjan questioned him about Post-Traumatic Stress Disorder. I am a reasonable person and can understand how good people who work in prisons can be radically affected by seeing a man hanging from a rope in a cell or seeing two men sticking each other with homemade knives. I can imagine how it feels to go to work and wonder if today is the day where something horrible happens to myself or someone else I care about. These people Mr. Godin represents go home at the end of the day and have a chance to decompress – they have a choice to return to work or go elsewhere. They also have better access to counselling than prisoners. When people who go to work in Canadian prisons are leaving sick, what outcome is expected of marginalized individuals who live in a prison for years without reprieve? Federally incarcerated people who have offended, who are reminded daily of an action as though it is the totality of their being or defining moment of their lives – people labelled 'offenders', for example, as opposed to people who have committed an offence – are expected to rehabilitate and reintegrate into a society they may not have adequate skills or resources to succeed within in the first place. These people do not go home at the end of a twelve-hour day. Every moment of their lives is dedicated to these issues causing Post-Traumatic Stress Disorder in prison staff. There is no such thing as safe and humane custody in a prison, and anyone who says otherwise is making money for saying so.

Matthew Hines' story, unfortunately, is not a single event. It was not the first and it most certainly will not be the last. Dorchester Penitentiary has incidents like this periodically. The last incident occurred with a prisoner who was falsely accused of smuggling in drugs or weapons into the facility, and after numerous regular frisk searches and x-rays, CSC along with a doctor took it upon themselves, under force and duress, to probe his anal cavity. Before that incident, it was keeping a man in a dry cell until he pulled back the foreskin of his penis while another man watched, badgering him through the process. CSC refused to consider how this man had been sexually abused by an older man as a child and how such event was absolutely traumatizing. Another event of staff molesting prisoners happened when the institution refused to acknowledge reports of its occurrence until it happened directly in front of them. The doctor and his crew still work in Dorchester. Imagine living in a place where you have to see, let alone give respect to, the man who stuck his finger in your bum? The molesting staff member still works in Dorchester. How about how the fella who traumatized the other man – relocated, perhaps given administrative leave at the most? Rapes, murders, assaults – covered-up behind thirty-foot high cement walls.

There was no trauma counselling given to prisoners regarding these incidents. Trauma counselling was available to the staff members who murdered Chubbs, as well as the staff members who watched and assisted a doctor stick his finger in a man's bum. Human rights? Mental health? These ideals, at best, are talking points to justify salaries and employment. How can this be said when prisoners are experiencing abuse like this?

The inefficacy of prisons, along with the statistical and empirical evidence proving it, has been known to the Canadian Government and parliamentarians, Senators included, for decades. Consider the irony in touting human rights, while using segregation and punishment to achieve justice. Instead of applying science and humanity, which often are not politically endearing when it comes voting time, we as a nation use the practice of imprisonment which has been around for hundreds of years. How many technologies, particularly relating to human behaviour and health do we continue to use which are this old? Disregarding the age of the practice, where is the proof that it accomplishes what it sets out to do with respect to rehabilitation?

Substantial concern has been recently given to mental health, especially as it relates to the federal penitentiary system. There is substantial testimony regarding how CSC is addressing mental health concerns in the Senate's current study on human rights in corrections. Just as in the latter half of the 20th century in Kingston Penitentiary, it took people dying or being radically abused before Canadians stepped up to address the issues plaguing our prisons. Ashley Smith, Matthew Hines and many others have paid the price, as have their families and friends for this indifference. Canada is not a human rights respecting nation behind its prison walls, despite the talking points of CSC officials. What is written on paper as CSC policy is not the reality of implementation on the ground! I and my peers live the daily experience of these disconnected policy makers. Where is the independent oversight in prison with teeth? The Office of the Correctional Investigator makes recommendations without any requirement for them to be implemented.

At what point in Canadian history did we develop evidence showing that the state is able to police itself? Indigenous women are being driven out into the boonies, sexually harassed and abused by police officers in Quebec. Officers manufacturing testimony and perjuring themselves after they murder a Polish immigrant with a Taser. These are things which occur in the open. Can you imagine what happens behind 30-foot high penitentiary walls where there exists no oversight mechanism with teeth? What happens when the policy and agenda are decided upon and moved by the very institution which implements it? Let me remind you: Matthew Hines, Ashley Smith, etc. CSC has not tempered its capacity to harm, nor formed the realistic insight to manage their own policy or direction. Yet they are one of the few organizations which deal with Canada's most marginalized people and somehow are allowed to manage themselves without authoritative check.

I am grateful for the Canadian health system, as I understand it. Doctors are trained for years in universities to ensure they understand the human body. They know about how medications and surgeries impact the human body, as well as how social conditions affect the healing process. Doctors do not generally use injections of mercury anymore to cure diseases as they did back in the 1800s because science has demonstrated it does not work.[1] Doctors now get their marching orders from an independent body, the College of Doctors and Physicians, rather than from some authority who decides practices solely based on politics or economic imperatives. As best as possible, respecting the dignity of every person involved, Canada has developed a health care system which is not based on ideology. If there is any direction taken by the government that does not include this concept with respect to the penal system, any consideration of human rights by anyone is a waste of money and time.

"Protection of society" is ambiguous phraseology. It suits the right-leaning 'get tough on crime' and the left-leaning 'get smart on crime' crowds. It is politically genius, but what does it do for a prisoner? That we are still having to debate human rights and mental health concerns today is indicative of the system's perpetual failure to correct itself.

There are precedents in Canadian history for entire system failures, most notably Residential Schools. It is generally accepted knowledge that Residential Schools were a complete failure. Back when these institutions were used it was about protecting society from a different demon: the 'Savage'. Again, since that time, we have discovered the problems – perceived to stem from Indigenous cultures and peoples – were actually produced from Canada's colonial institutions involved in assimilation. Canadian paternalistic, egotistical views were forced upon Indigenous peoples and as such, much was destroyed. The problem Canada thought it had was not even a problem and the resolution of this problem was the actual destructive force! Now, after seeing what institutionalization can and does do, we still rely on institutionalization to protect our society. We, as a nation, have learned nothing from our past. Clearly, truth and reconciliation takes time.

There are substantial issues which relate directly to the purpose of the Senate Committee on Human Rights. Recognizing that every individual incarcerated in Canadian federal penitentiaries is a person that struggling with their mental health, whether because of circumstances prior to their incarceration and/or resulting from it, is the beginning of a real discussion. Lock and key rehabilitation is not working.

The prisoners of Dorchester Penitentiary Medium Sector would like to discuss what penitentiary life is like. We believe you will see Canada's worst implementation of policy: the actual chicken-cooping of human beings (*sans melodrama*). We can demonstrate how the economy takes precedence over mental health and rehabilitation, how *Quiet Rage* (Zimbardo and Musen, 1992) is prevalent in today's prisons, and how what is written on paper or what you are being told by the Keepers is not accurate. We invite you to hear the accounts of murders, rapes, assaults and harassment perpetrated by your government, to see how an institution implements policy for their own preservation as opposed to the preservation of a just, safe and peaceful society, or to see how minority population prisoners are systemically discriminated against.

Standing together in solidarity (see *Appendix*) is the salutation you left us with in your correspondence. Perhaps there was a time when solidarity was a reality. As for standing, those days, too, are long gone. I am grateful for this opportunity to shed light on the issues prisoners face.

ENDNOTES

[1] Today, the problems are solved by sterilization and aseptic conditions. Penicillin appeared in the 1940s and chlorothiazide in 1957 and new effective agents have taken over in the treatment of diseases with mercurial. Please see Norn, Svend, Henrik Permin, Edith Kruse, and Poul R. Kruse (2008) "Mercury – A Major Agent in the History of Medicine and Alchemy", *Dansk medicinhistorisk arbog*, 36: 21-40

REFERENCES

Zimbardo, Philip and Ken Musen (1992) *Quiet Rage: The Stanford Prison Experiment.*

Dorchester Institution
David W. Threinen

I am a prisoner at Dorchester (medium security) and currently the chairman of this institution's seniors group. What really perturbs me about initiatives such as this collection is that a lot is said, but very little seems to come of it. You can publish in whatever journal you wish, but politicians do not read journals. I personally have been in this penitentiary system for 40 plus years without release and have engaged in several "studies" of various types concerning incarceration. I have yet to see any of them bare any fruit. But having said that and being the optimist that I am, I must go by the adage, "nothing ventured, nothing gained".

As early as the mid-1990s, people such as the then Correctional Investigator, started warning the powers that be that the federal penitentiary system was going to get bogged down by what was being called "geriatric inmates", which it could not handle. I am sorry to say that that prediction has come true. Health Canada and various organisations list a starting age of being called a senior at 50.[1] Using that as the starting number, we have approximately 100 seniors in this institution alone. This comprises approximately one quarter of the population. Of those, around 40 are 65 plus, in other words, retirement age. Among their many concerns, is that penal infrastructure continues to be built with a lot of stairs. A good portion of seniors have medical problems that make climbing stairs almost impossible. For the purposes of this report, I will be referring to prisoners of retirement age of which I am one. I just turned 69 this past March.

It is very hard for seniors to find employment on the street, never mind in a penitentiary system geared toward younger prisoners. The last government saw it fit to take away Old Age Security, so we basically have no income to purchase what we need to survive inside anymore. They tell us that we can get our pension back when we get released, but that means those lucky enough to get released, get released with nothing. We have absolutely no way to save anything for anything, let alone release.

That is just one of the problems that we face. Another, even more serious problem, is violence that is directed at us from younger prisoners. There was a time in the system when if you assaulted or in any way harmed a senior, you paid a severe penalty. I am afraid that those days are gone also. With all of the changes the previous government has made with the new sentencing laws and others, the violence level inside the prison has risen, especially violence towards seniors. The reason is obvious – we can no longer defend ourselves. In the last ten years, in this institution there have been at least six suicides, two murders, one suspicious death, one death due to falling, and three by natural causes such as cancer, and so on. With the exception of one of the murders, all involved seniors. Of every ten men walking around with black eyes and fat lips, eight are seniors and there is not anything we can do about it, especially when the "system" denies that it is happening.

As if the above two problems are not bad enough, there are two others, but they can be combined into one. They are the institution's health care facilities and the manner in which penitentiary units are being built. Most new units being built still have a lot of stairs in them, which results in seniors having to climb to get anywhere inside the penitentiary. As a good number of seniors are in wheelchairs or use things like canes or walkers, this makes getting around very difficult and, for some, impossible. When some still try to climb these stairs, many fall and hurt themselves. In some cases, as the previously mentioned death by falling, the fall can have serious consequences. However, it is not just seniors falling down and severely hurting themselves that is the only problem with health care. It is also the ailments that seniors have such as arthritis, rheumatism and other old age ailments federal penitentiaries are not equipped to deal with. Maybe I should not use the term "equipped", but instead use the word funded. As we know, dealing with seniors' ailments is more expensive than those of younger prisoners. As an example, in this institution, the only dental care we can get is to have our teeth pulled. There is no dental hygienist available at all. This part of the dental department was removed because funding was taken away by the government due to the rise of the senior population who, in many cases, require more serious dental care. And the mental health care is totally non-existent. In summary, the changes that effected this group of men are:

1. No funds
2. No mobility
3. More violence
4. More suicides
5. Less health care
6. No Hope (mental health issues)
7. Ailments
8. Released into society with no money

Having said all of that, please see the following proposal that would virtually eliminate all of the above. Of course, this is just a draft proposal and it is open to serious negotiation and change. It gives a base to start with to deal with the problems that seniors behind bars are facing. With new sentencing laws that promise to incarcerate more people with fewer release opportunities, things are not going to get better, they can only get worse.

PROPOSAL FOR ELDERLY PRISONERS

It is obvious that looking at prisons in general that they were never designed to handle geriatric prisoners. They all have stairs, which limits the mobility of those prisoners in wheel-chairs, using crutches or canes, or those who for various health reasons, have a difficult time getting around. And judging by the construction of newer institutions, the problem of geriatric prisoners is still not being looked at or being taken into consideration. Not only are the penitentiaries themselves not being built to accommodate geriatric prisoners, neither are the health care facilities. Virtually all of the health care facilities are geared towards younger prisoners. As an example, I use my current institution's Health Care Unit. It has five beds, three of which are already occupied, two by geriatric prisoners. Millions of dollars have recently been spent here to expand office space for the doctors and the nurses, but not one cent was spent updating the area where the prisoners are housed when necessary. That fact in itself proves that nobody is looking at the problem. There are various reasons why seniors are not being considered for release:

1. Their crimes
2. Family left to take care of them and no retirement home will take them
3. They have given up hope

Let us deal with each of these items individually.

Their Crimes
It is no secret that in their younger days, many of the men in question committed very serious offences. I use the term younger days because the majority of the men in this category have served well over 30 years without ever being released. There does come a time, when, regardless of

the offence, due to their age, they are no longer a danger to anyone. The federal government needs to seriously evaluate alternatives to incarceration for aging prisoners.

Reintegration Barriers

There are two main reintegration barriers faced by aging prisoners. One, the most prominent, is that residences for seniors are fearful of housing a former prisoner. The second, is that even if they are willing to take them, there is no bed space available. As I stated earlier, most of these men have been inside for thirty plus years and during that time, most if not all of their family has passed away. So, in effect, if they can't find a retirement home to take them, they have no place to go.

Loss of Hope

In far too many cases, the person in question has just plain given up. This leads to severe mental deterioration such as depression, which could lead to suicide. Since 2007, three seniors have committed suicide in this institution: one due to paranoia; one was a drug addict who was locked in a cell to go cold turkey; and one for depression. During this period, one senior was murdered by a younger prisoner.

On top of all this is the issue of mental problems such as Alzheimer's, dementia, Pick's disease, secondary dementia, senile dementia, and toxic dementia to name just a few. In the late 1990s, there was actually a case of a senior with Alzheimer's at Mountain Institution in British Columbia. For obvious reasons this man could not be left on his own so he had a palliative care trained prisoner assigned to be with him at all times. It should be noted at that time that there was an accredited palliative care training program in Mountain Institution. It was training prisoners to care for prisoners. Unfortunately, the program was discontinued for reasons unknown.

Mental health problems are not the only thing that seniors need to worry about. Previously, I mentioned that one senior was murdered by a younger prisoner. Seniors being assaulted by younger prisoners is an ongoing problem in the federal penitentiary system. Because they can no longer defend themselves they are beaten and robbed of their canteen and other personal items. In far too many cases, they are also sexually assaulted. In almost all cases, this activity is being either ignored by penitentiary staff or when it is serious enough that they have to take notice, it is swept under the carpet.

A Solution

Failing the implementation of more humane and less costly alternatives to confinement for geriatric prisoners, build them their own facilities. Pick a spot that is centrally located and build a single-story prison with cells and cell doors large enough to accommodate wheel-chairs and other devices that seniors may need.

Re-establish the accredited palliative care training program and have one wing built to accommodate prisoner orderlies. By doing this you would negate having to hire a large number of nursing staff. One orderly could be assigned up to six patients to care for depending on the seriousness of their problems. They would, of course, be supervised by nursing staff. By having prisoners like this, all the healthcare facilities would have to deal with would be geriatric prisoners.

Remember that we are only dealing with those aged 65 and older, and who are of retirement age. If you were to re-establish their old age pension you could make this almost self-sustaining. For example, the geriatric prisoners would need a pay level. The average payment is approximately $1200.00 per month. $350.00 of that would automatically be deducted for food and accommodation. Out of the balance they would be expected to pay for over the counter medications they may need such as items currently sold in our hygiene accounts and purchasing catalogue. They would also be expected to pay for cable just like in regular institutions. That should leave a large enough balance for regular canteen purchases and other expenditures. A certain amount would go into a savings account, but seeing as how many of these men will not be going any place given the nature of their offences which are unlikely to be swayed by positive changes when before Parole Board of Canada members during hearings, that account will not be necessary.

As for institutional maintenance, that could be done by those still able to get around. There will still be some able to do cleaning, work in the kitchen, handle a snow blower, general plumbing, and the like. An institution like this would not need as large of an administration as regular institutions. All you really need is a warden, maybe an assistant warden, head of security, and some guards, and maybe someone in finance to handle accounts. The outside perimeter could be medium-security, while inside could be minimum or at least low-medium. Remember that we would be housing geriatric prisoners, whose fence climbing days are long gone.

CONCLUSION

Seniors are getting tired of being beaten and robbed, raped, and murdered behind bars. It is time for the Government of Canada to do something about the problem of geriatric prisoners before things get out of hand and they have to start explaining why nothing has been done about a problem that was brought to their attention decades ago. While alternatives to confinement ought to be promoted, having our own penitentiaries is the next logical solution to the problem. Of course, having said all of that, transfer to this type of facility would be voluntary. There may be some seniors who still have family visiting or may have some kind of support in the community where they are. It is important that the decision be theirs.

ENDNOTES

[1] Office of the Correctional Investigator (2015) *Annual Report of the Office of the Correctional Investigator 2014-2015*, Ottawa. Retrieved from http://www.oci-bec. gc.ca/cnt/rpt/pdf/annrpt/annrpt20142015-eng.pdf

In the Community
Hyper A'Hern

INTRODUCTION

I am a federal prisoner currently serving six years on a first-time offence. I would like to make it readily apparent that this submission is not an unfounded or uneducated assessment of the penal system. I will be giving situational, emotional, and physical context and by extension, my biases, so that my words may not fall on deaf ears. Following this, I will give a detailed account of my individual experiences, the changes in prison I observed while serving time, and how they have impacted my life within a framework to express the priorities that I would like to see with respect to federal penitentiary reform going forward. These experiences include the dehumanization of prisoners, the traumatic events that occur in a hostile environment and the overwhelming sense of helplessness at the hands of the prison officers who have been given complete dominion over human life. Although the quantity of issues that need to change are numerous, I would say that the top ten on the list are the lack of pardons, the proliferation of mandatory minimum sentences, food inadequacies, health care issues, delays with regard to parole, the lack of intellectual stimulation from a lack of access to resources/hobbies/education, the broken prisoner grievance system, the lack of psychological resources, the lack of accountability, and the attitudes of prison officers.

BACKGROUND INFORMATION

To begin, I would like to provide both situational context and openly present any biases I may have. As we are all the sum of our experiences, I will leave it to you to reflect upon these biases as you read my account. I will begin the context with some background information. I am a Dalhousie University graduate with a double major in English and philosophy. I was accepted into both a master's degree in education, as well as Dalhousie Medical School. I have traveled the world teaching English as a second language to kindergarten, elementary school, middle school and university students. I have never so much as missed a bill in my life, never experimented with drugs and have never even been drunk. I have committed exactly one crime in my life, when I temporarily lost

80

the ability to feel emotion and had heightened suicidal ideations. Up to this point I was a fully law-abiding citizen with a $64,000 scholarship to medical school. Despite this, and no criminal record, I was denied bail twice, remanded for eleven months, and tried by the same judge that denied me bail. I was told by my lawyer that I would be given four years, but ended up with a six-year federal sentence due to a mandatory minimum sentence created by the Harper government. Three years later, I am up for parole and I am overwhelmed with anxiety at trying to piece together a life that has been shattered by not only my actions, but also the judicial and penal system. I am unable to ever get a pardon and pursue my dream of being a neurosurgeon for the IWK[1] due to Harper imposing longer time-frames and stricter rules for pardons. I cannot travel to many countries, be a teacher any longer or even get a job at McDonalds with a criminal record. Thanks to Harper's punishment agenda, I will forever be defined by a single action, not a lifetime of achievements.

As for the emotional context, I was diagnosed with "extremely, severe Post Traumatic Stress Disorder" as a direct result of this penal system. I would like to note that the psychologist thought that a single adjective was not sufficient to describe my diagnosis. I have been diagnosed with severe depression, severe anxiety disorders, and I have developed fibromyalgia as a direct result of the inhumane, traumatic, and dehumanizing experiences given to me as a gift-wrapped present from "Correctional" Service Canada. I am unable to function on a daily basis without excruciating pain and have a strong desire to end my own life as a direct result of this legalized torture every day of my incarceration. Thanks to Harper's agenda, an aspiring neurosurgeon will be reduced to living on welfare because I am unable to function as a normal citizen in the Canadian workforce with these mental and physical conditions.

Finally, I would like to provide physical context and the biases that are associated with this. I was remanded for eleven months in a super-max provincial jail, did the mandatory ninety days in a maximum-security environment at Springhill Institution, and was finally placed in a medium sector facility at Dorchester Institution with a strong indication that being placed in a minimum-security facility was in my immediate future. This never occurred. I have no institutional charges, thus I cannot speak about a segregation experience. I was deemed, and I quote, "too normal and socially well-adjusted for a rehabilitation program and it would do [me] more damage than good", so I cannot speak about the formal component of rehabilitation.

Therefore, it is with this prelude that I give you the situational, emotional, and physical contexts and biases already discussed as a basis to weed out the inevitable cynicism that will follow from my position. Despite this cynicism, I will try to the best of my ability to give a grounded and accurate account my experience of the Canadian penal system and the reforms that I would like to see.

ISSUES

Lack of Pardons
The first item that I would like to see immediately reviewed and changed is the pardon system. It was originally intended to allow people to not be defined by a single action and provide them with an incentive to work towards making amends by becoming a law-abiding citizen who contributes to society. Today's system is a mockery of those once proud ideals as the Harper government continually tore it apart so that it is nearly impossible to obtain. Many of the criminalized are no longer even potential candidates for a pardon and even if they are, the amount of time it takes to obtain a formal pardon would usually put one well into their golden years. In my situation, I would like to reiterate that not only did I once have grand dreams, but I am not a candidate for pardon. I have a schedule 1 offence with violence and so I am immediately precluded from a candidate position to obtain a pardon. This means that for the rest of my life, the best I can hope to achieve is mediocrity. Where is my incentive to contribute to society? Where is my incentive to not commit an offence again? Do we want a society where an individual is defined by a single action and their only deterrence for not committing harm is prison? Given that positive reinforcement works exponentially better than negative reinforcement, I would like to believe that if I do well and help my society that I could be forgiven by my country for what I have done and perhaps even be a doctor someday. If I am being bold, perhaps even a neurosurgeon. Therefore, what I would like to see change is a shorter time frame on pardons by at least half and, more importantly, no discrimination against particular types of offences so that anyone has incentive to work hard for their country's forgiveness.

A Review of Mandatory Minimum Sentences

Second, a review of the mandatory minimum sentences that the Conservatives imposed during their three successive mandates is sorely needed. We should trust our courts to be able to discern what level of punishment is appropriate and not have them bound to give someone a mandatory sentence for something that can be rectified in other more meaningful ways. We are sending a mixed message to the public by binding judges to these minimums. We are saying to trust the courts with applying the law, while at the same time undermining the judicial system by not allowing a judge to impose the sentence they deem adequate. In my case, what I needed was a psychologist and a friend, not six years in a traumatic environment. Had the judge been able to make the decision to give me a year or two, I would have experienced much less trauma and would have most likely not have developed the mental and physiological issues I have today as a result of repeated exposure to the prison subculture that I had never even known existed. Therefore, many, if not all mandatory minimum sentences should be abolished.

Food Inadequacies

Third, the food needs to be reviewed. On paper, we are eating chicken cacciatore and meat pie. In reality, we are eating shards of processed chicken in a sauce that could not be described as revolting due to the glaring inaccuracies of this statement and a pie that is 80 percent fake potatoes and some spaghetti sauce. I need not say much on this topic. In my personal experience, I have found numerous pieces of plastic and metal in my food, several bugs and have gotten food poisoning twice. I have also thrown up immediately after eating and as of now I eat almost exclusively bread, which consists of approximately 40% to 50% of our daily calorie intake. I do not need to express what this kind of malnutrition practice can do to a human body. We get fatter, while at the same time being malnourished. There are other animals in the animal kingdom that we do this to as well and their back fat makes a great burger taste better. What I would like to see moving forward are two things. First, I would like the food to be reviewed so that there are discernable pieces of meat in our food. Second, I would challenge the Attorney General of Canada Jody Wilson-Raybould and Public Safety Minister Ralph Goodale to eat a single lemon chicken or chicken cacciatore meal from this institution without vomiting. That action would only need to be done once to spur necessary reforms in this area.

Healthcare System (Inadequate and Delayed Care)

Fourth, the healthcare system or perhaps a lack thereof would be more accurate, needs serious attention. In my experience, it is nearly impossible to see a doctor, dentist or any specialist. For instance, it took me five months to see a doctor and an additional eleven months after seeing a specialist to get a diagnosis for fibromyalgia. Then, I waited an additional two months to be medicated. During this time, I submitted dozens of requests, complaints, grievances and final level grievances, placed calls to the Correctional Investigator, and wrote letters to human rights organizations, the Minister of Justice, and the College of Physicians and Surgeons. Only the College of Physicians and Surgeons responded. I was in pain every single day waiting for a diagnosis and now that I am medicated, I have not seen a doctor since to adjust my medication even though the neurologist specifically stated that follow-up with these substances was essential. The exact wording from the doctor when I finally did see him was "with the way this system is you won't get close to a proper treatment for your condition". I was and remain appalled. That statement alone says everything that is needed about the system when the people that work in it recognize its immense failure. Going forward, I would like to see more doctors that are easier to access, much more frequent dentist and optometrist clinics, and most importantly, a total scrapping of the necessity to see a nurse first before seeing a doctor. Nurses are not qualified to make a diagnosis or prescribe medications so this is simply job creation, creation of paperwork, and as a direct result, a drain on the system as a whole. I am a Canadian citizen, a human being and I am entitled to equal health care, but what we receive in here is not even a shadow of what health care should be.

Delays with Respect to Parole or
Escorted Temporary Absences (ETAs)

Fifth, postponements associated with parole and escorted temporary absences (ETAs) is getting to the point where most people only believe these things to be a myth. The Parole Board of Canada (PBC), as a neutral third party is rarely the culprit, but rather it is the parole officers and the lack of speed within the system that are the primary causes for delays. I would like to state at this juncture that I had a parole officer that was fairly decent and so I cannot speak personally to the kinds of horror stories that plague this institution. However, even I, with the best parole officer in this institution, was still subject to two postponements of my parole due to not being able to speak to a psychologist, which is now mandatory before a parole hearing. Most parole officers tell you to try for day parole on your full parole eligibility date and I myself have been told this, but does this not defeat the purpose of the eligibility dates? If you are only supported on your full parole date then why even have a day parole eligibility? I am sure you will be regaled with tales of parole officer nightmares, or as we call them stat officers, because many are kept until their statutory release dates once two-thirds of their sentences are served. Even though they have completed their mandatory programs, their parole keeps getting pushed back. I am inclined to believe the age-old wisdom that one or two people may lie, but when dozens are saying the same thing, there is probably some truth to it. That being said, my negative experiences were minor and I was lucky that only two small postponements happened, which should speak volumes about what the system is like. The CSC study R-193 titled "Waivers, Postponements and Withdrawals: Offenders, Parole Officers and National Parole Board Perspectives" states "The proportion of federal full parole pre-release decisions delayed or cancelled increased from 55% in 1998/99 to 62% in 2007/08".[2] These kinds of statistics are outrageous as it is well researched and documented that prisoners who are released on parole have a substantially larger chance of success that decreases proportionally with the amount of time spent unnecessarily incarcerated. This is colloquially known as "warehousing" and became a common practice under Harper's reign. The reality is that parole officers are overworked and cannot see everyone they need to or do everything they need to in a timely manner, while the mandatory psychology programs are often beyond capacity leaving people to wait to finish their programs before applying for the six months it takes to get a parole hearing. What I would like to see going forward is more prisoners getting out on or near their eligibility dates in order to facilitate rehabilitation by reducing time spent incarcerated and cutting down the more than $100,000 per year it takes to house each one of us in federal penitentiaries for men.

Lack of Intellectual Stimulation and Personal Development
Sixth, the ability to better oneself through access to resources, hobbies
or education is very near to non-existent. I cannot speak about other
institutions, but ours has not had a hobby shop in over four years. The
same can be said about resources such as access to the internet or access to
education. I realize that these may be three very different things, but they
all share at least two common threads: intellectual stimulation and the
ability to better oneself. Even though the Commissioner's Directives are
very clear about being entitled to "resources that are equivalent to a public
library" and the right to education, the reality is our library is infrequently
open, only recently have we been able to request heavily monitored
internet searches, and the "school" we have not only had unqualified
'teachers', but the curriculum past grade 9 is almost non-existent. As a
tutor for seventeen months at my institution, I observed how countless
students were fully prepared for a provincial exam based on the material
we had available only to nearly fail the exam because the 'school' had the
wrong book. This, along with other penitentiary school inadequacies, not
only undermines prisoner pursuits of high school diplomas, but also hurts
the chances of those who have the potential to go onto post-secondary
education. This, along with the fact that hobbies are non-existent make
an already dull and intellectually sterile environment feel like Dante's
final circle of Hell – frozen in time. How are prisoners supposed to better
themselves if the 'school' is a farce and there are no resources or hobbies
to improve one's mind or skills? Going forward, I would like to see
hobbies re-implemented full scale, better access to internet resources and
most importantly, a complete reform of the 'school' here to be coordinated
with the provincial curriculum and standards, as well as availability of
post-secondary education.

Broken Prisoner Grievance and Redress System
Seventh, the prisoner grievance system is broken. I will not put lipstick
on a pig and say anything other than the prisoner redress system is utterly
useless. To get a response, I frequently write two requests dated fifteen
days apart and a complaint dated at the end of those thirty business days,
mark those dates on my calendar, and wait several months for a response.
This is not an exaggeration. I have gone to the initial grievance level to

get deodorant from Inmate Supplies. I have waited nearly two years to be diagnosed with a problem that a quick Wikipedia search would have aptly provided an answer to. I have two grievances in now that, without any exaggeration once again, have had an extension filed for the extension taken to process the grievance. I was supposed to receive an answer in July 2016, the last extension I received was in December 2016 saying an answer was expected in January. It is now March 2017. This system is so broken that they cannot get an extension for an extension filed on time on two different grievances. Furthermore, I cannot file a final level grievance to Ottawa until the grievances at this initial level are responded to. I have tried to send one via government mail, but the mailroom opened the letter and returned it to me saying that prisoners are only allowed to put in final level grievances through the system after the procedure has been followed. However, if they control that process with no external accountability checks and refuse to answer, then we prisoners are completely at their mercy in the hopes that they will do their jobs without any accountability or consequences. What I would like to see going forward is a complete dismantling of the prisoner redress system and another system implemented by *third party* that is given some authority over at least a portion of CSC in an otherwise unaccountable system. This is a dream, however, because if Canada is not willing to sign the United Nation's *Optional Protocol to the Convention Against Torture and other cruel, inhumane, or degrading treatment or punishment* (OPCAT)[3] they are certainly not going to yield any of their totalitarian and tyrannical reins of power to a third party that allows prisoners to be empowered by expressing their concerns or fighting for their rights all while getting results. Therefore, a more realistic desire going forward would be to have a grievance clerk that is in an openly accessible area such as the library or the Inmate Committee office with a direct link to Ottawa that can be used once the initial level grievance has passed its expected response date so we are not entirely at the mercy of CSC's benevolence or lack thereof.

MAJOR ISSUES

Severe Lack of Professional Psychological Resources
Eighth, and the beginning of the three major issues I have identified, is the serious lack of psychological resources. At present, we only have three

psychologists and one psychiatrist for nearly 500 prisoners. Such lacking resources has consequences. For instance, I had a single objective on my correctional plan, which was to participate in psychological intervention. It took eleven requests (nine of which went unanswered), three complaints (two unanswered), one grievance which is still not answered despite having finished counseling in full, and several calls to the Correctional Investigator all within a period of eleven months to be able to be seen by a psychologist, which CSC said was what I needed to be doing to be rehabilitated. I did not qualify for a formal program and I was months away from my full parole date before I was seen by a psychologist. Moreover, I had to postpone my parole twice because it took so long. With numbers like these, why are there only a handful of psychologists and one psychiatrist, neither of which most prisoners ever see? This is an unacceptable system especially since the *vast* majority of prisoners either need or would benefit greatly from psychological intervention. Also, by extension, society benefits as we are spending less by releasing prisoners early, rehabilitating them which adds to public safety, and reducing recidivism rates, further improving both public safety and incarceration spending. What I would like to see moving forward is a *drastic* increase in mental health funding for federal penitentiaries so that every prisoner who needs it can benefit from personalized psychological sessions so the issues that caused them to commit offences in the first place can be dealt with. Also, to be clear, I do not want a half-baked attempt for political publicity so that each prisoner gets one hour with a psychologist. I want to see a devotion to genuinely helping prisoners by getting psychological intervention at least once a week for the duration of their stay for those who need and want access to such support. Psychological issues are not fixed overnight or in an hour and they are also not fixed by programs where unqualified facilitators give us abstract tools to use as the current Integrated Correctional Program Model ICPM (CSC's formal program)[4] likes to believe. We need professional psychological help to aid in addressing the issues that led us here to begin with, otherwise known as actual rehabilitation.

Zero Accountability from Correctional Service Canada

Ninth, and in my opinion the very foundation of nearly every issue I have discussed, as well as many more I have not, is the lack of accountability within CSC. What other Canadian government agency is completely self-governed, has its own set of laws, is veiled in shadows from the public eye, and is so close to above the law that they can kill human beings with little to no consequences? What other Canadian government agency is its own self-contained fiefdom that that needs not be accountable to any other organization? Who thought that any Canadian government agency having the ability to regulate themselves was a good idea? If you have not already, look at the Correctional Investigator's reports year after year stating that the system needs serious attention, which are all ignored by CSC. Look at the John Howard Society of Canada and Canadian Association of Elizabeth Fry Societies reports time and time again. Look at the senseless deaths of prisoners that could have been easily prevented or the millions a year in lawsuits against the institutions all without meaningful consequences and little to no media coverage as they sign non-disclosure agreements for settlements. All these organizations have no bite to back up their bark as CSC is accountable to nobody under the vague and ambiguous guise of "the interest of public safety". These words absolve them of any responsibility and people just accept this as standard practice for their protection. In other words, CSC is given dominion over human life and are beholden to nobody with no consequences or accountability to anyone but themselves for their actions. All these organizations recognize serious problems, but can do nothing other than make recommendations that CSC can choose to ignore. Could you imagine a company not being accountable to their shareholders? Could you imagine a government not being accountable to its people? I can – it is called Correctional Service Canada.

I was once asked by my friends what prison was like. Since I am the only person I have ever known that has gone to prison, I had to reflect a long time about this. The next time we spoke, I told them prison was like Chinese water torture. Any given droplet is of no concern, but 10,000 of them consecutively will drill a hole through your skull. Likewise, it is not always the murder and the covering up evidence before the RCMP investigate it that is the main issue, but rather the excessive use of force, the inhumane nine-day lockdowns without showers or phone calls, the 28-hour periods between meals on lockdown, the malicious act of leaving the lights on all night or kicking doors at 3:00am, the shutting off of water or toilets, the mysterious absence of video footage when an officer pummels a prisoner, and the mind-numbing lack of anything productive to do, all of which go mostly unnoticed and undocumented, which are the issues. What people do not understand is, like Chinese water torture, every condescending comment, every unanswered request, every time the phones are mysteriously shut off even though the guards have access to turning them off and on, every bite of uneatable food, every restless night on a half inch piece of foam on metal, every 'random' search, every 'Rec on the range'[5] for the third time this week without cause, every refusal to answer you by the guard when you need something, and every flashlight in the eyes every hour on the hour, are droplets that start to drill a hole through your skull. All the while, you have no real power to address any issue because no organization you contact – assuming the mailroom allowed the letter to go through as they do not like their secrets to leave the walls – can do anything but make recommendations. These 'minor' issues culminate together over years are the real culprit of insanity behind bars. This breeds a hostile, dehumanizing, traumatic, and helpless environment where most prisoners feel completely defeated, un-empowered to change their situation and devoid of any hope. As an example of this, when the Supreme Court of Canada made their ruling that physician assisted suicide was legal, several prisoners talked about it in a genuinely excited manner as a potential escape from the daily misery created by those droplets. It was such a large deal that the Inmate Committee actually looked into it and posted information on the walls due to the volume of people curious to see if they could qualify. Several letters were sent to *Dying with Dignity Canada*. None were answered. This is the hopelessness and helplessness that the lack of accountability breeds as the public seems to forget we are still humans and Canadian citizens too.

What I would like to see moving forward is a third-party organization that is not affiliated with CSC that has federal mandate to oversee at least some of the components of the organization and have jurisdiction to implement necessary changes. Ideally, there would be a process to formally petition this third party as prisoners to address issues as they arise. Secondly, I would like to see the veil of secrecy cloaking CSC lifted by allowing the media and public access to see the daily workings of the institutional life so they can be made aware of these serious issues.

Finally, I would like to see Canada not only sign the UN's *OPCAT*, but to be subject to surprise visits by the UN and this third party so as not to give them time to prepare a picture-perfect view of the system as is currently the case with the Correctional Investigator. The prisoners can always tell when the inspectors are here because the food gets substantially better and we get double portions. This is a running joke within the institution, which is why only surprise visits will suffice.

Attitudes of Correctional Officers
(Psychological Screening or Retraining)
Tenth, and finally, a serious screening process for correctional officer's psychological make-up or retraining for officers every few years is sorely needed. I would like to admit at this juncture that not every guard I have met is malicious or vindictive. In fact, there are four of them that are decent human beings. The other several dozen that I have encountered fall into exactly two categories which, after all you have read, I am sure you could hazard a guess. These categories are bullies and those who have been bullied. The bullies are tolerable. A few kicks to the door and some sneering usually fills their need to diminish or dehumanize others, and it is usually left at that. Those who have been bullied are something else altogether different. You would think after experiencing bullying themselves that they would be empathetic to those who have been stripped of their freedom, liberty and individuality. Yet it seems their need to expend all the years of repressed anger outweighs their empathy. These are the ones that are most dangerous. These guards go out of their way to belittle, traumatize and dehumanize as many prisoners as possible. They resort to violence quickly and prisoners cannot ask anything of them without walking on eggshells. I have personally been beaten for "being too smart" and therefore insubordinate. It was never written-up or documented, and to this day I am not even *known* to the security team in any negative capacity due to excellent behavior in the institution, yet I was a victim of an undocumented assault without cause. Two prisoners have human rights complaints in on this correctional officer and yet he is still on the same range as us working as if nothing is happening. If you look for the guards with the most frequent complaints against them, you will find those who have been bullied. According

to the CSC study R-44[6] titled "Attitudes of CSC Correctional Officers towards Offender" done in 1996, "23.3% of CO's [correctional officers] exhibit empathetic views of prisoners, 76.2% held punitive views of corrections, and 53.6% supported rehabilitation". That was two decades ago and before Harper's 'law and order' agenda implicitly supported the idea that you go to prison for punishment, not as punishment. This means that more than 20 years ago over three-quarters of correctional officers believed they were here to punish us and *over half* do not support rehabilitation! We cannot allow people who have such beliefs have unaccountable dominion over human life.

What I would like to see moving forward is a *clear* mandate for CSC to prioritize rehabilitation in practice, not just in theory, and provide the subsequent training necessary to implement this new shift in mindset. Our punishment is being stripped of our liberty *not* being beaten, physically or mentally, for any reason. We need to put the "correction" back into "correctional" officer. Secondly, I would like to see a battery of psychological tests for *every* officer before ever being allowed to set foot in a federal institution.

CONCLUSION

CSC implements barbaric practices of mental and physical torture in a dictatorship-like environment with zero accountability to anyone but themselves, and has a long way to go before it can confidently say it belongs in one of the most free and progressive countries on earth. Ideally, the system needs to be completely remolded as our intoxication with incarceration as a solution to our problems is outdated and detrimental not only to prisoners, but also to public safety as these people *are* getting out and often without being properly rehabilitated. Problems such as a lack of pardons, mandatory minimum sentences, food inadequacies, health care issues, postponement of parole, lack of intellectual stimulation from a lack of access to resources/hobbies/education, the broken prisoner grievance system, the lack of psychological resources, the lack of accountability, and the attitudes of correctional officers will continue to plague this system as captives are dehumanized, traumatized, and overwhelmed with a sense of helplessness all while CSC looks good on paper. CSC's mission statement states, "The Correctional Service

Canada (CSC), as part of the criminal justice system and respecting the rule of law, contributes to public safety by actively encouraging and assisting prisoners to become law-abiding citizens, while exercising reasonable, safe, secure, and humane control". It sounds pretty does it not? If Prime Minister Justin Trudeau and the Liberal Party truly believe in an "open and accountable government", they need to turn their gaze to where a blind eye has been turned for decades – the federal penitentiary system. I was once a proud, world-traveling Canadian wearing our flag everywhere, but I have been rendered unable to feel anything but ashamed of my country due to this experience and the knowledge that my nation will never forgive me with a pardon for what I have done regardless of how much I try to make amends or give back to society.

ENDNOTES

[1] The IWK Health Centre is a hospital in Halifax, Nova Scotia that provides care to women, children, and youth from Nova Scotia, New Brunswick and Prince Edward Island (IWK Health Centre, no date).

[2] Please see Shauna Bottos, Tammy Cabana, Tara Beauchamp and Karla Emeno (2009) *Waivers, Postponements, and Withdrawals: Offenders, Parole Officers and National Parole Board Perspectives*, Ottawa: Correctional Service Canada. Retrieved from http://www. pbcclcc. gc. ca/rprts/r193/r193-eng. Pdf

[3] According to the website of the United Nations Human Rights Office of the High Commissioner (OHCHR), Canada is not listed as a member of the human rights council. The OHCHR website also provides a map of all countries which are (a) state party, (b) signatory, and (c) no action. Canada is listed as "no action" as of April 2017 (United Nations Human Rights Council, no date).

[4] Integrated Correctional Program Model (ICPM), which was introduced as part of CSC's modernizing and streamlining of programs and services. This consolidated all of CSC's core programs into one ongoing program that is designed to target the "risk" of all prisoners.

[5] "Rec on the range" refers to a modified routine that CSC implements in incidents like lockdowns. Under this routine, prisoners are not confined to their cells, but must remain on the unit and are not permitted to attend the yard of have any other movement throughout the institution. This operating procedure was in keeping with the former principle of the *Corrections and Conditional Release Act* (CCRA) that the "least restrictive measures" must be used.

[6] Please see: Robinson, David and Michel Larivière (1996) *Attitudes of Federal Correctional Officers Towards Offenders* (Research Report R-44), Ottawa: Correctional Service Canada. Retrieved from http://www.csc-scc.gc.ca/research/092/r44e_e.pdf

REFERENCES

IWK Health Centre (no date) *Wikipedia*. Retrieved from https://en.wikipedia.org/wiki/IWK_Health_Centre

United Nations Human Rights Council (no date) Retrieved from http://www.ohchr.org/EN/HRBodies/HRC/Pages/CurrentMembers.aspx

Dispatches from the Quebec Region

Port Cartier Institution
T.B.

I have been incarcerated for over twenty years and have lived the changes that were enacted under the three previous Conservative federal governments. Below, I discuss what, in my view, are some of the most profound changes.

THE SHIFT TOWARDS AN AMERICAN-STYLE SYSTEM

I have watched this all play-out very slowly. I feel some of the changes that have been made are very un-Canadian and if ordinary Canadians actually understood this they would not tolerate it. The notion of rehabilitation has been replaced with the far-right leaning notion of punishment. The Scandinavians understand the difference between rehabilitation and punishment, and have bet very heavily on the former, working wonders for their penal system and society. The Germans have also gone the more humane and civilized way. And again, this had positive outcomes on their society as a whole. The American 'tough on crime', 'lock them up and throw away the key' approach is the equivalent of sweeping the dirt under the rug. It does not fix the problem, it just moves it around. What have the Americans gained by their dungeons and 'tough on crime' approach? A super angry, disenfranchised, poorer, more desperate and dangerous society. I think it to be true when it is said that a society's value can be measured by how they treat their prisoners. Look at the extremes. On one side we have Sweden, Norway, Finland and Germany. On the other extreme we can see Saudi Arabia, Iran, China, North Korea, Russia and the United States. Can we not say that the more freedom a country has, the more rights it affords to its citizens, the better society will look after their weakest? Anyone who says we should lock anyone up and throw away the key is basically saying they are too ignorant, too close minded, too hateful and too scared to understand the merits of rehabilitation. Human rights and prisoners' rights go hand-in-hand. This shift to a broken American-style system must stop. All studies show that harsher punishments do not reduce crime and that a more civil rehabilitation approach does work. Today, if someone is convicted of three murders in Canada he or she can be sentenced to life-75, meaning no parole eligibility before 75 years in prison. In Norway, the same conviction will result in a sentence of 21 years with first parole eligibility after 14 years. Is their society falling into murderous chaos? No, on the contrary their recidivism rates are the lowest in the world, because they stress the importance to rehabilitation, not punishment for punishment sake.

LAWS ARE THERE TO PROTECT THE ACCUSED AND/OR CONVICTED FROM A TOTALITARIAN STATE

In the last twenty-three years, I have noticed a shift away from protecting the rights of the accused and/or convicted, as if eroding their rights gives victims greater rights and standing. I can understand the need for the state to want to fight for the rights of victims, but that cannot and must not come at the cost of the rights of those in conflict with the law. This move undermines the whole justice system. Keep in mind as we continue down this dangerous slope, we will move closer to totalitarianism whereby citizens will be subjected to excessive state power. The *Charter* must take precedence and inform law-making in this country.

MULTIPLE LIFE SENTENCES ARE UN-CANADIAN

Most experts will agree that a life sentence is a bad thing. It causes too much damage to the life of the prisoner, making rehabilitation much harder. That is why the many progressive countries,[1] have removed the life sentence from their sentencing and have replaced it with a 21-year maximum no matter the crime. Canada has made a great mistake by going in the other direction and sentencing people to multiple life sentences. Life-25 was a bad enough trade-off when the death penalty was abolished in this country. Increasing parole eligibility beyond this offers little hope with respect to rehabilitation. Why would this prisoner with nothing more to lose not act out in the most violent and desperate way possible behind bars?

It is inhumane to give such punishment. A civilized society offers its people a chance to correct an error, a chance to improve one's life, a chance to rehabilitate. An emotional eighteen-year-old can make a terrible mistake and because of a life-sentence their whole life is ruined. People change. Any psychologist will swear that a man at eighteen or twenty is not the same man at forty or fifty. But now with multiple life sentences, the notion of rehabilitation has been eroded of its meaning for many prisoners.

PRISONER PAY NEVER ADJUSTED
FOR INCREASED COST OF LIVING

It is incredible to see how bad the federal penitentiary system has fallen. In the last few decades, I have seen the income of correctional officers go up every few years. Prisoner pay has stayed the same for the whole time I have been in the federal penitentiary system and now CSC even cut our pay by a third, so we can pay further room and board costs.

About 20 years ago, CSC made a small change to try and help prisoners with the cost of living. They added $4.00 extra on a hygiene account so people could clean themselves properly. When given a choice of food or soap, people will choose food. So, the creation of a separate hygiene account where every pay an extra $4.00 was given whether the prisoner worked or not, just to have the extra money to buy soap, toothpaste, shampoo and the like. And this hygiene account can only be used to purchase hygiene items. Well, that was more than twenty years ago. What do you think $4.00 every two weeks can buy for personal hygiene? Behind the walls, deodorant costs $5.78, toothpaste $3.85, a toothbrush $4.25, and so on. Basically, you make a choice, one time you buy deodorant, two weeks later a toothbrush, two weeks later shampoo, two weeks after that toothpaste, and if you need to buy soap for $1.25 a bar that just means you will not have deodorant for a month. Is this how it should be? People choosing what they need to clean the most?

Prisoner pay is just as bad. It has never been adjusted for cost of living. People who have no families and rely only on their pay inside can take up to two years just to buy a television for themselves to occupy their minds. It is beyond ridiculous. It is shameful. Basically, the only way around this, is to sell drugs, steal and sell things from the prison kitchen, basically go to the prison black market to make ends meet. Some people who never stole a thing in their lives are working in the kitchen so they can steal extra food, sell it and use the profits to purchase basic necessities. The only solution, and it would fix dozens of spin-off problems, would be to make a long overdue pay correction. The best way would be whatever the national minimum wage is, that should be our daily pay. When the national average is raised to meet cost of living and inflation, then the prisoner pay follows. That is why mirroring the national average minimum wage makes the most sense. It can be used as a base. Most people here make $5.80 a day, a very few make $6.90 a day, and a lot more make less than $5.80 a day. From this, they remove about a third for room and board, then there is cable cost, committee costs, the Inmate Welfare

Fund, and so on. We are lucky to have $2.50 from the original pay received. Then keep in mind whatever we buy we pay taxes on as well. So, money that does not go very far to begin with, goes nowhere once CSC tacks on room and board. This ridiculous notion of room and board needs to end, and pay must go up to meet inflation and the cost of living. Otherwise, problems stemming from this will continue to persist.

INSUFFICIENT HALFWAY HOUSE CAPACITY AND BUILDING SUPER-PRISONS

Halfway house space continues to be insufficient given the demand.[2] A halfway house is an essential block in a prisoner's rehabilitation plan. With so many waiting to go into halfway houses, it makes it hard to believe that the government wants prisoners to rehabilitate, especially when we witnessed hundreds of millions of dollars spent on transforming existing penitentiaries into super-prisons. Why does Canada need larger federal penitentiaries?

CENTRAL FEEDING SYSTEM

The central feeding system[3] must stop. Prisoners are human beings and should be treated as such. The very name itself is insulting, like we are animals. Asides from this, the logic to abandon the current food delivery system is very simple. Central feeding systems remove the nutritional value of the food. The second strike against this system is the loss of food quality and taste. If the government wants to feed us cardboard, then that should be part of our sentence. At present, it is not, and being fed this fare is an added punishment. There have been reports of people getting violently sick over the food. Another important issue is that kitchen work and training provide prisoners with more job training. Some people in the past have been released and got stable well-paying kitchen jobs based on what they learned in prison kitchens.

RETURN TO POLICIES AND PRACTICES THAT PLACE A STRONGER EMPHASIS ON REINTEGRATION INTO SOCIETY

There should be stronger emphasis and training for prisoners who are on their way out. I have seen job training cancelled, along with special school programs and even basic job skills training come to an end over the years. This must change. More money must pour into these types of programs. What are people who have been in penitentiaries for decades to do when they get out? It is very important for our society that prisoners have the necessary tools they need to get out and stay out. A violence prevention program will not have the same value to a prisoner as a kitchen training program or programs teaching computer skills, marketing, business management, and the like. Having the means to provide for yourself is a first and necessary building block to achieving the stability necessary to live safely in the community.

ENDNOTES

[1]   These countries include France where prisoners who receive life sentence are eligible for parole after serving 18 years. In Germany, a life sentence is 15 years. In Denmark prisoners can receive a pardoning hearing after serving 12 years. It should be noted that "life" sentenced prisoners serve an average of 16 years (Mock, 2015).

[2]   According to the 2014 spring Report of the Auditor General Michael Ferguson which examined how CSC is managing public resources in accordance with its mandate, the organization was not preparing prisoners for a timely release into the community and many prisoners were being warehoused at higher security levels where the costs to incarcerate are much higher. In this assessment, the Auditor General found that: "We also asked CSC officials whether offenders were transitioning to community facilities once they had been granted day parole. The officials explained that the number of community accommodations available for offenders released on day parole had declined. Available beds in community facilities are taken by a growing number of prisoners on statutory release or subject to long-term supervision orders. These offenders are required by the Parole Board to reside in community facilities as a condition of their release, and have priority over prisoners released on day parole. As a result, some prisoners who were granted day parole stayed in the penitentiaries while they waited for accommodation to become available in the community" (Office of the Auditor General Canada, 2014).

[3]   The central feeding system is the "modernised" delivery of food services to federal prisoners wherein the food is cooked at a central location and then flash frozen and shipped to the institution where it can be re-warmed before being served. This is referred to in common parlance as "cook chill" technology and while the program has been introduced as a cost saving measure since it was introduced in 2014, the system has been fraught with complaints from prisoners regarding the quality and quantity of the food provided. See for example (National Post, 2017).

REFERENCES

Mock, M. (2015) "Fact or fiction: Not all "life sentences" around the world are actually for life", December 18. Retrieved from http://www.robertreeveslaw.com/blog/life-sentences/

National Post (2017) "'Yuck!' Hungry offenders bartering sausages as prisons try to cut costs with new menu, ombudsman says", *National Post* – March 21. Retrieved from http://nationalpost.com/news/canada/prison-food

Office of the Auditor General Canada (2014) "Chapter 4—Expanding the Capacity of Penitentiaries", in *2014 Spring report of the Auditor General of Canada*—Correctional Service Canada, Ottawa. Retrieved from http://www.oag-bvg.gc.ca/internet/English/parl_oag_201405_04_e_39335.html

Port Cartier Institution
Anonymous Prisoner 6

I am in my forties and have been serving a life sentence since the early 1990s. This being the case, I have observed and experienced the real impact of the Harper government's changes to Correctional Service Canada (CSC) policies and practices. In my twenty-five plus years of incarceration, I have resided in many federal penitentiaries located in Quebec and have directly witnessed many of CSC's machinations in the fleecing of the Canadian taxpayer. I will try to be as concise as possible, limiting my comments and observations to a few short sentences per topic, because it would be far too easy for me to go on and on, and get lost in the details when my goal is to make specific arguments.

The first and most obvious change relates to *prisoner pay*. The new Commissioner's Directive 730 *Offender Program Assignments and Payments*,[1] in conjunction with a parole officer's 'discretion' and/ or 'professional opinion' gaining more credence, allow them to enter information into Inmate Performance Evaluations, whether accurate or not, that deprive prisoners of their rightfully deserved pay level, which can in turn lead to mistrust and hostility between the prisoner and the case worker. From personal experience, even if a prisoner has done everything humanly possible to fulfill every aspect of their Correctional Plan and has the paper trail evidence to demonstrate this, the parole officer retains 'discretion' to report that they have low accountability, motivation and engagement.

When a prisoner uses the *complaint and grievance system* to remedy a situation like the one just mentioned, it now takes a ridiculous amount of time to receive a response. At every level, the answers are nonsensical and tow the organizational line. I can still remember when the Complaint and Grievance system actually worked, albeit this was a long time ago. Under Harper, CSC removed the second level grievance, but this did nothing to reduce the delays in processing complaints or the collusion between staff members at the different levels within CSC.

After an eighteen-month to two-year wait for the third level response to the grievance, the only course of action for a dissatisfied prisoner is the Federal Court. Obtaining provincial Legal Aid services to fight the federal penitentiary system is often next to impossible. Once a mandate can be obtained, often there are no lawyers available or they are too busy to take the case. In reality, they are not paid enough for the work they have to do. Meanwhile, the Attorney General has unlimited resources to fight prisoner petitions. During this process, CSC frequently continues abusing their 'discretionary powers', which go unchecked and often violate the constitutionally protected *Charter* rights of prisoners.

Self-represented litigants before the courts get no help from CSC, despite what the Commissioner's Directives would lead a naive reader to believe. There are no "computerized resources comparable to those in community libraries" (Commissioners Directive 720 *Education Programs and Service for Inmates*).[2] The paltry list of "judicial" resources inside is insufficient to direct a self-represented litigant anywhere. There are no photocopying services in the library here in Port-Cartier and most of the legal books are not on the shelves, but are hidden away.

From personal experience, while embroiled in a battle with CSC before the courts, on several occasions after having consulted a legal book that was on the shelf and accessible to all, when I subsequently returned to the library to consult the same book it had been removed from sight and had to be requested. Moreover, as unbelievable as it may sound, after Port-Cartier Institution purchased a *French Annotated Criminal Code* and I had made several complaints via the broken and corrupt complaint and grievance system guaranteed by the *Corrections and Conditional Release Act* (CCRA) to no avail, I had to fight for a year with the assistance of Language Rights in order to obtain an *English Annotated Criminal Code*.

Returning to the issues with the pay, there are the *new deductions* for "Room and Board" and the "Inmate Telephone System" (ITS). Both of these deductions would be ridiculous if they were not so cruel. They cut our pay with these new deductions, imposed vague and discretionary objectives in our Performance Evaluations, while severely diminishing the quality and nutritional value of our food. They also diminished our medical and dental care. Under our old pay system, a prisoner could barely get by, especially when they had to help pay for phone calls to family and/or Private Family Visits. Should one get sick, they have to pay for very expensive cough syrup, cough drops and aspirins that are no longer supplied by CSC.

The deductions for the ITS are a big CSC deception. I know a couple of different prisoners who have challenged the ITS deductions because they do not use the service. When prisoners inquired to find out how much money exactly was in the account to repair it, as we were lead to believe, we were told that no such account exists. In fact, the money is re-funneled back into helping defray the overall cost of the telephone system.

Another CSC rip-off is the new "Prototype" *catalogue for prisoner purchasing*. We used to be able to purchase from any store that would put up with CSC's payment scheme. Now, the only option we have is to purchase items through this new catalogue. Items that we had been purchasing from one specific supplier are now two and three times the price in this new catalogue. The company that runs the catalogue appears to be purchasing these items (e.g. the exact same models of shoes) directly from the same companies or suppliers we once dealt with and charging us outrageous prices. You would actually have to see and compare the previous and current catalogues to fully appreciate this.

Furthermore, we had for years been allowed to deal with a well-known store that sells music on Compact Disc and shipped them through the mail. Now we have to purchase all our music through this new supplier at a flat rate per Compact Disc. We are no longer allowed double-CD's and if it is more expensive than twenty-five dollars we will pay more. If it is less we still have to pay the minimum twenty-five dollars. The end result is that not only do prisoners pay more for products, with less pay then they had before, it impacts the overall number of items that can be owned within the allotted fifteen-hundred-dollar limit set by CSC.

Returning to the new Commissioner's Directive 730[4] in relation to the Correctional Plan and *education*, it is often applied in such a fashion that it borders on cruel and unusual punishment. There is a waiting list for seats in the schools, because there is a lack of jobs in the prisons. Most of the prisoners who are there do not want to be or are there through coercion by their parole officer. Where does this leave the few that actually want an education? On a waiting list or in a classroom where it is so noisy or disrupted by people that do not want to be there or should not be there as they would rather be working. Those present have difficulty concentrating and getting any work done in such an environment.

Back in the day, CSC used to offer actual job training skills for trades such as brick layer, carpenter, plumber, draftsman, electrician, welder, small engine mechanic, barber, gardener, as well as kitchen jobs. If CSC's actual objective was to rehabilitate prisoners, instead of guaranteeing the momentum of their revolving door, they could be teaching guys skills that they might actually use once released. Instead, they spend a ridiculous amount of money creating new 'rehabilitative' programs and the only jobs created are the ones for the new guards they hire. A cynic would come to the conclusion that their real objective when creating a 'new' program and coercing prisoners into taking it is to justify the continued position and salary of the guard turned 'Program Facilitator'. I just finished a "maintenance program" given by a former guard and it was 'recommended' that everyone in my program do the course again, if available. Talk about fleecing taxpayers! How about computers for job skills training? This is where the future is headed. Computers had a moratorium put on them just before the Harper-era. The main reason that prisoners are no longer allowed to own computers was, and continues to remain, bogus[3] – institutional security. Yet, we still have a limited access to computers owned by the institution. So, if they are so dangerous to the security of the institutions, why do we still have access? Their reasoning is completely flawed and applied inconsistently.

Last, but not least, there is the new five-year waiting period between Parole Board hearings for Lifers. This is troubling, particularly for all those that diligently try to fulfill their Correctional Plan despite the overcrowding in schools and the waiting lists for 'rehabilitative programming', the parole officer's 'discretion' when it comes to Inmate Performance Evaluations and the like. To be told "you can try again in five years" extinguishes hope. How can CSC continue to pretend they are trying to rehabilitate anyone, when by all appearances it would seem they are really just trying to guarantee the perpetual growth of the federal penitentiary system?

ENDNOTES

[1]   Correctional Service Canada (2017a) *Commissioners Directive 730 Offender Program Assignments and Inmate Payments*, Ottawa. Retrieved from http://www.csc-scc.gc.ca/acts-and-regulations/730-cd-eng.shtml

[2]   Correctional Service Canada (2017b) *Commissioners Directive 720 Education Programs and Services for Inmates*, Ottawa. Retrieved from http://www.csc-scc.gc.ca/acts-and-regulations/720-cd-eng.shtml

[3]   According to Commissioners Directive 566-12-*Personal Property of Offenders* in effect 2015-10-19: "Inmates who have approved personal computers, peripherals and software, which were authorized as personal effects prior to October 2002, will be permitted to retain this equipment until the time of their release from the institution or violation of the conditions...". That said, owning a computer is now considered a security risk (Correctional Service Canada, 2017c). Correctional Service Canada (2017c) *Commissioners Directive 566-12 Personal Property of Offenders*, Ottawa. Retrieved from http://www.csc-scc.gc.ca/lois-et-reglements/566-12-cd-eng.shtml

[4]   See *supra note 1*.

The following are the issues that are important to me, with access to computers being top of mind.

COMPUTERS FOR PRISONERS

Prior to prison, I worked as a computer professional for over thirty years. I believe that the most important necessity for prisoners today is to update the technologies we have access to, starting with computers for prisoners. If computers are not a security concern in common areas of the institution, they should be allowed in our cells as well.

I cannot think of any bit of information that exists today that you will not find available in digital format. The number of software applications available cover almost every topic, from any kind of self-help (physical, psychological or emotional) to a complete range of educational topics and on through to professional training. I have been personally thinking about taking one of the programs for Alzheimer's memory improvement, but it is only available on computer.

It used to be that digital content was harder to find than hard copies. Today, the reality is reversed as digital/electronic content is everywhere and paper copies are harder to find. This situation is not going to improve for prisoners. Out-of-print books are being brought back in electronic format only, and more and more companies are communicating electronically. Those behind bars are left searching for a physical location to address our correspondence.

Even today's social and educational programs are putting greater importance on technology/computer-based problems and solutions. When we see that coding programs are beginning to be taught in schools, starting in elementary school through to Grade 12, it is clear that it is socially unconscionable to keep prisoners in the stone age and/or in the dark. I would also like to point out that the only way for a prisoner to access higher education and fulfill their potential is to have almost unlimited access to a computer system.

When we look over the technology that they (i.e. the prison administration) do allow us to have and use, it is all surely out of date to the point where we are being forced to make due with obsolete technology (e.g. diskettes/disks). Here, we have a technology that was wracked with problems when it was in full use, at the top of its game. My point is clear when one looks at the speed with which the industry moved to improve, repair and replace this technology. We are working on out-of-date machines. The Commissioner's Directive 566-1[1] clearly allow prisoners who do have personal computers the right to keep and use the tools that come with the operating system (i.e. Windows). The Directive that allows computer owners the right to have 20 diskettes and non-owners 5 diskettes is an example of inversed logic given that those with the hardware can save their files on it. It is dreadfully clear that computer professionals were not included in the talks about computers and associated technologies during the period in CSC history when these Commissioner's Directives were written.

PRISONER PAY AND TAXES

The prisoner pay has not been adjusted for many years. We continue to pay outside prices and taxes for items just like every other citizen, while earning a woefully inadequate salary. I may be here in a federal penitentiary against my will, but I still pay rent (i.e. food and accommodation), with 30 percent of my pay taken for this alone. This leaves me with $28 in take-home pay every few weeks, which does not go very far.

DOUBLE STANDARDS

I would also like to have addressed the double standard that exists in Canada's federal penitentiaries. Whenever a prisoner does something towards an officer or the CSC in general they, along with their fellow captives, pay the price. I have things taken away because of what another prisoner has done. However, it is inappropriate for me to take out my frustrations on one staff member due to the actions of one of their colleagues.

Why are there two systems in place concerning prisons, them and us? If we act out, the response is swift and hard, even when we are innocent. When staff members act out, we are more likely to be told to make a complaint, as they know that little if anything will come of it. If we threaten legal or criminal action we are threatened and coerced, beaten into submission, sometimes literally. Meaningful accountability should apply to all who live and work behind the walls.

PURCHASING

We are now being forced to pay twice as much on items that are of such a low quality that some items are forced to be returned to be replaced three or four times before the prisoner finally refuses to accept delivery. We are often receiving items that are clearly "slightly-used" and are expected to accept what they offer. When we do not and subsequently complain, we are accused of behaving in bad faith in the transaction. Case in point would be computer diskettes. When we order a box of ten they arrive loose in a Ziploc bag. To add insult to injury, the diskettes are clearly of different models. Some still have the glue from previous stickers. In the case in question, CSC technicians checked the diskettes and responded with the verdict that they were clean, hence new.

Items in this new catalogue that are marked as being acceptable in maximum-security facilities are refused here for no apparent reason. I find this hard to accept. In addition, why can we no longer purchase items from Walmart, Sears, Canadian Tire and the like? Our funds are supposed to be held and administered by CSC. How can they not be able to dispense them to different companies? Why are we forced to give our families financial information to send money home? This whole system around money promotes an underground economy, a black-market. They take enough of our cash to pay for listening services for our phone conversations, now they want direct access to our family's information. It is a violation of their privacy.

FARMS FOR FOOD

I have heard that the government is already looking into the possibility of bringing back the prison farms. Bring them back to offset expenditures for food, as well as provide hands-on training for the prisoners working there. This makes sense, both fiscally and with respect to rehabilitation.

OTHER OBSERVATIONS
AND RECOMMENDATIONS

We have very little access to the library and reading materials. Many reading materials (e.g. legal) are kept out of our hands. When the issue is forced, they allow us thirty minutes to look through a title and to write any notes we might be interested in. How can we ask for a book that we do not know exists? Many of the books are out of date and while trying to find information, we may find old case law or points of justice that are no longer useful. We need access to information about everything from religious background, ancestral information for those who wish to learn where they come from, music lyrics for guitar to pass our time, and information for school work.

Video conferences between the prisoner and their family are needed when distance between us makes visitation prohibitive. I know that in a limited sense this already exists in other prisons, but the stupidity of how it is currently arranged with a person having to present themselves to the institution where their loved one is held is awe inspiring. There are more churches spread out around the world then there are halfway houses or parole offices. Arrange the connection through the penitentiary chapel and outside churches located close to the families. The priest/pastor is always present, as well as a guard also. Communication between priest and family could precede services, just to make sure everything goes smoothly and there are no incidents. Thank you for your time and your interest in our thoughts and plights.

ENDNOTES

[1] For more information please see Correctional Service Canada (2017) *Commissioners Directive 566-12 Personal Property of Offenders*, Ottawa. Retrieved from http://www.csc-scc.gc.ca/lois-et-reglements/566-12-cd-eng.shtml

Établissement de Cowansville
Comité des détenus / Maxime Guillemette, Guy Tousignant, Daniel Loyer, Mario Ethier et Ricky Hankey

Nous vous soumettons ce qui nous semble les points les plus importants à nos yeux au sujet des changements apportés au Service correctionnel du Canada (SCC) par le gouvernement conservateur sous le règne du Premier-Ministre Harper. Le gouvernement conservateur de Monsieur Harper a fait de son programme électoral la nouvelle philosophie du SCC l'approche « *tough on crime* ». Avec l'aide des médias, qui dirigent l'attention vers certains types d'incidents ou d'événements et clament qu'il s'agit des plus grands problèmes, des plus grands dangers actuels, la réalité en ce qui concerne le déclin général de la criminalité est ignorée. Les conséquences pour les prisonniers sont nombreuses.

En ce moment, il y a une absence complète de suivi psychologique, sauf en cas de détresse. Le budget a aussi été réduit pour les ressources en matière de santé incluant un accès réduit aux dentistes et optométristes.

Nous pouvons aussi identifier deux grands types d'impacts découlant de la restriction des revenus des détenus. Le premier est d'ordre psychologique (ex : diminution de la motivation au travail, sentiments de colère et de frustration, une certaine anxiété, etc.), le second est d'ordre matériel qui n'est pas sans incidence sur l'ordre psychologique (ex : garder contact téléphonique, climat négatif à l'intérieur de l'établissement, manque de fonds à la sortie qui nuit aux efforts de réinsertion sociale, manque de fonds pour le soutien financier de la famille et les moyens pour maintenir une communication avec celle-ci, un manque de financement pour la majorité des projets de sortie nécessitant un minimum de dépenses comme les activités sportive ou sociales). D'après l'ancien gouvernement du Canada les ponctions effectuées sur les revenus des détenus s'inscrivent dans l'objectif de les responsabiliser. La responsabilisation correspond au niveau de participation du détenu à son plan correctionnel. C'est la seule responsabilisation. Il nous faut conclure que le concept de responsabilisation, tel qu'il est exprimé par le SCC, se limite aux aspects « judiciaire » du crime, ensuite aux comportements sociaux lié à la politesse et à la conformité aux règles de l'établissement. Il est donc présomptueux de prétendre que la ponction de 30% supplémentaire imposées sur les maigres revenus des détenus qui travaillent ait un lien avec la responsabilisation des détenus Les résultats du changement de philosophie du SCC est que nous sommes moins bien placés pour notre réintégration dans la communauté.

La recherche menée par le SCC a elle-même ciblé la famille comme étant l'un des facteurs atténuant le risque de récidive. Il n'existe presque plus dans les établissements à sécurité médium de programmes structurés qui permettaient aux détenus de se préparer adéquatement pour le retour progressif à la vie en société.

Il est aussi important de souligner que l'emploi est l'un des besoins criminogènes les plus fréquemment ciblés en matière de traitement pour la réussite de la réhabilitation sociale des prisonniers. Or, il existe peu de formations professionnelles afin d'inciter les prisonniers à acquérir des compétences pour une future sortie. De plus les ponctions de 30% font en sorte qu'il n'existe aucun incitatif pour les détenus d'acquérir une certaine somme d'argent pour leur sortie. Des restrictions ont également été imposées sur les diverses formations post-secondaire et à distance qui étaient offertes et qui sont payées par les prisonniers eux-mêmes. Nous encourageons le SCC à bonifier l'accès à des postes informatiques avec accès à Internet sécurisés pour recevoir ces formations afin que les détenus à leur sortie ne soient pas des incompétents en informatique.

Les fermes agricoles (ex : Westmorland, Pittsburg, Frontenac) n'existent plus. Elles étaient une excellente source de valorisation pour les prisonniers au travail (ex : contact avec des animaux) et elles devraient encore exister aujourd'hui.

CONCLUSION

Définitivement, à la lueur des lectures et des consultations que nous avons effectués auprès de la population de l'établissement de Cowansville, nous constatons que les politiques du dernier Gouvernement conservateur n'ont fait que punir les détenus. Les ponctions de 30%, le resserrement des critères pour l'obtention d'une libération conditionnelle, l'absence de programmes de formation académique, l'absence de programmes de formation professionnelle et d'autres mesures ont fait que les détenus ont été laissés à eux-mêmes. Ils n'ont quasiment plus de soutien à la réinsertion dans la société, ce qui est un non-sens.

Dispatches from the Ontario Region

Bath Institution
Josephy Joseph / Inmate Committee Chairman

To provide feedback to the federal government about current problems with criminal justice laws, policies, and practices enacted during the 2006-2015 period under the previous government, as well as future directions for penal policy and practice, the Inmate Committee at Bath Institution conducted a facility-wide consultation. Below, is the feedback we received on what should change, with much of the focus on reforms to Correctional Service Canada (CSC) penitentiaries.

ANONYMOUS BATH PRISONER 1

Group Food Drives
Group food drives have been eliminated. Group food drives enabled us to maintain community contact and raise money for organizations such as the Make a Wish Foundation. I would like to see a return to the previous policy and for CSC to allow groups to raise money through pizza and chicken sales, cultural food drives, and the like.

Prisoner Purchasing
CSC staff are no longer allowed to purchase items for prisoners through the institutional purchasing program. For example, the position of "purchasing officer" has been eliminated. With the elimination of this program the cost of purchasing has skyrocketed to way above what is reasonable. The new program has only one supplier and they charge way too much. I would like to see a return to the program of having a purchasing officer who has the authority to shop for each prisoner.

Institutional Food (Cook-Chill)
The food served on the line is no longer edible due to the new procedures such as freezing. Due to the change in food services I must now purchase extra food at the canteen, which is far from ideal as these items are not healthy. I would like to see that the government make kitchen work a job training program. This would assist with employment outside of the prison that would teach marketable skills, while providing nutritious food to prisoners.

Ion Scanner
The ion scanner is reading for *possible* contact with narcotics, which often results in the loss of visits and Private Family Visits. This puts a lot of

strain on marital relationships and also restricts elderly parents who are on medication from visiting the institution, which results in loss of family and community contact. I would like to see that the CSC use all tools available to staff. Instead of restricting the visit on the basis of a scan, a positive reading must be followed by a secondary or dog hit to justify this. I would like to see more done to promote family contact.

Escorted Temporary Absences

Escorted Temporary Absences (ETAs) for family contact and personal development granted from medium-security facilities are rarely granted. This prevents prisoners from doing important things like renewing their driver's license. It also takes away an opportunity to lower their security rating and restricts them from showing progress in their correctional plan. I would like to see that medium-security institutions be directed to start approving ETAs to get prisoners out to visit family, attend NA, AA and church outside of the prison.

Personal Effects

There is a $1,500 cap on the total value of all personal cell effects (i.e. property), which also includes stored effects. This extremely limits my ability as a long-term prisoner to save clothing, music and other items. I would like to see a return to the policy of issuing the full $1,500 dollars of valued cell effects.[1]

Group Accounts

Religious groups like Buddhists, Pagans, Jewish, Catholics and other persons of faith are no longer allowed to form group accounts. My religious group is now falling apart because we cannot purchase specific feast foods or buy basic items for our group coffee gatherings. I would like to see that each group is allowed to create an account as was the practice in previous years.

ANONYMOUS BATH PRISONER 2

Incentive Pay

The $2.20 per hour incentive payments that prisoners received for the productive labour that they carried out for CORCAN have been eliminated. I will no longer work for any CORCAN project. I believe this is slave labour. I would like to see a return to the former policy and that incentive pay be reinstated for honest labour.

Additional 30 Percent Deduction for Room and Board

There is now an additional 30 percent deduction from prisoners pay to cover the cost of "room and board". I can no longer send money home to my family, pay for telephone calls or afford private family visits. I can also no longer afford stamps for letters to stay in touch with my family. I would like to see a return to the policy of additional room and board only being imposed if the pay surpasses $69 in a two-week period as was the policy in the past.

Escorted Temporary Absences

ETAs from a medium-security prison must have two armed guards. Prisoners cannot afford to pay for the costs of an armed escort when going out on an elective ETA. As a result, they will not be granted the ETA. I would like to see a policy where they do case-by-case judgements. Not all ETAs require two armed guards, that is a ridiculous policy.

Life Line

The Life Line program has had all of its funding cut. This has resulted in the elimination of what were formerly trusted escorts for the purposes of Escorted Temporary Absences from the prison. We can also no longer access the counsellors that Life Line provided. I would like to see the Life Line program brought back and expanded as it was a successful program.

ANONYMOUS BATH PRISONER 3

Access to Medication

In August 2015, CSC National Headquarters ordered that the drug Gabapentin be removed from the drug formulary. This drug was used to treat non-diabetic neuropathy and other disorders. In being restricted access to this formerly prescribed medication I am in pain every day and it gets worse in the winter. I suffer from severely reduced productivity and it has hindered my legal work that I am doing to get out of prison. I would like to see that CSC eliminate and rescind the policy of restricting access to this medication, allowing doctors and specialists to prescribe medical treatment that meets the standard found in the community.

Least Restrictive Measures

The law stating that the CSC must use the least restrictive measures to protect society has been eliminated and reworded. The change allows security reclassifications on a whim by CSC employees. This has frustrated my attempts to get to lower security and therefore parole. I would like to see that the previous law be reinstated requiring that CSC impose the least restrictive measures required to protect society.

Prisoner Purchasing

CSC now forces all prisoner purchasing to be done through one supplier nationally. This policy took effect on 1 April 2016. As a result, the supplier now has a monopoly and we are given trash quality items at prices that we cannot afford. This is a rip off. For example, a pair of size 13 poor quality socks now costs $11. I would like to see that the monopoly be eliminated, and that prisoners be allowed to resume making purchases from the local suppliers with competitive prices and good quality items.

Prisoner Pay

In October 2013, CSC cut incentive prisoner pay. They are also now double dipping by charging us for "room and board" when our previous pay levels already accounted for such expenditures. This policy change has made the purchase of food and vitamins unaffordable so one cannot compensate for the cuts to food quantity and quality. One can also no longer save to hire lawyers and get medical care. I would like to see that the pay cuts be reversed and that instead prisoners be given a pay increase as has been recommended by the Office of the Correctional Investigator and many others.

Food Services (Cook-Chill)

The food is now made at one supply factory and cook-chilled. This has further reduced the nutrient supply, quality and quantity of food. It has made most meals unidentifiable as products do not have any labelling. We do not even know what we are eating. I would like to see that CSC resume having the prison kitchen cook meals for us.

Access to Programs

CSC is not allowing programs to be accessed before a third of a sentence is served. They are timing access to programs to coincide with statutory release at two-thirds of our sentences, which makes parole eligibility meaningless. This makes parole at the one-third mark next to impossible and allows the parole officers to force the waiver of hearings. This is changing and worsening the sentence imposed by the judge. I would like to see that CSC schedule program completions before the earliest parole eligibility date.

Access to Computers

CSC has restricted computer access and eliminated most of the remaining prisoner-owned computers. This has made things such as resolving disagreements with staff on legal issues impossible. I would like to see CSC allow the use of tablets on wireless networks to allow us to do legal and other work.

Prison Farms

The prison farms have been closed. This has degraded our food supply quality and eliminated the valuable experience of working on the farms. I would like to see that they rebuild the farm camps, preferably, even better than before in an effort to expand available jobs.

Second Level Grievances

CSC has eliminated the second level of the grievance process. This has resulted in an increased delay of responses at the final level and reduced the amount of evidence produced for later use in the courts. I would like to see that an independent grievance system be installed to solve all the problems associated with CSC investigating themselves.

Personal Cell Effects

CSC has changed the policy on cell effects. The total value of cell effects both stored and in the cell, must not amount to greater than $1,500. Many prisoners, and in particular, Lifers, are told that they are above the limit and have had to send out property or lose use of it in order to be allowed to make new purchases. I would like to see a return to having the cell effects limit apply to only what is being used in the cell with the ability to store items beyond the $1,500 limit.

ANONYMOUS BATH PRISONER 4

Gladue Principles

Under the previous government, CSC had policies to work around *Gladue* principles in an effort to maintain the status quo for Indigenous prisoners (i.e. criteria to detain prisoners past their eligibility dates, culturally insensitive risk assessments designed to purposefully keep us incarcerated, etc.). Under the guise of public safety and fuelled by fear-mongering in the media, the previous government gave the false impression that it was adhering to the *Gladue* rule when in fact it was not. This has an impact on me and all Indigenous prisoners who have been affected by residential schools, colonialism and the 60's scoop, because CSC staff and Parole Board Canada (PBC) officials say that they have considered *Gladue* principles when in fact they have not. I would like to see that the new government review all policies that the previous government installed that had an overreaching effect that consequently engulfed Indigenous prisoners. Denunciation is not valued among Indigenous people, yet it exists in sentencing as a means to ridicule. This denunciation segment has to be removed for Indigenous people in the courts.

ION Scanners

The ion scanners are not reliable. This often results in visitation being terminated. CSC needs to evaluate and implement alternative visitor screening processes that are more reliable and do not contribute to the dehumanization of prisoners' loved ones and volunteers from the community.

ANONYMOUS BATH PRISONER 5

Parole Eligibility for Lifers

The Conservative government changed the eligibility criteria for Lifers and 'dangerous offenders'. Under the new policy a parole hearing is only allowed every five years, which contributes to a sense of hopelessness. I would like to see that the policy be changed back to allowing parole hearings every two years.

Institutional Services

Institutional Services are not issuing enough clothing for release. This has affected me because I have no effects on release and all money that I possess is needed for incidentals, not including rent. I would like to see Institutional Services issue enough proper clothing for release.

Health Care – Medication

Health care is both changing and denying our medications. This has resulted in pain and suffering. I would like to see health care professionals act as such, not as CSC enforcers.

Grievance/Complaint Process

The grievance/complaint process has changed. This has resulted in massive delays in CSC responses. I would like to see an independent process and complaint procedure. This would ensure consistency across the system.

ANONYMOUS BATH PRISONER 6

Prisoner Accountability

The way "offender accountability" is unreasonably defined conflates accountability and motivation woven within the correctional plan and assessment process. This has resulted in lower pay and negative reports.[2]

Pay Deductions

The introduction of the additional 30 percent pay deduction has reduced my ability to save for release. I would like to see that the pay deduction be rescinded and that the pay increase recommended by the Office of the Correctional Investigator over a decade ago be implemented.

Medical Expenses

Institutional Services is offloading medical expense onto prisoners with recent policy changes. This has resulted in a lack of access to medical supplies and made it difficult to prevent dental issues. I would like to see that CSC allow more frequent medical and dental check-ups, as well as make available the recommended medical supplies instead of forcing prisoners to order at their own cost and with increased delays in delivery.

Purchasing

CSC has changed the purchasing policy and we are now required to purchase items from a single supplier, which are highly over-priced. The products are of poor quality with misleading advertising and poor selection. For example, under the old policy a television that cost $119 plus taxes. With shipping the price was $143. The same television now costs $243. I would like to see CSC allow other suppliers or deal with a supplier that is fair and honest thus ending the monopoly. The government should investigate political ties to this company, if any.

Drug Strategy

With changes to the CSC "drug strategy" I now have a lack of contact with family because of dubious policies. I would like to see that when it comes to the enforcement of the policy of a "hit" by the dog or an ion scanner that it is only considered a possible contact rather than a reason to deny visits or access to families. Do not punish the prisoner's family for a hit that is not substantiated by solid evidence.

Phone Deductions

With the policy of charging prisoners for the costs of administering the Inmate Telephone System I am now paying the costs of a phone that I may never use. There are also major delays for adding a number to a telephone list. I would like to see that the pay deductions end, along with streamlining of the approval process for adding telephone numbers to a pin list.

Access to Computers

With the current policy regarding access to computers I have lost mine. I need it to teach myself basic skills as I lack any experience on the Internet. I would like to see CSC allow the purchase of personal laptop computers with Internet access using the European model of restricted access to websites.[3]

ANONYMOUS BATH PRISONER 7

Prisoner Pay

With the change in pay rate, including the additional 30 percent deduction to cover the costs of room and board, I am no longer able to save any money for things I would like to buy, such as new clothing, a television, stereo or new PlayStation to pass the time, and food items when they come available. I would like to see that the 30 percent deduction be removed and that the pay upgrade be reinstated.

Food Nights / Socials

With the removal of food nights and socials where we used to be able to invite the warden, members of the public, military, police, lawyers, MP's and the like, and cook them up a meal, we can no longer generate this type of contact with the outside world. This type of contact assisted with our reintegration into society. I would like to see that this order be rescinded and that they give us back our social night.

Parole Hearings
With recent policy changes, "Lifers" no longer have the opportunity to see the PBC face-to-face and are sometimes forced to have a parole hearing via a television screen. For instance, I have been informed that my next parole hearing will be in front of a television screen. As such I have decided not to attend. I would like to see that that parole hearings mandatorily take place face-to-face, rather than through a TV screen as this is not humane.

Prisoner Pay
Prisoners' pay has not increased with the costs of inflation. This has resulted in not having any purchasing power at the prices that vendors are currently charging. I would like to see our ability to purchase from stores that we had before with reasonable prices be restored.

Access to Technology
Our access to technology is very restricted. As it stands right now, games or computers are not available or are only available when grandfathered in. This makes it difficult to get games for older systems, which cost as much as current game systems. Computers in cells are not available at all. I would like to see that CSC change the policy and allow technology that is available in other jurisdictions.[4]

CSC Staff Culture
As it stands there is no accountability by CSC. Record keeping of meetings with parole officers is unfair as staff seem unaccountable for their actions and inactions. This affects us because low trust inhibits our rehabilitation and breeds resentment. There is too much emphasis on punishment and not enough on rehabilitation. I would like to see this changed.

Job Training
There is currently limited job training. This results in lower chances of getting a decent job after release. I would like to see more current and useable training for jobs.

ANONYMOUS BATH PRISONER 8

Life Line Program
Life Line has been removed. Many Lifers and 'dangerous offenders' may need an Escorted Temporary Absence to lower ratings and move to a minimum. Formerly, Life Line would take part in these escorts. I recommend that CSC bring back this successful program.

Cell Effects
With the change in personal property allowances to a $1,500 maximum value, including stored effects, it has affected my ability to make purchases for things that I need. I came in with $1,500 dollars in effects and I need to destroy or send out 2-3 shirts in order to buy one thing. I would like to see that CSC take into account inflation and raise cell effects to a higher level, while allowing extra seasonal-wear to be stored in personal property.

ANONYMOUS BATH PRISONER 9

Room and Board
CSC is now charging prisoners additional "room and board". This has taken away my ability to save for release. I would like to see CSC remove this charge to promote safe prisoner reintegration.

Administration of the Telephone System
CSC is now charging prisoners 8% of their pay for the costs of administering the Inmate Telephone System. I hardly use the telephone, yet CSC deducts $132.52 per year. I only spend about $10 to $20 per year for phone calls. This reduces my ability to save. I would like to see CSC remove this charge and implement a per minute or percentage of phone time brought towards this cost.

Non-Essential Dental Services
CSC no longer provides non-essential dental care including cleaning of teeth. We now do not get treatment unless it is an emergency. Good hygiene and regular care by a professional is recommended. I would like to see that CSC change this policy to allow for regular cleaning and assessment, which will save taxpayers money in the long-term by helping curb emergency dental treatment.

Prisoner Purchasing

CSC has instituted a centralized purchasing program. This has affected me because I have purchased different items of which two were defective and two were the wrong size. I was told that I could not send them back despite the guarantee in the front catalogue. I think that this is a "bait and switch" and that is illegal. If I order something it should not be substituted by the supplier unless they are willing to take it back if it is not acceptable. CSC has allowed a monopoly for prisoner purchasing and it should be changed.

Food Services

CSC has changed its method of providing food to prisoners. The cook-chill method of central production is not very good. Many prisoners complain of bloating after eating certain meals. As well, we believe the amount of dairy in our diets is of concern. The answer to this concern from Bath staff is that they give us powdered milk three times per day. A large percentage of prisoners will not consume this milk. They also do not put milk on their cereal and thus they do not eat cereal. Powdered milk and below standard food does not promote good eating habits. We have requested meetings with the regional dietitian. At the time of writing, it has been two months since the request and no response. Prisoners should be consulted about menus and changes to it. A full and impartial audit of the menu for prisoners should be done with changes reflecting the findings that emerge.

ANONYMOUS BATH PRISONER 10

Dangerous Offender Policy –
Commissioners Directive 705-7
Security Classification and Penitentiary Placement[5]

It is near impossible to ever get your file up to the Assistant Commissioner, Correctional Operations and Programs for a final decision to minimum. You have people making decisions solely on your file and much of it relies heavily on static risk factors which are calculated when you first come into the system. Static factors never change and the dynamic risk change that people like me make through programs will never lower our risk levels enough to attain a minimum-security rating so you will always be denied if your file ever makes it to the Assistant Commissioner, Correctional Operations and Programs. Some men are pushed towards volunteering to take the antiandrogen medications whether they truly need it or not because they feel that they will never get out without doing it. Yet they are still turned down for minimum for whatever arbitrary reason the decision maker feels fits this policy. I feel that it is being used as a de facto "life means life" sentence even though I was never sentenced to life in prison. There have been revisions to the dangerous offender provisions in 2012 where judges can now declare a person a dangerous offender and give them a fixed sentence. Individuals like myself who received an indeterminate sentence back in the early 2000s and have attended more than a half-dozen parole hearings, completed all programs successfully, including maintenance programming, have no realistic avenue to get to minimum, let alone ever getting out.

I would like to see a return to the decision making powers being placed in the hands of the institutional head, the same ones who can make the decision to send a prisoner serving life for first degree murder or any other sentence to minimum. They should be qualified to do the same for prisoners serving an indeterminate sentence like myself who was not given a life sentence.

There should be specific criteria and periods outlined advising CSC parole officers and institutional heads when a person serving an indeterminate sentence should be moving along, especially when a prisoner is complying with all aspects of their correctional plan. I am coming up on 20 years incarcerated and my only hope seems to be when my static risk factors are reduced in my sixties and that is a few decades from now.

Parole Reviews

One of the safeguards for someone like myself serving an indeterminate sentence, was an automatic parole review at two years to ensure that every case is being tailored to the specific needs of the prisoner for a successful re-integration back into the community and to ensure that a prisoner is not being unreasonably warehoused. I will be up for another parole hearing in summer 2017 with all programs including maintenance having been completed. Unless CSC moves me to a minimum, PBC will not consider me for parole until I have spent some time in such an environment. I have already listed two problems above that are blocking me from achieving this goal. I can apply before the five-year period, but the PBC can refuse to see me if there is no significant change in my casework, which as you can see there will not be any. Therefore, I can never satisfy any criteria to actually obtain parole. I am in fact serving a life means life sentence, which is not what I was sentenced to. I am a first-time federal prisoner and I was incarcerated in my early twenties. These policy changes have ensured that I will likely never gain parole under these current guidelines, no matter how much programming I will have participated in.

The parole review should be reverted back to a two-year review period. PBC is the final decision maker for release and I feel that they should exercise that power. After someone like myself has been in front of the PBC several times, even in front of the same board members, two and three times, they should stop passing the responsibility back onto CSC whose current policies will never give them what they need to grant me a parole release.

Access to Licensed Psychologists

It is now harder for prisoners like myself serving an indeterminate sentence to qualify risk change after programs. The facilitators are no longer able to make risk estimates in our program reports because they no longer teach the program alongside a licensed psychologist who would supervise them when they would complete actuarial risk measurement tools such as the Stable 2007 and the static 99-R.[6] The facilitators do complete the actuarial measurements for your file, but they cannot legally be used. We are then sent to see a contract psychologist for risk assessments and they bring their own battery of assessment tools which they rely on and these do not include the Stable 2007 nor the Static 99-R. In their final report, they make mention that they can only assume that my risk may have gone down because I have completed the program, yet no risk estimates or Stable 2007 and the Static 99-R were used in my final program report. When I inquired into this problem, the answer that I was given was that the institution has no say in what assessment tools these contracted psychologists use. Also, actuarial measurement tools such as the VRS-SO which is a tool used specifically to measure risk changes after programming are not used, only actuarial measurement tools that measure static risk. My most recent psychological assessments are still quoting comments from my intake assessments nearly a decade and a half ago. They tell the parole officer the information (static risk) they already know and not if I can be currently managed in the community. Thus, people like myself are stuck in limbo and our parole officers have a hard time justifying moving you along.

Licensed psychologists specialised in specific program treatments should be brought back into programs to assist the facilitators in doing complete treatment assessments after program completion so that when risk assessments for transfer to minimum are done by a review of your file, the most current and up to date information is provided for decision makers.

ANONYMOUS BATH PRISONER 11

Dangerous Offender Parole Reviews

Several years into my sentence, the mandatory every-two-years parole review was changed to every five years after my sentencing. This retroactive change to my sentence arguably goes against the rule of law that requires that whenever a new law, legislation or policy is enacted, that it only affects those who are sentenced *after* the measure is introduced. Accordingly, this has now done away with the "grandfather clause" and is an infringement of my *Charter* rights.

During my dangerous offender hearing, it was made very clear to me and the court that I would first have to serve four years before being eligible for day parole and seven years before being eligible for full parole. After which a mandatory review for full parole would be conducted every two years, indeterminately, until such time as I have proven that I am no longer an unmanageable risk to public safety or I die therein.

With this sudden change in policy, I will now have to wait every five years for a mandatory parole review, missing two reviews in the process. This has caused an extreme amount of internal emotional stress for those designated as dangerous offenders. It further adds feelings of hopelessness to an already disheartened sentence.

Statistics have shown in the year 2015-2016, of the 565 (and counting) dangerous offenders with indeterminate sentences across Canada, only around two dozen or 4.2% are serving the remainder of their sentence in the community (PSC, 2017, p. 59). Very few of those designated as dangerous offenders cascade down to a minimum-security institution.

The dangerous offender regime gives little to no hope to the prisoner with the D.O. designation that they will ever get out as there is no statutory or warrant expiry release dates. It has essentially labelled D.O.'s as incurable, giving us little to no hope for a better future.

The remedy for this policy change should be that the dangerous prisoner regime should be revamped to include a determined period, no matter how long that may be. It should also include that the prisoner serving under the dangerous offender regime be reviewed every two years, as it was at the time of his/her sentencing and that strict long-term-supervision-orders in a supervised community setting be offered to those prisoners who display a long period of good time. This should be based upon successful programming and behaviour, allowing us to cascade down in security ratings should no new charges or misconduct arise, coupled with good institutional adjustment and genuine display of change, thus offering the dangerous offender the opportunity to return to society and their families.

Incentive Pay for CORCAN Employees
and Cuts to Regular Pay Scheme
Under the changes made in the pay schemes for CORCAN employees, CSC is essentially operating legalized sweatshops. CORCAN employees are paid a maximum of $6.90 a day on A level Pay, $6.35 a day on B level pay, $5.80 a day on C level pay, $5.30 for D level pay and $2.50 a day on E level (or welfare) pay. This pay regime is also before deductions that cut at least half of that pay out. It essentially tells prisoners that it is okay to employ a worker for pittance. Furthermore, the remainder of the non-CORCAN job's also pay under the same pay schemes. Prisoners are scratching by to pay for Inmate Telephone System Phone card expenses, legal and library printing and photocopying, group dues, food drives, prisoner purchasing, canteen, and the like. It is almost impossible to send money home to our families who are in need and lacking the income provided by an imprisoned family member. Debts and reimbursements for the crimes they committed continue to go unpaid as arrears build. This leaves the prisoner to be released to greater fines, penalties and debts upon their return to the community. In the case of Lifers and D.O.'s, who are very unlikely to get out at all, it also leaves the debt completely unpaid and the persons or companies who are owed, out of the money that is due to them completely.

With a 30% cut in our pay for room and board three years ago, prisoners are forced by necessity to find other ways to make our end meet and in some cases, this causes certain prisoners to break institutional rules and protocols. A person on E level pay will net about $12.50 every two weeks. How can one be expected to maintain their expenses on such a low pay rate?

This 30% cut in pay for room and board is currently being contested across the nation. When these pay scales were originally established over thirty years ago, room and board was already taken into account. It is unfair for CSC and by extension the Government of Canada to double dip for funds from prisoners who already have so little. Also, since the establishment of these pay scales prisoners have not had a raise in pay since the 1980s, despite the fact that inflation has raised the price of so many items that we have need to purchase.

Would it be legal for an employer to employ a person, house them in a 6 by 10-foot space that has a single bed, desk, chair, shelf, toilette and sink, basic cable TV, and make them work a fulltime work-week for the daily wages we make and the poor meals we receive? The remedy for this is to not only return our 30% back, but also a raise in pay to reflect the minimum wage of the respective province they are serving time in, in order to keep up with the rising costs of inflation.

ENDNOTES

[1]   What the author is referring to here is that the total value of all personal effects cannot exceed $1,500. Under the old policy this $1,500 cap applied only to personal cell effects that were issued and not those that were being stored at Admissions & Discharge. If a prisoner requested to exchange an item they could put in a request.

[2]   For instance, former Correctional Investigator Howard Sapers is quoted as saying: "Several other principles were muted or abandoned such as proportionality and restraint in the use of imprisonment gave way to other objectives, usually framed in terms of the "pre-eminence" of public safety. The reference to inmate "privileges" was removed from correctional law. Other long-standing principles, such as the least restrictive measure, were replaced with more ambiguous and elastic language that included "proportionate and necessary measures." The notion of "offender accountability" became political shorthand for a series of legislative initiatives that effectively increased the severity of the sentence or the length of time spent in custody" (Office of the Correctional Investigator, 2016).

[3]   For Instance, according to the Learning Infrastructure for Correctional Services *Report on E-Learning in European Prisons*: "In several European countries network solutions for e-learning in prison exist – most of those how- ever not covering all regions and prisons – and in many countries at least projects and pilots in this respect have been or are carried out. While we cannot assume to know about all activities and initiatives on network based and elaborated use of e-learning in European prisons we know about respective activities in Austria, Belgium, Denmark, France, Germany, the Netherlands, Ireland, Norway, Spain, Sweden and the UK. This means that e-learning in fact is already quite spread in Europe and it is to be expected that this development will continue. In fact, there already is a "community" of e- learning

and knowledge management focusing on prison education and training in Europe" (Hammerschick, 2010).

4   According to the most recent report of the Office of the Correctional Investigator: "Since 2002, incoming inmates have been prohibited from bringing a personal computer into a federal penitentiary. It is increasingly challenging and expensive to repair the ever- diminishing number of personal computers still in use in federal facilities. It is difficult to see how such information-deprived environments can be considered purposeful or rehabilitative. There is simply no remaining rationale or logic behind CSC's position on these matters. There is still not even limited and supervised access to the Internet or email for federal inmates, even as many other jurisdictions, including the Federal Bureau of Prisons in the United States, allow restricted forms of electronic communication, as well as use of tablets to promote contact with the outside world. These initiatives help inmates maintain familial and community connections while incarcerated, thereby serving larger reintegration aims" (Office of the Correctional Investigator, 2016).

5   Correctional Service Canada (2017) *Commissioners Directive 705-7 Security Classification and Penitentiary Placement*, Ottawa. Retrieved from http://www.csc-scc.gc.ca/acts-and-regulations/705-7-cd-eng.shtml

6   According to Hanson and colleagues (2007): "The STABLE-2007 and the ACUTE-2007 are specialized tools designed to assess and track changes in risk status over time by assessing changeable "dynamic" risk factors. "Stable" dynamic risk factors are personal skill deficits, predilections, and learned behaviours that correlate with sexual recidivism but that can be changed through a process of "effortful intervention". Should "effortful intervention" (read: treatment or supervision) take place in such a way as to reduce these risk-relevant factors there would be a concomitant reduction in the likelihood of sexual recidivism".

REFERENCES

Hammerschick, W. (2010) *Learning Infrastructure for Correctional Services: Report on e-learning in European Prisons – Concepts, Organisation, Pedagogical Approaches in Prison Education*, European Commission. Retrieved from https://ec.europa.eu/epale/sites/epale/files/report_on_e-learning_in_european_prisons.pdf

Hanson, K. R, J. R. Andrew, T. L. Harris, and L. Helmus, L. (2007) "Assessing the Risk of Sexual Offenders on Community Supervision: The Dynamic Supervision Project", Ottawa: Public Safety Canada. Retrieved from https://www.publicsafety.gc.ca/cnt/rsrcs/pblctns/ssssng-rsk-sxl-ffndrs/ssssng-rsk-sxl-ffndrs-eng.pdf

Office of the Correctional Investigator (2016) *Annual Report of the Office of the Correctional Investigator 2015-2016.* Ottawa. Retrieved from http://www.oci-bec.gc.ca/cnt/rpt/pdf/annrpt/annrpt20152016-eng.pdf

Public Safety Canada [PSC] (2017) *Corrections and Conditional Release Statistical Overview 2016*, Ottawa. Retrieved from https://www.publicsafety.gc.ca/cnt/rsrcs/pblctns/ccrso-2016/ccrso-2016-en.pdf

NIGHTMARES UNDER THE CONSERVATIVE REGIME

Here are a few of my thoughts on, or nightmares experienced under, the Conservative regime. Specifically, I focus on attacks to Correctional Service Canada's (CSC) mandate to make our communities safer through rehabilitation. Originally, I had intended to list ten of the most damaging reforms, however, the list expanded as other prisoners approached me with suggestions for inclusion in order to protect their anonymity.

As way of background, I have been serving a life sentence in the Canadian penitentiary system since the 1980s, with a brief hiatus in the American federal system for a few years in the early 1990s following a walk-away from Collins Bay in 1988. I was returned to Canada under the *Transfer of Offenders Act* in the mid-1990s and was in Millhaven until late-1997. From there, I was sent to Joyceville where I remained until early 2016. I was sent to Beaver Creek Medium later that year and transferred to Beaver Creek Minimum since.

Least Restrictive Measures
The removal of the "least restrictive measures"[1] priority from decision-making in the *Corrections and Conditional Release Act* (CCRA) with "measures that are consistent with the protection of society, staff members and prisoners and that are limited to only what is necessary and proportionate to attain the purposes of this Act", has introduced a subjective standard permitting arbitrary decisions without specific criteria. It permits the prolongation of imprisonment, while permitting harsher, more punitive decisions to be made with respect to the movement and treatment of prisoners while they are confined behind bars and supervised in the community. If imprisonment is to be a measure of last resort in Canada, the "least restrictive measures" principle needs to be restored.

National Drug Strategy
Within Commissioner's Directive 585 *National Drug Strategy*,[2] the standard of review for triggering "administrative consequences" was replaced with a standard of review of "reasonable belief". That means that should a prisoner be charged or convicted under section 19 of a drug-related offence in the institution or where there are reasonable grounds to believe that they have been involved in drug-related activities, a reassessment of risk and

131

needs shall be completed, and a number of administrative consequences shall be considered. This policy could merit a full review on its own as it is a perversion of all of the *Charter* provisions to ensure decision-making bodies engage their duty to act fairly before losses of liberty ensue for the criminalized. The shift to "reasonable belief" does not require proof. This standard means the decision-maker does not need to provide evidence and denies the prisoner the chance to appear before an independent chairperson to adjudicate the matter. The language of section 19 equates a charge to a conviction, imposing punishments that usually have the same effects as sanctions requiring a formal charge to be laid with an independent chairperson hearing evidence and the protections of duty counsel being present for the hearing. Under this directive, there is not even a requirement to have a hearing. A "reasonable belief" can then be used to deny pay raises, employment opportunities, transfers to lower security units or penitentiaries with their increased liberty, access to releasing mechanisms like escorted temporary absences (ETAs), unescorted temporary absences (UTAs), work releases, and supervised release opportunities like day and full parole. All of these effects can occur on a say-so, without the protections of due process guaranteed under the *Charter* and embedded by law in other CSC policies.

Parole
If the punitive or deterrent part of the sentence is the parole eligibility (see Attorney General of Canada v Whaling, 2014 SCC 20),[3] then for Lifers in particular, why after ten, or twenty, or thirty years behind bars are they not ready for parole? The Conservatives put in place barriers to access rehabilitation programs and release mechanisms. They pushed all of the releasing mechanisms involving community participation down to the minimum-security level through practices, while maintaining the guise of potential access at medium-security levels. They did not change the legislation or policy to directly deny access at medium-security levels, just the practices. Such practices include system-approved catch phrases such as "It is likely the prisoner would take the opportunity of placement in minimum security to escape", expressing opinion as fact, with the effect of denying cascading opportunities. The arbitrary, untestable "reasonable belief" standard of decision-making spread beyond the drug strategy into concepts like accountability that require such things as pleading guilty to access Parole Board Canada (PBC) hearings. Reforms are needed to put in place more objective standards for release.

Unescorted Temporary Absences
and Escorted Temporary Absences

The *CCRA*, section 115(1)(a), has been changed to restrict access to UTAs and mandates successful UTAs over the period of a year before a Lifer can make supported, successful, day parole applications. This legislative change establishes time limits for frequency of access and duration. As a matter of practice, CSC asks for a year of ETAs, followed by a year of UTAs. This ensures a Lifer cannot gain day parole until eighteen months after their eligibility date because applications for a hearing can routinely take five months to process. I do not have access to the legislative archives, but simple online research should show the changes to access over the Conservative regime had the effect of extending imprisonment. Moreover, statistical analysis of incarcerated time spent in excess of day parole eligibility for Lifers, during the reign of the Conservatives, should show statistically significant increases across the entire country. The creation of practices ensuring an extended, expanded progression of community access increased the time Lifers (and others) spend excluded from the community.

If sentence release was represented by a temporal continuum, and releasing events like ETAs and UTAs were represented by nodes on the continuum, the Conservatives generated a demand for more nodes, before parole release was possible, while increasing the space between the nodes, often without the knowledge of prisoners themselves. Often excluded, but always the subject to a Case Management Team's created correctional plans flowing out of these hidden policies, the prisoner is left to suffer prolonged separation from loved ones and the community at large. The Conservatives did this without any proof that the public good was actually served in any way. While selling the public on their desire to protect 'public safety', the Conservatives sacrificed proven methods of reducing that very risk.

Compassionate Escorted Temporary Absences

In Commissioners Directive 566-6 *Security Escorts*,[4] section 15, it notes that at least two escorting officers, both armed (except for incarcerated women), will be deployed for ETAs. This can make the availability of ETAs difficult, if not impossible. Particularly as the policy under the Conservatives was to make cost considerations a factor in approval decisions. Also, the practice of mandatory minimum staffing practices restricted the number of staff available for escorts. Significant numbers of approved ETAs were not completed due to "staff shortages". This practice continues. We just had an Indigenous man denied a compassionate ETA because staff were not available. The pass was so he could attend the funeral of a man that was like a brother to him. The two men had grown up in and out of the system, from the juvenile system to present day, with the dead man having been able to stay out for years, while this fellow still struggles with his issues. Even though approved by the deputy warden, on the morning of the funeral the fellow was told he was not going. He had to call the daughter of his closest friend and tell her, as she cried, that he would not be coming. "But everyone is waiting for you", she said.

Volunteers
The oppression of volunteers has resulted in their reduced numbers and limiting activities including them. Boundaries became a hot topic and method by which to exclude volunteers. Huggers were removed from volunteer lists. Excessive screening practices for drugs and negative comments during visitor screening discouraged others. Negative comments might include, "Why do you want to help murderers and rapists?", "They are only using you", "If this machine goes off we are going to tell the police", and the like. How does such rhetoric that undermines the ability of prisoners to build bridges into the communities where most of them will return to contribute to CSC's promotion of rehabilitation and safe reintegration?

Prisoner Pay
Through claw-back methods such as "room and board", pay has been reduced to pennies per hour. The federal penitentiary system does not respect labour laws. We are being paid pennies while more and more costs of imprisonment are downloaded onto the prisoner population. It will cost me five cents a page to print this letter and a dollar for the stamp. Further, for our work there is no vacation time, no pension and no health care package above the "essential" limits. There is no overtime, no extra pay for working federal or provincial or religious holidays, no protections against being punished for quitting jobs hazardous to health or unsuited to the physical, mental or emotional realities of the individual. When prisoners work they should be afforded the same protections as every other worker in Canadian society.

Health Care
The shift towards "essential health care" means that prisoners are continually forced to a lower standard of care than in the community. Prisoners addicted

to nicotine are expected to pay for substitutions like Nicorette gum, because tobacco is now against the law inside prison. Thirty chicklets of gum are costing Beaver Creek prisoners over fifteen dollars. Two weeks work at pay level C ($5.80 per day) nets $28 and change. Nicotine addicts can starve trying to meet their addiction needs if they want to remain viable minimum-security prisoners. When the ban on cigarettes came in to being, cessation products were supplied by CSC for a period of three to six months, depending on the penitentiaries. Lifers are in real trouble. If anyone there knows of some kind of financial support program for those so severely addicted to nicotine they are now addicted to the gum, please let me know so these prisoners do not have to spend all their wages and some of their food money to support their nicotine habit. Health care is worthy of its own study. The removal of Gabapentin from the treatment of nerve pain other than diabetic neuropathy or post-pain shingles is a study in the corruption of the medical profession and its ethics by the bureaucratic dynamics of a security-driven environment that is a CSC institution. Dental care is the barest of the most minimal standards. As I write this I have had a broken filling for three months. I can eat on one side of my mouth, for which I am thankful. Bridgework that I had done before coming to prison cannot be repaired or replaced unless I pay for it myself, which would be acceptable if I was paid minimum wage for my labour. As it is, it would cost me $800 or every penny I can earn over a fourteen-month period at my present rate of pay. That would mean I could not replace clothing or shoes or subsidize my food allotment. I must survive on $35 per week for groceries. As such, my teeth and other preventative health care steps must take a back seat to the daily round of punishment I and others endure.

Prisoner Transport
While not a federal reform, there is presently a failure to protect safety during transit of prisoners. Ontario law has included an exclusion for prisoner transports that violates the intention of seatbelt laws as it does not require transported prisoners in the province to wear them. Handcuffed and shackled prisoners are locked inside a metal box inside a van, which prevents the spread of feet to balance the prisoner against the g-forces of turns and being able to use one's hands to protect against being thrown against the front or back during rapid deceleration and acceleration. This is an accident waiting to happen.

Correspondence
Current correspondence practices within CSC facilities do not follow the
Post Office Act. Mail deliveries have been reduced to two or three times a
week, if lucky, when the Act still requires delivery within twenty-four hours
of receipt.[5] Issues with mail also include search and seizure violations, as
correspondence is routinely intercepted and returned to the sender often
without notifying the intended recipient of the interception or providing
written reasons to the sender for the return of the correspondence.

Old Age Pensions
The removal of access to Old Age Pensions for prisoners over the age
of 65 in the name of denying Clifford Olsen benefits, means prisoners
cannot accumulate savings that would contribute to their reintegration to
communities. Of what benefit is it to Canadians as a whole to discriminate
against prisoners in this way? More importantly, if the aged prisoner cannot
work, which is often the case when a person gets older, their income is
reduced to a net sum of $13 every two weeks. The Old Age Security pension
would allow the prisoner to supplement their income and permit them to pay
for things like shoes, clothes and non-essential health care items. Denying
such benefits to prisoners can also mean further destitution for their spouses
or dependents who previously relied on these funds to make ends meet.

Institutional Parole Officers
Institutional Parole Officers (IPOs) have become increasing risk averse in
their decision-making. Decisions are delayed until other mechanisms force
their decision. This way, the IPO can claim they did not have any choice
in the matter. They avoid responsibilities and protect against being held
accountable. A review of the governing policies and the practices of the
entire Case Management Team, would be helpful. For example, even though
COII's are supposedly a member of the team, they almost never attend case
conferences. One of the things the Conservatives did was remove timelines
from decisions. Rehabilitation and reintegration requires a positive mindset
and goal setting. Moreover, according to upper management, all of the
IPOs in Beaver Creek have psychology backgrounds and are trained risk
assessment evaluators. We know one was a nurse. One has a degree in
biology. One was a graduate in social work. And I could go on. I do not
know that a degree in these fields qualifies as sufficient to replace those hired

to work within the psychology department. Should trained psychologists not be the ones making accurate, in depth use of psychological assessment tools to measure the progress of the prisoner in adapting to a pro-social community as one progresses through the steps of gradual release? If the concern about a gradual release that reduces the risk to public safety is so great, should there not be attempts to qualify and quantify character traits engaged in each step such that there can be an objective understanding of how the stressors of adaptation to outside communities may be managed more easily? For example, long-term prisoners may suffer from temporal dislocation. The pace of decision-making on the street appears to be at light-speed after years of having to wait days for simple decisions to be made by staff. What resources need to be in place to help the prisoner cope with this? Could we speed up decision-making inside the prisons? How do psychologists address temporal dislocation in therapeutic settings? Incarceration can exacerbate attention deficits. How would we treat this in such a way as to improve the releasing prisoner's chances of successful reintegration? Do we even bother with a base line test for any of these elements of "adaptability" potential? Not to my knowledge. As for training, should there not be manuals and materials made available to prisoners outlining objective measurements of successful completion of each step so the prisoner may move on to the necessary successive step without delay? What does each step measure and how does it measure that step (e.g. ETA, work release, UTA, day parole)? What social skill-sets does each step require of the prisoner? How is attainment of these skill-sets measured? But when questioned about just how, or with which criteria, decisions are made with regard to accessing the prisoner's progressive steps toward release we are left to depend on self-disclosure and self-reporting to the IPO, which can be subject to minimization or even denigration.

Social Programs

The reduction of budgets and staff associated with social programming has resulted in one staff member covering two or three positions. This was only possible through changes to policies, practices, and their implementation that had the effect of crushing social programming activities. Social programming in this sense would be recreation, hobby craft, music, some socialization programs and group activities. Group activities include having guest speakers in. Social activities are a necessary part of rehabilitation for people suffering from social dysfunctions. There used to be a community volunteer coordinator who would also function as an educator on prison realities for the community in the sense that, while visiting universities, colleges, vocational schools and other collections of peoples (e.g. Rotary Club, the Optimists, the Loyal Order of Moose, and churches, etc.) they would dispel myths about prisoners and prisons. Some would result in an awareness of restorative justice. There used to be a day, in the summer months, called "volunteer appreciation day" where family and people on the prisoners' visiting lists, as well as volunteer's active with the prison cultural and social groups could all come together. What this meant to the prisoner and the family, along with the volunteer, was a level and degree of communication impossible any other way. A prisoner can tell his or her family they are working on release. A prisoner can tell the volunteer about their relationship with family or friends. However, when all three meet a lot of that discussion is unnecessary. Families can be reassured that their incarcerated loved one is working toward release. The volunteer can see with their own eyes the support the family is willing to give. At the same time, networking and more effective efforts can be made toward release. This day needs to be restored in federal penitentiaries across Canada.

Room and Board
If we have to continue to pay extra room and board then we should be shown how to claim our payments under the *Tax Act*. If we make under a certain amount in the community we are able to recover the payments from the government. The current setup reminds me of stories from the 1800s where in one-industry towns the company would also setup a store where workers would receive wages in chits only good for redemption at their store.

Multi-Level Institutions
The clumping, lumping or amalgamation of institutions into multi-security level penitentiaries represents the best of collective failures under one umbrella. Conservatives made security God. The trouble with this is that security does not co-exist peacefully with any other mandate within a penitentiary setting. Security is expressed by force. Security is best served when risk is reduced to zero. Unfortunately, because to live is to risk and to risk is a matter of choice, reductions in risk translate into reductions of choice and a crushing of life. Witness the life of the four-year old child whose

mother never lets go of their hand. While she does it to keep the child safe, is this child developing life-skills? Can this child cope outside of the sphere of influence of the mother? Personal experience says the child will lack vitality. Without the liberty interests invested in lower security, the prisoner cannot grow positive socialization skills or prove trust necessary for release. In prison settings, security can easily become a monster. Domineering, armed with tear gas and lethal force, there are those whose desire to employ the tools at hand overcomes any consideration of alternatives. The guidelines for use of force exist because murder by staff is a historical truth. Almost every *Charter* right embedded by law in the policies and practices of CSC have tombstones in their shadowy past. Multi-security level institutions do not function at the lowest security-driven common denominator. The security practices of the more severe, more oppressive security levels seep into what are intended to be less restrictive environments. The systemic practice of operating at minimum staffing levels continuously within the institutions means that staff routinely float across barriers, where previously there was separations between security levels. Staff bear the burden of this as well, where they encounter poor planning and incomplete knowledge-sets about job-related performance needs, which constrict and conflict with their duties. Even though a job may bear the same title at differing levels of security, the functions, behaviours and concerns can change dramatically. Yet the demands upon the staff may not be adjusted accordingly. This is unfair both to staff and prisoners.

Parole for Foreign Prisoners
Parole for foreign prisoners with a removal order have become exponentially more difficult because they are not offered the same privileges to prove low risk as prisoners of this country. There are no mechanisms or tools in place to prove trust. This is especially problematic for those serving indeterminate sentences (i.e. Lifers).

The Grievance System
The grievance system is nothing more than lip service with a toothless watchdog. I have liked, on a personal level, most correctional investigators I have met. But the office is an offense to common sense. The Correctional Investigator's office is permitted to make endless reports year in and year out about the abusive situations within CSC, while being denied the least bit of

power to change the inner workings that generate and/or permit the abuses. The grievance system is worse than useless. It generates frustration and hostility. Even if the prisoner gains an admission that someone somewhere has behaved inappropriately in action or interpretation of policy, the grievance itself has no power to enforce proper behaviour. I am reminded of the prisoner buried in the hole who would endlessly explain, to anyone who came along, how he did not belong in the hole. Yes, after listening, they would agree. He did not belong in the hole and then they would explain to him why they could not change his status. They were only the dishwasher or the clerk or the turn-key. You need to speak to so and so, and he would say he had. Well, they would say, that is just not right. Something needs to be done about that. And I, buried next to him, would listen to them walk away.

Green Initiatives
Last but not least, the Conservative government dismantled a number of green initiatives like recycling and composting that were taking place in the penitentiaries. It is extremely difficult to be green in the penitentiary setting if this environmental understanding is not supported by administrative decisions. In fact, the practices may actually be actively discouraged by the decisions made. This needs to be looked at as another element of rehabilitation. Building consensus and improving practices would mean prisoners returning to their greater communities would carry with them a more earth-friendly approach to life.

ENDNOTES

[1]   Of note, the Liberal government's latest act to amend the *CCRA* includes the following: "The Bill proposes to reinstate the CCRA guiding principle "least restrictive measures" in Part I of the Act. For consistency, the guiding principle of "least restrictive determination" would be reinstated to deal with conditional release in Part II of the Act" (Canada, 2017).

[2]   See Correctional Service Canada (2017a) *Commissioners Directive 585 National Drug Strategy*, Ottawa. Retrieved from http://www.csc-scc.gc.ca/lois-et-reglements/585-cd-eng.shtml

[3]   Canada (Attorney General) *v.* Whaling, 2014 SCC 20, [2014] 1 S.C.R. 392.

[4]   Correctional Service Canada (2017b) *Commissioners Directive 566-6 Security Escorts*, Ottawa. Retrieved from http://www.csc-scc.gc.ca/lois-et-reglements/566-6-cd-eng.shtml

[5]   According to Commissioners Directive 085 *Correspondence and Telephone Communication*, paragraph 13: Distribution of mail: "Under normal circumstances,

incoming mail shall be distributed to inmates and outgoing mail forwarded to the Post Office within 24 hours of receipt" (Correctional Service Canada, 2017c). Correctional Service Canada (2017c) *Commissioners Directive 085 Correspondence and Telephone Communication*, Ottawa. Retrieved from http://www.csc-scc.gc.ca/ policy-and-legislation/085-cd-eng.shtml

REFERENCES

Canada, P. S. (2017, June 19) An Act to amend the Corrections and Conditional Release Act (CCRA) and the Abolition of Early Parole Act (AEPA). Retrieved September 12, 2017, from https://www.canada.ca/en/public-safety-canada/news/2017/06/ an_act_to_amend_thecorrectionsandconditionalreleaseactccraandthe. html?=undefined&wbdisable=true

Canada (Attorney General) v. Whaling, 2014 SCC 20, [2014] 1 S.C.R. 392

In the following, I outline a few key problems that emerged within the federal penitentiary system during and after the rule of successive Conservative governments.

ETA ELIGIBILTY PROCEDURES

It is now a requirement that all "Lifers" are required to apply to the Parole Board for a single Escorted Temporary Absence (ETA). No Lifers are excluded from this requirement. In my case, I have been in for over a quarter century with a good institutional record and all programs completed. In addition to this, I had been granted many ETA passes to my brother's home and to a halfway house. Suddenly, I was required to apply to the Parole Board for a single ETA. This unnecessary delay not only kept me from seeing my family for almost two years and penalized me for no reason, but also harmed my nephews, nieces, grandchildren and other family members. It also tied up the Parole Board to do a hearing for something that was previously under the authority of the Warden. For all the antipathy some politicians direct towards 'red tape', why impose such hoops with respect to ETAs?

TIMELINES FOR ETA / UTA / DAY PAROLE
OR FULL PAROLE APPLICATIONS

Last year, I applied for a package of UTA passes, along with a Day Parole. I was granted all of the UTA passes I requested and was told to take them over a nine-month period. I successfully completed all UTA passes with excellent reports on each and automatically applied for Day Parole. I received a letter from Parole Board Canada wherein they advised that they would be denying review of my application due to regulations stating I could not apply until a 1-year wait period was completed. I found this rather confusing in that I was told to take my UTA passes over a nine-month time span. The delay is only three months, however, seems quite unnecessary given the fact I complied with their nine-month time frame. It would seem that warehousing is once again being structured into the system, whereby rules and regulations that lack common sense are contributing to the population figures.

PAROLE OFFICERS

It is common knowledge that new parole officers are assigned to prisoner's time and time again, often resulting in failures to follow through on the progress made by those behind bars under the supervision of previous colleagues. The standard answer to most is that, "I am new here and it will take about a year to get to know you and familiarize myself with your case". Not only has this delayed a person who has been working towards their rehabilitation and release, but it somewhat degrades them, taking away any incentive to go forward. In a system that is already bogged down, it also adds to the warehousing factor and the crowded penitentiary environment.

COMBINED WORKFORCES

CSC has combined work forces of medium- and minimum-security penitentiaries. In our case, Fenbrook Medium has been combined with Beaver Creek Minimum, and employees are not sure on which side they will be working when they show up in the morning. It is understandable that employees from the medium side, when stationed to work on the minimum side, are mentally incapable of adjusting their attitudes and insist on implementing rules that are from the medium side.[1] We are no longer in the "camp" setting as a result of this. Additionally, most of the staff on the minimum side has a caseload to look after. Time and time again, we are unable to contact our CXII for days or weeks, as they are posted elsewhere and not available to us.

PENSIONS

The Old Age Security funds were taken away from prisoners under the Harper government. Even though a person may have been a Canadian born citizen who worked their entire life and paid their taxes, they are now denied the pension funds. I have seen many fellows, whose wives were dependent upon the income to maintain a roof over their head and food on their table, no longer being able to contribute to their family's well-being. They are also no longer able to afford their prescription drugs due to the high cost of same. They have, in some cases, lost their homes and ended-up either on welfare or eating at a soup kitchen post-release. With no funds to establish themselves properly into society, what are their prospects of success and what will be the impact upon their communities?

COMPLAINT PROCESS

There is a process in place wherein if management or staff has wronged a prisoner, the latter is entitled to have their problems reviewed and corrected through a complaint and grievance process. In my case, we had a Warden here who was short-lived and created a lot of problems before being removed. He left a path of destruction before moving on and many of his actions were of a nature that they affected caseloads in a very serious way. I issued a complaint and received a letter stating that my case would be assigned and reviewed in approximately three months. Since that time, I have now received many of such letters, advising that they still had not assigned the case and giving a new date of three months down the line. This standard form letter has become standard issue and after a full three-year period I am still receiving them. The former Warden has moved on without being held accountable in the least. The complaint and grievance system is badly broken, and needs to be investigated with the thought in mind of improving the review times. The system as it now stands makes a complete mockery of the notion of redress.

CONCLUSION

I trust my submission and input will be of some assistance as part of the review of the criminal justice system by the federal government.

ENDNOTES

[1] See Shook, Jarrod (2015a) "Collins Bay Institution: A Cluster F*#k", *Journal of Prisoners on Prisons*, 24(1): 49-51.

On 15 January 2016, I wrote a letter to the Honourable Jody Wilson-Raybould, Minister of Justice and Attorney General of Canada, concerning the discontinuation of the Old Age Security (OAS) payments to persons serving sentences in prisons across Canada. I received a letter acknowledging that my letter had been received and that it had been redirected to Honourable Jean-Yves Duclos, Minister of Families, Children and Social Development. The acknowledgement letter stated that this would be the proper place to deal with such issues. The response letter from the Honourable Jean-Yves Duclos noted:

> Since an prisoner's basic needs-such as food, shelter and medical care are supported by public funds while they are incarcerated, there are no grounds to provide the additional income of OAS benefits during the period of incarceration.

I submit to you that although there is support for a prisoner during their incarceration, there is the issue of having funds to rely on at the end of their period of incarceration. As well, there is in many cases the issue of their spouses out in society having needed the OAS funds provided by their incarcerated spouse only to have these funds withdrawn and suffering the loss of that income. This loss can have a very negative impact and may lead to a spouse having to go on social assistance or even worse to maintain their lodging. Worse still, they may be forced into the street. In any case, sufficient monetary resources need to be available at the time of a prisoner's release. It would be less burden on all levels of government if the prisoner were able to provide for their families during incarceration and upon release into the community.

I was accepted to receive OAS in the months leading up to its termination for imprisoned persons. Before the termination, it was my intention to send my OAS to my wife to help her to carry on in the community. My wife at the time of the termination of OAS had been my steadfast support out in the community for nearly twenty years. She had countless number of times visited me and spent time in Private Family Visits, all at her own expense. My point of view was that it would only be right to help to repay her for all she had done for me. For almost two decades, my wife worked at a company until she walked in one day and was laid off. Being in her late sixties, it was very hard to find employment and, in the meantime, she used up the money she had managed to put away. This is just one other example of how my OAS would have been useful in helping my wife to weather the storm out in society until my release from prison.

I truly hope this will help you to understand the position of many prisoners affected by the former government's very irrational decisions during their time in power.

The reason I am contributing to this *Dialogue* on penal reform in Canada is because I am in my sixties and my crime was an isolated incident, resulting in a sentence for second degree murder in the 1990s. I did 15 years inside as a model prisoner and was paroled in 2008 to a halfway house. Once there, I spent two years in the community without incident and was subsequently given full parole. However, in 2013, I was revoked for a negative urine sample. I have been back inside since, incurring unnecessary costs to taxpayers as my breach did not constitute a danger or threat to the public.

Prior to my incarceration, I was never a burden on society. With several skilled trades under my belt, I owned a home and business. Ever since Harper's 'tough on crime' and 'life means life' approach to imprisonment, a lot of us Lifers were revoked with no new criminal charges and with no help from our parole officers. This leaves us with no light at the end of the tunnel. There should be a time limit that restricts revoking parolees who have committed no new crimes once they have completed a significant portion of time under supervised release.

Beaver Creek Institution
Anonymous Prisoners

Having served more than a decade in federal penitentiaries, I have seen many things change for the worse. Below, is a list of recommendations that a number of us at Beaver Creek Minimums who meet regularly to discuss how we can atone for our actions with our victims and communities compiled during one of our meetings. However, before getting to this list, we wish to emphasize that given the time we spend behind bars and our will to succeed, there is such a wasted opportunity for educational training, including post-secondary trades. If offered in a more expansive way, it would make all the difference in the world. It is also important for us to have the chance to make money, to send funds home to help out and to have some resources upon release. The lack of incentive pay for working for CORCAN really hurts. I hope the Liberals make good on their promise to help make us better citizens.

Here are our ideas for change:

- Put in place opportunities to gain employable skills that reflect today's jobs
- Offer more trades and work training
- Streamline the grievance process
- Ensure consistency with respect to how parole officers apply policies
- Ensure that program assignments can be available and completed before major decisions like parole hearings (see the Auditor General's recent report on not preparing male prisoners for reintegration)
- Reintroduce accelerated parole review for first-time, non-violent prisoners
- Reinstate rules limiting double bunking and address crowding
- Encourage family support by making it easier to visit prisoners
- Lift the 2002 computer moratorium and allow personal computers as is being recommended by the Office of the Correctional Investigator of Canada
- Repeal the pardon legislation passed by the previous government
- Review pay cuts related to prisoner accountability issues

- Increase the possibility of release through Escorted Temporary Absences and Unescorted Temporary Absences
- Make funds and courses available for post-secondary education
- Reinstate incentive pay for CORCAN assignments
- Increase the grocery allotment
- Reinstate Old Age Security for prisoners to promote their safe reintegration
- Abolish phone charges for people who do not use the phone

Beaver Creek Institution
Salomonie Jaw

My name is Salomonie Jaw from Nunavut Territory and I have been a federal prisoner for the past 16 years. I have served all of my time behind bars in Ontario. When an Inuk person from Nunavut is convicted and sentenced for a term longer than two years they are sent down to southern Canada to serve it. That is because there are no federal penitentiaries in Nunavut. As the Nunavut population is growing, I think it is time the federal government start considering to build a federal penitentiary there if it will not put in place viable alternatives to incarceration for Indigenous peoples as Prime Minister Justin Trudeau mandated Minister of Justice and Attorney General of Canada Jody Wilson-Raybould to look into.

The things that I would like to see done by the federal government, which in my view are very much possible to implement, are the following:

1. Assist our families and loved ones to visit us, providing an escort so that they will be safe and not get lost during travels. Presently, many Inuit prisoners do not get to see or spend time with their loved ones the whole time that they are incarcerated, which undermines their reintegration.
2. Allow Inuk prisoners to attend the funerals of their relatives. It is mentally straining both to the prisoners and survivors of death when the former is denied this opportunity.
3. Reinstate the two-year wait for a parole hearing after a prisoner has been denied parole.
4. Restore prisoner work pay to where it was before. We prisoners started paying more for our own food and accommodations some years ago and as a result our take home pay was considerably decreased.

Thank you for this opportunity. I sincerely trust that you and others will seriously look into these very important points.

PROGRESSION OR REGRESSION?

I would like to offer my observations on some of the changes that have occurred within Correctional Service Canada (CSC) penitentiaries in the last ten years following the release of *A Roadmap to Strengthening Public Safety* (Sampson *et al.*, 2007). I have been incarcerated for more than 20 years. I spent almost 5 years in pre-trial custody in solitary confinement and over a decade and a half years in the federal penitentiary system. After several months in the Millhaven Assessment Unit I was moved to Kingston Penitentiary. After approximately 30 months, I cascaded to Warkworth Medium Security and within a short 18 months I was sent back to maximum-security where I spent an additional 4 years. I cascaded once again to medium-security at Fenbrook Institution, following almost 5 years. For the past few years, I have been in Beaver Creek Minimum.

When I first entered the federal system in 2001, CSC was espousing the mission statement set out by Ole Ingstrup. It appeared to me progressive, with a focus on rehabilitation as opposed to retribution. There were certain individual liberties that I felt were conducive to personal growth and responsibility. For example, you could own or purchase a personal computer, post-secondary studies were easily accessible if you could pay for it, you were allowed almost any type of personal item that fell under the institutions security guidelines and there was a general air of progression with attention to quickly cascade to lower security levels. Additionally, there was a focus on CSC "Core programming" (i.e. anger management, substance abuse, etc.). At that time, vocational training programs were non-existent, except for menial institutional jobs and limited CORCAN industries work assignments.

In 2007, the report *A Roadmap to Strengthening Public Safety* was released and five key areas were addressed: "offender accountability, eliminating drugs from prison, employability, physical infrastructure, and eliminating statutory release". With the implementation of the recommendations, "offender accountability" resulted, in most cases, in a drop of our pay levels, usually from level A ($6.90 per day) to level C ($5.80 per day). The reduction in pay was to motivate prisoners to either actively pursue their correctional program or acknowledge their culpability (in cases that convicted prisoners maintained their innocence) or involvement in an organized crime group. Under the guise of "offender accountability", more stringent cascading parameters to lower security levels were enacted, creating bottle necks for prisoners following their correctional plans. This also resulted in the implementation of paying additional room and board, as well as a flat rate for the telephone maintenance beyond the per minute cost paid by prisoners in full. "Offender accountability" through the reduction of institutional pay has resulted in demotivation, rather than motivation for good conduct and responsibility.

Eliminating drugs from prison has been fairly successful, however, at a great cost to personal dignity to our visitors and ourselves. The drug interdiction program still uses antiquated ion scanner technology that produces many false positives that are reported in the Offender Management System (OMS), which casts a suspicious light on prisoners, which may affect future transfers, as well as access to escorted temporary absences (ETAs) or unescorted temporary absences (UTAs). Moreover, the visitors and prisoners are dog searched when an ion scanner hit is recorded and even when the dog search that follows is uneventful, the false positive is still recorded on OMS. Often there is a physical roadblock in place before visitors enter institutional property, and their vehicles and persons are searched. As you can imagine this is a high price to pay to maintain family and community contact. Eliminating illicit drugs from penitentiaries is important and helps with the overall rehabilitation of those who have drug use issues. However, it is important to uphold and maintain the dignity of visitors and prisoners, including those who are not part of this subculture.

In the area of employability not much has changed. Meaningless jobs still prevail and there are few opportunities to gain consequential job experiences or developing marketable skills. The introduction of basic workshops at minimum-security such as Small Engine Repair, Horticulture, and Basic Carpentry are okay, providing a modest amount of information, but does not give enough accreditation for prisoners to apply to an apprenticeship program. What the focus of employability has resulted in is greater internal restrictions on prisoner movement during the workday. Depending on the security level, and as was just recently implemented at Beaver Creek Minimum, if you do not have an institutional job or are gainfully employed elsewhere as in the case of work release, you must stay in your cell or on your range. Previously, you were allowed to go to the library, the gym, hobby-craft or walk the grounds. Further work is required in the area of employability, through concrete training programs that provide prisoners with government accredited certifications or professional licensing. The gaining of marketable skills and educational upgrading are assurances to reduce recidivism and controlling long-term costs associated with crime.

Physical infrastructure changes have resulted in amalgamating different level security institutions in the same area, as well as decommissioning Kingston Penitentiary. While there maybe cost savings associated with fewer senior and administrative staff positions, when two institutions are combined like Fenbrook Medium and Beaver Creek Minimum, the higher security ethos is adapted for the entire multi-level institution. Security staff from both levels are used and the higher security staff have a tendency to use a harsher style in the lower security setting. We have earned our way to minimum or camp as it was once referred to, we are on the cusp of re-entering society, and it is important that we do so in less institutionalised ways. Multi-level security facilities on the same premises do not seem to work. Instead of ramping up the prison-industrial-complex, it would be wise to study the Norwegian model and implement the elements that work there.

The fifth key area outlined by Sampson and colleagues (2007), the elimination of statutory release, was never implemented. It should stay that way, especially given the costs of incarceration and the benefits of gradual release in terms of safe reintegration.

With many of the changes that have occurred in the intervening years, much discretion afforded to wardens has been removed, translating into a larger role for Parole Board Canada (PBC). For example, if you are serving a life sentence and housed in a minimum-security you are eligible to participate in ETAs, whether for personal reasons such as maintaining community contact or to offer to volunteer work through a community services volunteer group (CSVG). Your ETA application is presented to the PBC, after having been exhaustively reviewed and approved by the various levels within the institution. A ruling by the PBC is made and an ETA is granted. The length of the permit is usually six months and has to be renewed thereafter with another application to the PBC. It costs the system more money by adding these types of redundancies and greatly slows the progress of a prisoner's reintegration. The removal of warden's discretion also undermines their role and part of the dynamic security element they bring to the office. The warden or their designate walk the institution regularly, observing prisoners first-hand under a variety of situations. They often know the prisoner on a first name basis, which gives them key information on their true conduct, which in addition to formal reports, contributes to a more accurate evaluation of a prisoner's prospect for success in the community when it is necessary to make a decision on an application. This style of corrections is humane and effective, and was previously practiced with successful results. A return of warden's discretion is efficacious in reducing costs and streamlining decisions.

From a Lifer's perspective, UTA and day parole eligibility dates have been delayed due to the lack of streamlining. Although the prisoner reaches an eligibility date, it is virtually impossible to get day parole on that date. The system would like to see a series of UTAs first, before considering the idea of day parole. It is a catch-22 – without the possibility of demonstrating that one is a manageable risk by participating in UTAs or work releases it would then preclude them from having a remotely reasonable chance at day parole. The current wording of the *Corrections and Conditional Release Act* (CCRA) does not allow Lifers to participate in work release before their UTA date, despite being housed in a minimum-security penitentiary. In addition, the idea of a federal prisoner having the wherewithal of earning any measurable monies to support their reintegration is very slim. As mentioned earlier, Level A pay is $6.90 per day. After deductions that were not in place before, the pay is $3.40 per day. These are additional impediments to a successful release and reintegrating back into society. In the recent Conservative era, streamlining of decisions was lost through the increased use of PBC decisions resulting in a bottle-neck that slows the prisoners' eventual release. In the case of Lifers, UTAs and day parole eligibility dates are moving targets that keeps an otherwise eligible prisoner from becoming a full-fledged, taxpaying citizen.

Mental health concerns are still issues that have not been resolved. Crisis intervention is marginally satisfactory, while on-going treatment to deal with issues are paltry. In addition to the myriad of problems developed from incarceration, especially mental health issues that arise because of privation, predation, isolation and marginalisation, the result is further trauma that usually goes untreated. We need to have more mental health professionals, as well as guides and mentors, to assist in our rehabilitation. I feel in many cases the index offences are a result of cognitive aberrations and an imbalance in a person's mental, emotional, spiritual and physical well-being. We can address this area by not necessarily throwing money at it, but by including our stakeholders – the community – through the promotion of outside volunteer participation, making our penitentiary walls permeable. Penal castigation and isolation does not work, but further exacerbates the challenges facing our society.

Along with mental health issues, physical health issues have arisen because of funding cuts. Preventive health programs like dental care have been seriously curtailed, with only emergency cases being seen. A return to dental hygiene and regular checkups are a cost saver in the medium- to long-term. Effective physiotherapy is almost non-existent and the preferred way is to medicate rather than to treat the underlying issues. With an increase in medication, there is also an increase in the potential for abuse of medication that may reinforce problematic drug use. Holistic and other preventative types of medical care should be implemented.

Double-bunking and crowding is an ongoing issue. Many of the ranges are designed for a certain amount of people and when you begin to exceed those limits problems arise that usually result in additional stress, depression, violence and isolation via segregation placements. You must remember that a person goes to a penitentiary as punishment, not for punishment. Being double-bunked for any length of time is punitive and undermines the elements of rehabilitation.

The quality and quantity of food has always been an issue in penitentiaries, which has been further exacerbated with the introduction of a central food preparation centre. The meal is prepared at a central site, packaged, frozen and shipped to the receiving institution. The institution then reheats the meal which is served to the prisoners. There has been a huge increase in the use of mechanically separated meats. Previously, each institution had its own kitchen where staff and prisoners worked together. The prisoners learned valuable skills that could easily be transferred to the community through the example set out by staff. They learned alternative ways of proper comportment. The good news is that some institutions, generally camps and some medium institutions implement the Small Meal Preparation Model. This is where prisoners, select from a list of approved food items, prepare, and cook the food that they eat. It is a fantastic program where prisoners learn to cook, bake and apply the principles of food safety, nutrition, and budgeting. The food per diem is five dollars, which is a challenge, yet the meals are generally nutritious meeting Canada's food guidelines and certainly tastier. Prisoners who have never prepared a meal in their lives have become quite proficient at it and this program instils in them a variety of skills that they can take with them when they re-enter the community.

Education and gaining marketable skills are the hallmarks of reduced recidivism. Currently, federal prisoners have little to no access to the Internet and as a result cannot access online post-secondary education programs. It is virtually impossible to get affordable and quality paper-based post-secondary studies any longer, and I believe that measures can be taken for limited electronically monitored access to educational sites. One of the goals shared by prisoners is that upon release they can hit the ground running by being prepared in advance through educational upgrading. Currently, CSC's educational mandate is to complete Grade 12, which is woefully below par. Easier access to post-secondary studies and limited Internet exposure will assist in a prisoner's safe reintegration into society, as well as reducing the costs to the system.

With the release and implementation of much found in the report *A Roadmap to Strengthening Public Safety*, CSC has become insular rather than forward-looking. The effective corrections that were practiced previously had a demonstrable drop in recidivism. Mental health issues continue to plague the federal penitentiary system and require a concerted effort to address the deficiencies with perhaps an additional focus on incorporating holistic health techniques. Double-bunking does not contribute to a person's well-being, and is detrimental to good and respectful behaviour, and this practice should be stopped. Finally, the quality and quantity of food has sparked numerous riots in the past, and it appears that we are going down that same aisle again. Decentralising food preparation not only provides respectful institutional work for prisoners, it gives them marketable skills that can be transferred upon release, while supporting the local community with contracts to provide supplies. A return to responsible and humane corrections will add to the progression of our society.

REFERENCES

Sampson, Robert, Serge Glascon, Ian Glen, Clarence Louis, and Sharon Rosenfeldt (2007) *A Roadmap to Strengthening Public Safety*, Ottawa: Public Safety Canada

I am a first-time prisoner and came into the federal penitentiary system a few years ago. Upon arriving to the system, I quickly learned of the slow, punitive and non-rehabilitative mentality under the Conservatives. There is no incentive to be rehabilitated or change, because no matter your efforts to do so, there are constant roadblocks to discourage you like:

(1) *The elimination of APR (accelerated parole review) and programs.* I have made a relentless effort to see what programs I can do that would be recognized, to have a fighting chance, so that when it is time for me to go before the Parole Board I can show my progress, what I have changed, how I can be successful. The reality is I do not have much to offer except all the volunteer programs which are not institutionally recognized, along with my honesty and transparency. There are no core programs for me as I do not qualify because I am a first-time prisoner. There used to be in my opinion a second chance, an incentive prior to 2011, an early release for first-time, non-violent prisoners, who if they behave as role models in the institutions they could be granted release. This was taken away by the Conservatives and APR needs to be reinstated.

(2) *Opportunities for post-secondary education, employable skills and trades have declined.* I have tried to upgrade my post-secondary education for the past two years with no success. I was able to have a bursary for 1 out of the 8 courses in Construction Management available at the time. After I completed the first course, they told me I could not continue due to the fact the course was no longer available through correspondence, only online, which meant that the option for me to upgrade my education in the field I want and will be working after my release was gone. Prisoners need options to gain employable skills or learn a trade.

(3) *Family and support via visits has been undermined.* I understand and agree there has to be security measures to eliminate the attempt for any type of contraband in the institutions, but the measures have to be consistent and unbiased. When it is solely relied upon, the ion scanner has been proven to be inaccurate, due to so many things that can influence its accuracy like medication, creams, colognes or just the fact of having a job that puts you in contact

with many people. All these things and many more can impact the accuracy of the machine. Screening measures need to be in place that are accurate and do not deter visitation that promotes prisoner reintegration.

I do not have much else to contribute as I have not been in the system that long, but I do see how only punishment and no rehabilitation can bring only negative outcomes. All I, along with other prisoners ask for, is for an opportunity to help ourselves become productive, contributing members of society, as we will be released one day into the community and will be your neighbours.

I am serving a life sentence for second degree murder with no full parole eligibility for 10 years. I started my federal sentence in 2011 at Millhaven Institution and am now in Beaver Creek Minimum where I have been since 2014.

A few things that I would like to see changed are to have the Old Age Security payment to qualified people be returned to them with back payments and interest. This was taken away from me and others by the Harper government because of remarks made by prisoner Clifford Olsen.

Secondly, my day parole and Unescorted Temporary Absence (UTA) dates are both set to the same date in fall 2017. The problem with this is that our parole officers always want us to have UTAs to our halfway house prior to being granted day parole, which makes it impossible to receive day parole on our eligibility date. UTA eligibility dates ought to be six months prior to the day parole eligibility date to facilitate this.

Beaver Creek Institution
A.C.C.L.

I received a life-25 sentence in the late 1990s and was imprisoned in the Pacific Region until recently, where I transferred to Collins Bay and then Beaver Creek Medium, followed by a placement in the minimum. Below, I offer my observations on the detrimental changes to the federal penitentiary system and what reforms are required to enhance correctional outcomes.

CSC'S APPROACH TO
CRIMINALIZED DRUG USERS

While residing at Collins Bay I was fortunate to be part of a group that met 50 judges from across Canada. I was amazed at how much they did not know about the federal penitentiary system they send people to. Repeatedly, they expressed that they thought that the people they were sending to federal penitentiaries would get the help they needed. They were horrified, you could see the look on their faces when prisoners spoke up and told them the realities of Correctional Service Canada (CSC) institutions. The bare minimum for employment and skills, and programs to help drug users, were the same program set everyone takes. There is no real help for those addicted to drugs behind bars. CSC will argue that they give them methadone and that they can take a program. CSC will say they are combating the 'war on drugs' by fortifying the walls and fences, adding drug dogs and searches, using ion scanners, which is outdated machinery. CSC believes the problem is with drugs coming into the penitentiary, yet you will notice that the union of guards does not allow the ion scanner to be used on their members. CSC does not adequately help the addict whatsoever and before coming to Ontario, I was in British Columbia where there is a great need for drug intervention and harm reduction because so many people die from overdoses every year, on the street and inside. The lower East Side of Vancouver is indescribable and saying it is the poorest neighbourhood in all of Canada is not saying enough. Fortifying fences and pushing family away, is only compounding the problem.

While I was in British Columbia, Greg Hanson and I got to sit down with Minister of Public Safety Stockwell Day to discuss recidivism. This was as the federal government was going from penitentiary to penitentiary interviewing prisoners and staff creating a report called *A Roadmap to Strengthening Public Safety*. I also took a course called "Prison Legal Advocate" with Michael Jackson from the University of British Columbia and other lawyers. They opposed this roadmap to no avail.

At that time, prisoners who did two-thirds of their time would go home, on parole and have to abide by rules and stipulations until their warrant expiry. These days, those same prisoners often have to reside in a halfway house and the system is backed-up immensely. Prisoners who get parole are often waiting for weeks or months for a bed to open. The beds taken by those who do not need them are preventing others from accessing the resources they are seeking. For instance, a prisoner who was addicted to drugs and had no family did not want to be released from prison unless he could go to a halfway house so he could have a chance. CSC would not let him reside at a halfway house, so on the day of his release he locked and barricaded himself in his room, refusing to come out. CSC initiated a lockdown, fragged him (used a bomb), and smoked him out of his cell. They then proceeded to pepper spray, hand-cuff and escort him out to the street. The next day, while they were packing up his cell, the prisoner now on the streets took his own life as he said he would do because he was tired of the struggle. I have a lot of stories like this one and I have developed a lot of empathy for drug addicts. They need help and the program module (i.e. the Integrated Correctional Program Model – ICPM) we have now by itself will not help.

With this said, the ICPM program is the best I have ever taken because it made me think not just about my index offence, but all my offences and what led me to them, challenging my behaviour and helping me learn about myself. CSC used to have violence prevention programs, family programs, drug programs, alcohol programs and the list went on. The problem was that prisoners would have to take sometimes between two and six programs during their stay and could not get them done in time for a parole hearing. Thus, the prisoner would be stuck in the penitentiary until the programs were complete and in most cases, were let out at statutory release. This ICPM is supposed to help prisoners address their programming needs and free up the facilitators so all prisoners can take a program. However, in practice, this is not the case, as CSC only has one program to offer with a huge waiting line to take it. The other problem with the ICPM is it addresses our problem needs in intervals. It has been awhile since I took the program, but weeks one and two would be about associates, weeks three and four would be about crime for gain, with weeks five and six about drugs and alcohol, followed by weeks seven and eight about something else. There is only a two-week entry into the moderate and a one month entry in the high ICPM that talk specifically about drugs. If you are addicted to drugs that is not enough support for your entire sentence to prepare you for the street and not consume drugs.

Years ago, CSC had Drug Free Units and they were somewhat a relief until they kicked prisoners off the unit for using, rather than helping them when in need. Security imperatives took over, as more searches, urinalyses and control became the norm. Previously, these units gave support to prisoners on the unit with a 24-hour toll free hotlines for help and daily circles. Prisoners also somewhat policed themselves and staff were specially trained for the needs of those on the range. When a prisoner was released and stayed off drugs they were an inspiration to all.

ON "FAINT HOPE"

As I already stated I am a Lifer. It took me more than a decade and a half to reach a minimum-security setting, and I made it there the day after my 15-year review pre-screening hearing for parole under the "Faint Hope Clause". The Harper government took away the "Faint Hope Clause" or 15-year review, which allowed Lifers to go through a pre-screening by a judge who determines if your case could go before a jury who could reduce your parole eligibility date. The criteria for it was stringent, requiring that all your programming be completed and that you demonstrate progress such as being in a minimum-security institution at the time of your application for pre-screening. Having ETAs and UTAs under one's belt is also an expectation. Given that I was in a medium and did not pass my pre-screening, I cannot apply again for five years. Under the old system it was two years. This change, along with many other penal reforms put forward by the Conservatives, were done in name of Clifford Olson and other exceptionally troubling prisoners, who were never getting out because necessary protections were already in place in our laws. The news media had a responsibility to mention this in their coverage of the punishment agenda, but often failed to do so as Conservative laws, policing and practices were implemented.

In my case, CSC would not send me to a minimum saying that if I received a bad decision in my hearing that I could be an escape risk, so they waited until after my hearing date to send me. The court says it is a prerequisite that I be in a minimum to apply and pass the pre-screening.

When CSC transferred me the very next day after my failed hearing suggests that I was setup to fail. When I came to minimum listening to the words of the judge and Crown, I sought to apply for ETAs and UTAs only to find out that I cannot get UTAs until I am eligible for day parole, which is three years before my full parole eligibility date. I am essentially being barred opportunities to prepare myself for release and the way the system is setup for Lifers, it seems that many of us that can safely re-enter the community will be incarcerated beyond our full parole eligibility dates.

ON THE SECURITY THREAT GROUP

The Harper government and CSC brought in what they call STG (Security Threat Group) claiming that the face of Canadian prisoners is changing. As the Canadian population has become increasingly diverse so too has the federal prison population, and by diverse CSC means gangs and people with gang affiliations. This label is inappropriately applied to many prisoners sometimes on the basis of the neighbourhood where arrested in, where they sit and eat at a table in the penitentiary cafeteria, if they work out in the gym with a "known gang member", and the like. It is very easy to be labeled and tremendously hard to be removed from the list.

Prisoners labeled as part of the STG are prejudiced with respect to the delivery of institutional services. STG prisoners cannot access pay higher than level "C" and are reported as not following their correctional plan. Furthermore, they cannot have jobs of trust within the institution. CSC more or less labels them a social pariah by telling others if they continue to associate with you then they too will be listed. This all has an impact on one's security classification as well and one's ability to access gradual release mechanisms.

It needs to be noted that for most, *if* a person belongs to such a party when they are arrested, they no longer belong to the party – they are "hung up". While awaiting trial, one who manages to get bail is required to follow non-association stipulations that prevent such relations from being maintained. The same goes for parole following a conviction and serving time behind bars. The STG label limits options for affected prisoners, which undermines their rehabilitation and reintegration. To respect procedural fairness, the STG has to be changed and stop being abused.

MIXING POPULATIONS

I am not an advocate for prisoners who choose protective custody. For years, I did not know how they lived and did not care. However, now all the penitentiaries are mixed and the lower you go in security, the more susceptible you are to having dealings with protective custody prisoners.

CSC institutions used to be general population or protective custody. Years ago, CSC decided to mix both and here is what I have noticed over the years. These protected prisoners are protected for a reason and that reason varies such as their offence, things they have said, but mostly their behaviour. What I mean by behaviour is such prisoners are the ones who bud in lines, who feel entitled to everything, who have the "I don't give a shit" attitude, and are rewarded for their bad behaviour because they become sources for security intelligence officers. Most of them are drug users who run from penitentiary to penitentiary owing money and telling security intelligence what they want to hear.

I am a grandfather and an uncle to about dozens of children. When I was in Beaver Creek Medium I was surrounded by prisoners who previously harmed children. These prisoners were verbally abused every day in one form or another – and I mean every day. That made me think about their rehabilitation and how they can move forward with all this abuse in a positive way. They must hold onto a lot of resentment and the people that will suffer are people on the street, and that could be one of my children, grandchildren or relatives. So now I pay special attention to what help CSC is providing these prisoners. Unfortunately, CSC only offers up a program and if completed then they are following the correctional plan. These prisoners have different needs than others such as counselling, therapy and all sorts of things that are not provided to them since the two populations amalgamated. This needs to change for all of our sakes.

When there was Protective Custody, these prisoners would be better positioned to get the help they needed and to not be abused every day. While I am not their advocate, I do not want to see people harmed on the outside or go through the trauma these people inflict. I feel that if I say nothing then I am a party to the damage they could cause once released. The General Population and Protective Custody facilities have to come back.

INCENTIVE AND REGULAR PAY

Prisoners lost the incentive pay that they made at CORCAN. This is a big deal especially in these times when the cost of living has gone up for everything. The incentive pay helped parents send money home to their families, pay the phone bill to keep in touch with their loved ones, gave a prisoner a sense of satisfaction while they were working all day. That CSC took away the incentive is damaging, both to the work program and to the rehabilitation of prisoners.

Few work opportunities provided by CSC lead to the transfer of meaningful skills and certifications. There is always an exception to the rule and Collins Bay has the best welding CORCAN program I ever been to with the chance to get a ticket every three months. A prisoner can get up to I think twelve tickets for welding. These tickets are only good in Ontario, but this is better than not being qualified at all. Here, at Beaver Creek, CORCAN has prisoners making tents and tool belts for Home Hardware, leaving us with absolutely no skills unless of course one wants to make the same amount of money outside as inside working for a sweat shop.

Prisoners need the incentive pay back, and all vocational and work programs need to provide prisoners with marketable work skills for employment. While on paper, Commissioner's Directive 720 *Education Programs and Services for Inmates*[1] promises this, CSC only offers the bare minimum at most of its institutions, leaving prisoners with minimal skills. This needs to change.

THE CONSTRUCTION OF NEW UNITS AND ITS IMPACT

In the context of declining crime rates, the Harper Government built units inside the fences of existing penitentiaries almost everywhere, despite owning property beyond them. Did they build these ridiculous penitentiary units on the inside of the fences to circumvent having to tell the public in town hall meetings and avoiding opposition to having multi-level facilities in their neighbourhood?

The pitfalls of these new facilities are numerous. Our yards have shrunk to nothing. Some of the buildings are unused eyesores (e.g. they have a 56-

bed unit here at the minimum and it has not been opened yet; they also have a program building that has never been used for programs, and it sits there empty with the heat and lights on). Since these buildings have been built, prisoners have been paying additional food and accommodation fees, while the cost of living inside (e.g. canteen, groceries and vending machines) has gone up. As already stated STG only get level C pay, and it is extremely hard for a prisoner to get and maintain level A pay.

We prisoners are basically paying for new units that should have never been built that have consumed our yards, taken from us our free time and space, created additional crowding problems in process via double-bunking, and made the environment more dangerous. We have paid for this with the violation of our rights and freedoms, including the right to be treated fairly.

We used to have socials and food nights. The Conservative government thought it was too much that prisoners could order and eat takeout food from local restaurants that occupy space around the penitentiaries. The guards' union said drugs come in through socials so they were cut, our groups and ethnic groups were cut and yes also religious groups such as Wiccan were cut. All of these cuts are undermining community connections that facilitate safe reintegration. Moreover, the food night CSC cut off local MA & PA restaurants we once helped, which also promoted a good working relationship between them and the community. Who does not want to make $30 times hundreds of people in one afternoon? Socials were a way for us to visit our families for a few hours in a nice setting and a chance for a family to see that things are all right for their parent in prison, and a good time for parole and correctional officers to meet and see their case load in a family setting. It is as-if anything that contributed positively to the lives of prisoners had to go under the previous government, consequences be damned.

POST-SECONDARY EDUCATION AND COMPUTERS

While prisoners, before and after Harper, can take post-secondary courses if they pay for them, the problem we are facing now is that all courses are online. The colleges and universities used to send books and that does not happen. The guards' union and CSC are going to have to get with the times. We are living in the dinosaur age. We need computer and Internet to gain an education on our own dime. Computers are a big part of the outside world and people like myself who have been in since the 1990s do not have the experience with email, texts and so on. Computers are used in all places for everything and not knowing anything about them puts us Lifers at a great disadvantage. The fact we are not allowed to have computers in our room is nonsense. At the very least, we should have limited access to the Internet and learn how to use it. Considering that most banking and payments are done electronically, it would make sense that we would know how to do it. While all attempts at advancement in these areas are thwarted, CSC and the guards' union tell the public they are preparing us for the future. We are being prepared for failure and job insecurity, and that is not right.

PURCHASING IS BEHIND THE TIMES

As part of the previous Conservative government's Deficit Reduction Action Plan, CSC's Executive Committee decided to standardize purchasing and procurement practices. Consultation on the list of personal effects was conducted in late spring 2013 with regions, institutions and prisoners. When they say consulted prisoners, they meant they sent a memo telling us what will be happening. Prisoner purchasing and allowable item limits have to be addressed. Right now, the purchasing system is being monopolized by one company. Before the Harper government, we were able to order allowable effects from local venders helping the community we lived in, at the same time keeping our own identity. Not long ago, prisoners wore the same clothing and numbers, which, along with many other deprivations, dehumanized the incarcerated leading to riots among other things. From the riots of yesteryear, the CCRR and CCRA came to be. This was seemingly forgotten by the Harper government, the guards' union and CSC who brought us backwards.

ON ACCOUNTABILITY

With *The Safe Streets and Communities Act* which received royal assent, several changes were made to the CCRA, including several measures put in place in the name of accountability. The problem with CSC's new version of accountability is they always hold us accountable for our actions and hurl labels upon us arbitrarily (e.g. STG), while not being accountable for fulfilling their own obligations. This antagonistic approach is not helping in rehabilitation and in fact are doing the complete opposite. Moreover, when the legislation sought to clarify that the "protection of society" was to guide CSC decision making, it made it sound as if this goal was not a chief priority before. We all know that the safety of the public has always been first and, to this end, a more collaborative ethos needs to be put in place inside Canada's federal penitentiaries to work towards this outcome.

CONCLUSION

I have covered many issues above that I am extremely passionate about. I believe people can change. I believe in rehabilitation and that people are genuinely good. Even as I am surrounded by negativity, constantly pounded, and put down by CSC, I have to believe in what people on the outside and parolees tell me when they say to hang in there, that when I am out things will be different and people are good.

ENDNOTES

[1] Correctional Service Canada (2017) *Commissioners Directive 720 Education Programs and Services for Inmates*, Ottawa. Retrieved from http://www.csc-scc. gc.ca/acts-and-regulations/720-cd-eng.shtml

I am serving a life sentence. I have been incarcerated for 14 years. From my perspective, the Harper government made reforms to the federal penitentiary system that will manufacture criminals.

Correctional Service Canada (CSC) removed many opportunities for prisoners when they reduced the workshop programs and opportunities to gain tickets for things like welding or carpentry. There are no apprenticeship hours or trades to be earned. When a person such as myself learns a trade, it provides me with options and the confidence to know I can learn and work, making me feel prepared to seek employment. CSC programing is crucial and it also works. It is good to look within yourself and have insight into why you do what you do no matter what walk of life you are from. However, despite the need or desire for change, a person needs confidence and education in regard to employment. This requires community support, in addition to employment skills, they can fall back on. It is with this in mind that I make the recommendations below.

BRING BACK TRADES

The demographics of prisoners are changing. Many of the prisoners receiving sentences are younger and the crimes committed are changing. There needs to be more programing geared towards street oriented crimes similar to a brand-new group/program named *BREAK AWAY* introduced by Life Line in-reach counsellor Rick Sauvé.

GIVE GREATER ACCESS TO COMPUTERS

The technology available to prisoners is obsolete in comparison to what is in the outside world. Windows 2007 and floppy disk is what I am currently working from and it was recently updated to this. For prisoners to be able to reintegrate into society they need greater access to computers.

REPLACE THE NEW AND FAILING MODEL INTRODUCED AT JOYCEVILLE ASSESSMENT UNIT

Prisoners sentenced to terms of four years or less have the opportunity to complete their core programing in accordance to their correctional plan while housed in the assessment unit. This is supposed to speed up the opportunities for such prisoners to apply for different forms of release by their scheduled eligibility dates. However, despite finishing their programing and being transferred to lower-security institutions, they are being warehoused and restricted due to lack of support from their new institutional parole officer (IPO). No matter what, prisoners are held back due to the caseloads the IPOs have. There should also be more program facilitators for other prisoners. Positive gains with respect to your correctional plan often comes down to how busy your IPO is and the current approach is failing many prisoners who are kept behind bars longer than necessary.

BETTER SUPPORT FOR PRISONERS
WHO USE DRUGS

Several months back, a prisoner known to us here at Beaver Creek was released to a residence. He had previously been denied day parole at a halfway house. He wanted to be released to a place and have the support of being monitored. This young man lacked community support and family. He was an addict, yet you would not be able to tell he had such struggles. He played sports, was charming and funny, polite, respectful, stayed away from the subcultures and he presented as social. Following his eventual release without adequate supports he himself sought, he overdosed just ten days later and passed away. He should have been released to a halfway house or a treatment centre. This is a tragedy! This was on CSC's watch. R.I.P.

Dispatches from the Prairie Region

Stony Mountain Institution
William Allan Beaulieu

The following is my personal experience with respect to Correctional Service Canada's (CSC) human rights abuses under the Harper government's punishment agenda. The way I discerned this punishment agenda developing was similar to how other countries in the past would centre out a powerless and branded segment of society to oppress. They incite vicious hatred against the group and categorize them into one group of 'enemies'. This method conveniently separates them from the rest of normal society.

Once the Harper Conservatives were able to instill this into the public whenever some tragedy occurred in the communities, it would beat the justice and public safety drum loud. Often leading the correctional oppression against the criminalized was Mr. Vic Toews, who was Justice Minister from February 2006 to January 2007 and the Public Safety Minister from January 2010 to July 2013. He seemed to dislike all the federal prisoners whom he labelled as 'offenders', contributing to the division between the Canadian people and the incarcerated. He especially seemed to dislike the prisoners serving life terms for murder, which are sentences that can leave one behind bars indefinitely. He stated, along with many other Conservatives, that Canadian people convicted for murder should never be out in the community on parole, which sent the message to all community parole services across Canada to revoke and return to prison as many Lifers they could get away with under the guise of public safety. Not satisfied with the re-incarceration of many of these prisoners, the retribution continued. He dismantled Life Line, the only program CSC had for prisoners sentenced to life under some form of state supervision. His office then created policies to make it more difficult for Lifers to attain any form of release. First, the policy of requiring Lifers to go before the Parole Board Canada (PBC) panels for Escorted Temporary Absences (ETAs) contributes to the unnecessary delays and is used as a punishment stick. This practice also stripped the power of penitentiary wardens to approved ETAs to eligible prisoners who earned it. Re-incarcerating all those paroled Lifers also clogs up the rehabilitation and release process for the ones still working for freedom. It is bizarre to require a Lifer to repeat the ETA process when they have been in the community for extended periods of time. This glaring punishment policy needs to be removed, with wardens again having the power to approve medical, compassionate and re-socialization ETAs.

Another punishment policy against Lifers is the requirement to wait for five years to apply for parole after every hearing when you were denied it. The previous policy was all Lifers were to be reviewed every two years once they were eligible for supervised release. For example, when a prisoner was granted day parole to a halfway house and adjusted to society well, the next step for him or her after seven to eight months is full parole. The five-year waiting policy means the decision to deny you full parole will result in one having to reside at the halfway for another four to five years. Halfway houses should not be used in cases where Lifers have a home to live in and sustainable incomes to feed themselves. Reducing the periods between parole hearings would free up much needed bed space for paroled prisoners who need the help. For those still inside the joint, you can be warehoused for years. The institutional parole officers often fail to review and update Lifer files for parole review.

My next observation with respect to Harper's punishment agenda has to deal with the parole supervision in the community and parole preparation inside the institutions. This factual information is gleaned from my personal experience and from listening to other prisoners recounting their experiences of having their human rights violated by the staff working inside the Canadian prison gulags.

When I was on parole in the community, the Winnipeg parole service was quite determined to have me back behind the walls of Stony Mountain Institution. I have fought off several attempts to return me to the penitentiary by successfully overturning alleged parole breaches. However, I have also been returned to prison nine years past my parole eligibility date for failed drug tests associated with using my doctor prescribed medication and for having friendly chats with someone I was in a halfway house with that resulted me in being labelled as someone associated with a gang member. At Stony Mountain minimum, I am not allowed an ETA to pay and keep my driver's licence current.

As it is, federal prisoners can be returned to penitentiaries for minor breaches of parole. The various minor parole breaches could be for drinking a bottle of beer, being late for curfew or talking to anyone with some type of conviction or accusation. This social behaviour is the norm in a free and democratic society. Only if alcohol or drugs were involved in the offence(s) that landed you in prison is a parole breach appropriate. Instituting parole breaches for associating with accused or persons with criminal records when most people I know have been in conflict with the law sets people up for isolation or failure. After all, it is not likely for many prisoners to get to hang out with the elites of society that have not been criminalized. This policy should only apply to those involved in gangs or criminal organizations. Parolees should be allowed to socialize with real people.

Under the Conservatives, I also witnessed parole breaches occurring because of a 'deteriorating attitude'. This is such an ambiguous label that allows a community parole officer to fabricate any reason to terminate your legal release. If you are an assertive and low-maintenance type of individual, your parole officer can resent that and assume they have no control over your life. They may think you are displaying an entitlement attitude to be treated with respect and dignity. These are some of the personal parole experiences I had and from what other prisoners related to me. For instance, if you disagree or stand-up to the parole officer for abusing their power over you, the end result is a negative parole report that states you have 'deteriorating attitude', which justifies revocation and re-incarceration. For my example, I took a higher paying job, a behaviour that was – for reasons unknown to me – perceived as a symptom of a 'deteriorating attitude' for simply making a positive change.

I was told by an institutional parole officer that their bosses instructed them to slow down the release process for Lifers. While I was sceptical when I heard this, I believe this is also true from what I saw in minimums. I did time in Saskatchewan and Manitoba penitentiaries mostly. Some guys wait excessively long time to start ETAs. I know one fellow who has waited for over five years for one. In other cases, paper work has been lost or misplaced. Sometimes, the institutional parole officer fails to follow the guidelines of their duties. In the process, proper rehabilitation procedures get put on the back burner and prisoners stay locked up unnecessarily. I have seen and heard of institutional parole officers taking a prisoner not serving a life sentence before the parole panel about thirty days before their statuary release date to give the illusion that prisoners are being paroled efficiently.

What needs to change are current parole case work procedures, which ought to be recorded to ensure that the rehabilitation process is being facilitated by CSC, as well as engaged in by prisoners. As it is now, institutional and community parole officers are given too much trust and power to assess and manage prisoners and the case files. There should be a deterrent to prevent them from abusing their power and duties of their office. Also, these recordings would serve to protect the parole officers from unfounded grievances from prisoners, while safeguarding the human and legal rights of the criminalized. The current setup is one whereby you have the prisoner versus the parole officer's word whenever revocation or any case management decisions have to be made. Due to bias that sees trustworthiness given to a CSC official over a prisoner who is labelled as untrustworthy, most of the time, people will automatically take the word of the former. Both parties have to be held accountable and be responsible in the rehabilitation process for it to work properly and fairly.

Lastly, I wish to touch upon the deteriorating situation with respect to human rights and the rule of law within CSC institutions where guards have total control over different facets of penitentiary life. When you go inquire about a matter at the visits and correspondence (V&C) department you often find a guard working there who does not have the time of day for you. It would be akin to going to your community post office to find a disgruntled uniformed postman working there. They have opened my privileged correspondence (e.g. letters sent to the House of Commons in Ottawa and legal offices). Papers associated with a human rights complaint were lost. I can only assume this takes place across the federal penitentiary system, whether in V&C or elsewhere in institutions. The unspoken policy is to treat us merely as 'offenders' that the rest of society despises. The obvious contradiction with this hateful attitude and general mistreatment of prisoner is, on one hand, they appear to be part of the correctional treatment process with programs and case work to get us ready to part of society and to uphold the values of it. On the other hand, these abuses and their mistreatment defeat that noble aim. When you are being disrespected and viewed as something less than a human being, the motivation to change and accept the social and human values of society can be difficult. The carrot should be put back, alongside the stick is my point.

In conclusion, the stern operating message that is needed from the current government to all its employees is that this hateful behavior towards prisoners must stop immediately. They are paid to be impartial, uphold the laws and not abuse our human rights. The guards need to return to their proper roles of preventing escapes and violence. Bring back regular staff to retain other operational positions of the institutions. This will remove the current police state mentality. Also, it will provide the opportunity for prisoners to interact with other community members from society. The managers of parole officers and general parole officers have to be better monitored to insure their offices are fair and properly assisting those that are part of their caseload. In fact, the current government needs to weed out all the staff refusing to follow or uphold the policies and guidelines of the correctional treatment process. The current abusive policies left over from the previous government are hindering the rehabilitation process, creating an unhealthy penitentiary environment, which makes it toxic for all concerned to do time or work there. Things have gotten so bad, CSC's mission statement that once hung at admissions and discharges was tossed into the trash can at Stony Mountain minimum. This is not how things should be.

I am an Indigenous prisoner serving a life sentence in Saskatchewan Penitentiary past my parole eligibility date. Years ago, I was diagnosed with cancer. After the operation to remove a tumour I was left with disabilities, including loss of memory and sight. I was in a wheelchair for several years. After a lot of physiotherapy, today I can walk with some balance issues. I cannot run.

While I was at Bowden Institution in Alberta I was granted cultural escorted passes by the warden. I had many successful Escorted Temporary Absences (ETAs) for a year. Then the Harper Government brought in a law requiring Lifers to have approval by the Parole Board of Canada (PBC) before being able to go on passes. I have been waiting for almost two years for approval to go on passes, with one excuse or another preventing me from continuing my healing journey. Why can the warden no longer be allowed to approve ETAs? They did it before Harper's punishment agenda was upon us with successful results the vast majority of the time.

I accept my life sentence for being involved in murder. For the past number of years, I have changed my life – no violence, drugs or involvement in prison subculture activities. I have dealt with my childhood trauma, my residential school abuse issues – the violence, drug use, negative thoughts and feelings that were symptoms of my sickness arising from my childhood trauma. I am involved in my culture, I am spiritual and I pray every day. I hope that I am able to take advantage of the cultural ETAs provided by the Elders without being assessed by people at the PBC who do not know me.

Saskatchewan Penitentiary
Anonymous Prisoner 16

It is my understanding that the Government of Canada has begun to assess the criminal justice system as a whole. There are many problems with the system as it is now, and while I understand that no human-made system of action is completely without problems, I feel that the number of problems within it and their impacts are considerable, and could be avoided. Problems plague this system all the way from the first moment of arrest up to the end of parole on the street.

I am doing a relatively short period of incarceration, but the stories and instances that I have heard described to me from a multitude of differing sources lead me to believe that almost the entire system is corrupted, from the abuses of power by law enforcement to administrative abuses of power once incarcerated. The problem is that such stories rarely get through the mail as all correspondence is read – as this letter no doubt will be – with the chance of it adversely affecting your period of incarceration being very high. Not many will take the threat lightly, and those whose stories you desire to hear the most are the most vulnerable to abuse. Those prisoners serving life sentences can be given serious setbacks for seemingly arbitrary and petty reasons.

If you are serious about evaluating and subsequently changing the nature of the criminal justice system then I implore you to visit each prison and have closed-door interviews with prisoners as this is the way you will receive the most unbiased and uncensored information. There are stories to be heard and tales to be told, which the medium of pen on paper does not do the reality of our accounts justice. I ask that you come to Saskatchewan Penitentiary and interview prisoners from the maximum-, medium-, and minimum-security units. Only then can you get a full picture of life behind bars.

Thank you for your time, consideration and the acceptance of this task. It is a worthy one.

I will begin by stating the obvious. Since all correspondence, except those of a legal nature are scrutinised, you should expect, on some issues, responses may be muted. For this reason, I will keep my observations and suggestions targeted to larger thematic areas. I am sure that you will receive many letters addressing issues with guards, the medical system and so on. As such, I am bringing other ideas forward.

Imprisonment is a business, and as such, those towns, cities, and municipalities which derive a net benefit from the proceeds of incarceration are more interested in their benefit rather than rehabilitation. This then turns our justice system into political football. There is hardly a politician out there who would stand up and try to find ways to reduce our prison population by fifty to seventy percent. Yet, that is what we should be looking at doing, particularly when a good number of prisoners are people with addictions and psychological issues. These issues are dealt with primarily through medicating prisoners. What we need are holistic rehabilitation centres, rather than penitentiaries. Those centres would revolve around addressing addictions (i.e. alcohol, drugs, psychological, etc.), and preparing prisoners through education and vocational training to reintegrate into society. Those centres should be considered for any prisoner, especially for those where violence is not considered to be a concern and for anyone returning to the community within five years.

The parole system is broken. Far too much power rests in the hands of Parole Board Canada (PBC), and its dependence on the bias and prejudices of its officials.[1] PBC should either be removed or its power diminished greatly (i.e. to issues related to those serving lengthy sentences), so that parole officers and psychologists who are professionals, and spend their time directly with prisoners are empowered to release them conditionally. As it stands now, a prisoner who has positive reports from all members of their CMT (Case Management Teams) can be denied parole after a thirty-minute parole board assessment. Considering that little professional training exists for PBC members, it hardly seems appropriate to empower them as much as we do. Another area where the PBC could be utilised is to act as a review where a prisoner feels that an error has been rendered by their CMT who would, under my proposal, have more responsibility with respect to the granting of parole.

I am also troubled by the number of restrictions placed on those who are granted parole. Often people wind-up coming back into the penitentiary system for breaching their conditions. I can understand the desire to keep prisoners away from environments that may cause them to re-offend, but when conditions are arbitrarily applied several years after release the likelihood of breaching one's conditions goes up. Perhaps a change in thinking is required. My suggestion would be that one's conditions can only include restrictions that are directly related to the offense. For example, if alcohol was not attributed as a cause of an offence then why put a restriction on a parolee that they cannot consume alcohol?

We as a society must understand how fast technology is moving and how it affects each of its segments. Consider that in today's world any criminal record against someone will live on forever. There is no 'pulling up stakes and restarting' somewhere else as you could have in the pre-internet age. In my case, the police tweeted my arrest and the charges within eighteen hours of being charged. Part of rehabilitation must allow a person the opportunity to not have their worst actions follow them forever. For this reason, I am advocating that on a first offence that does not include violence and is punished with a sentence of less than five years that no record can be accessed by the media once the warrant has been completed. These records should be frozen, that is to say that no one can access those records unless they are related to another offense and are required for sentencing. Essentially, the first offence is a non-recordable if it meets the parameters noted above.

The penal system places far too much emphasis on punishment, choosing to spend its resources on warehousing prisoners, rather than rehabilitating them. A change in philosophy is required directed to exiting prisoners slated to re-enter society capable of finding jobs and understanding how to deal with stress. We need to consider a simple overhaul. The longer we keep an individual in prison the less chance that we have of reintegrating them functionally into society. Everyone in prison has some level of depression, anxiety and stress. It is not only the confinement, it is the treatment. Guards have a master-slave view of their position. As such their own psyche can make for adversarial conditions. For example, after 9:30pm stand up count the guards come around every two hours. On paper, these rounds are to ensure that prisoners who are sleeping are not in need of immediate health care. So, as you are sleeping, it is not unusual for a guard to shine their flashlights into your face and kick the door. They say that this is necessary in order to apply CPR if necessary. This is ludicrous of course since they would actually have to arrive at the exact moment that you expired in order to have any realistic chance of applying CPR and saving you. What this policy does is wake people up every two hours, thus depriving them of a good night's sleep. At the same time as the penitentiary claims this as a safety protocol, they would not equip each housing unit with an AED unit.

At this point, it may be best to continue with this letter in an abbreviated fashion, otherwise I would fill pages upon pages. Here, then, are the points to consider:

- A "different" type of prison situation is required for dealing with gangs. Mixing these prisoners within the general population needs to be reconsidered.
- Rather than mandatory minimum sentences, our justice system needs to consider alternative options. Persons who have not committed violent crime would be better off being referred to mental health, addiction or similar services as required. Prisons offer little in terms of correcting behaviour related to these issues.
- I suggest that, as part of the review, you should focus on looking at other penal systems that treat prisoners with a level of dignity (e.g. Norway).
- Guards should be required to undergo a psychological assessment at least once a year. Honestly, I have seen too many guards who are bullies who enjoy berating and belittling prisoners. I cannot imagine any other workplace that would tolerate such behaviour. Regardless of my current imprisonment, I am a citizen and deserve to be treated as a human being, not as a punching bag or a whipping post.
- I will end with a broad statement in regard to health care and mental health care. Both are in serious need of overhauling. There are insufficient psychologists available to handle the needs of prisoners. They seem to exist only for the purpose of serving the institutions requirements, not ours or those of the communities to which most of us will return.

I trust you will find my observations useful. I do not believe that much, if anything, will change. However, I have honestly added my thoughts in the hope that other voices have spoken as well.

ENDNOTES

[1]   According to the 2014/2015 performance monitoring report for the Parole Board
of Canada, parole grant rates for the various regions are as follows: In 2014/15, all
regions reported increases in their federal conditional release offender populations:
the Atlantic (+5%), Quebec (+4%), Pacific (+4%), Prairie (+2%) and Ontario (+1%)
regions. However, in the Quebec region, the federal day parole offender population
decreased in 2014/15 (-5%), the federal full parole population remained relatively
unchanged (0.3%), while the statutory release population increased significantly
(+16%) compared to the year before. In 2014/15, the highest proportion of Aboriginal
offenders was in the Prairie region: 47% of federal male prisoners and 64% of
federal female prisoners in the Prairie region were Indigenous. By comparison, 33%
of federal male prisoners on conditional release and 42% of federal female prisoners
on conditional release in the Prairie region were Indigenous (Parole Board Canada,
2015). Parole Board of Canada (2015) *Performance Monitoring Report 2014/2015*,
Ottawa. Retrieved from https://www.canada.ca/content/dam/canada/parole-board/
migration/005/009/093/005009-3000-2015-en.pdf

First of all, I would like to take this opportunity to thank those who are making efforts to bring positive change to how the justice system treats people convicted of an offense. I do appreciate it. In my humble opinion, there have been many changes in how the Correctional Service Canada (CSC) treats the individuals that are entrusted to their care and those changes have not been to our betterment.

The increase in the penitentiary population has greatly affected all operations within the institution where I am housed, from security to recreational activities. As the population has grown, institutions are struggling to fulfill their responsibilities in meeting the individual's needs with respect to health care, mental health care, programs, recreation and so forth. For example, when this institution had a population of four-hundred, the waiting list to see the dentist was maybe three months at the most. Now with a higher population, the waiting list to see the dentist is closer to twelve months.

While the increase in the population has resulted in the hiring of more security personnel, other resources have dwindled, including with respect to parole preparation and social programming. As the per diem that is allotted to feed us has not increased in many years, the cost of food has continually increased. This has led to a couple of issues – the quality and portions of food have decreased.

There has not been an increase in the prisoner pay system since the 1980s, yet we lose a substantial portion of our remuneration to cover our food and accommodations, which sometimes need to be shared. On top of that we have to pay for the prisoner telephone system, stated as an administration cost. I know of some guys who never use the telephone or have a phone card, but they are still deducted 8% of their pay every two weeks for this service. I have heard many guys complaining about going to sleep hungry. Less money to spend in the canteen, along with the poor quality and quantity of food serviced in kitchen, has led to short tempers with violence erupting from individuals being hungry. This has increased the number of guys being muscled for their canteen or "taxed".

Another issue is that there is a lack of halfway houses in the communities. There are guys who are waiting anywhere from three weeks to two months before a bed becomes available for them to start their day parole that has been granted by Parole Board Canada. Here, we have part of the justice system stating it is okay for you to be back in the community, but the community does not have the resources for this.

Where relevant, I believe that there needs to be a balance between programs to help one become an emotionally balanced person and educational opportunities to become employable. Over the years, CSC's focus seems to be to fix the individual (i.e. their emotional or addictions issues) to the detriment of training for work that will allow them to survive upon release. To me, this makes no sense – I can control my emotions, but if I cannot put food on the table, I am put in a position where I may need to turn back to crime to put food on the table, but I will be polite about it! I remember thirty years ago when a prisoner could become an apprentice in many different fields and received more than just a high school diploma.

While CSC states the community support is important, it seems that correctional and parole officers try to discourage citizens from being a support in our lives. I have heard many stories about the poor treatment visitors experience at the hands of staff, and how parole officers describe an individual (prisoner) to family and potential employers affecting those relationships in a negative way.

The central purchasing system is a monopoly and is problematic. I wonder how all communities where federal penitentiaries are located have been impacted by this, and whether local stores and employees working in them have lost income as a result of it. As a Canadian citizen, I have lost my right to choose which company I would like to support or the brand I would like to wear. To my understanding of the law, as a prisoner I have only lost my right to freedom, but I retain all my other rights as a Canadian citizen. For Conservatives who promote the free market, I ask, what happened to competition? The change was passed as a way for CSC to enhance institutional security, however, that makes no sense as everything is subject to search (e.g. by a dog) when arriving at the institution.

In conclusion, I pray and hope that this information will be helpful in correcting some of the issues federal prisoners face on a daily basis.

W ith many decades of life experience in the Canadian penal system, I was encouraged by others to outline my life journey with Correctional Service Canada (CSC) and the Parole Board of Canada (PBC) to highlight some of the shifts that have occurred in the federal penitentiary system over the years.

ON CONDITIONAL RELEASE

I was convicted of murder as a teenager. After a decade behind bars, I was released on full parole, enrolled in university and got a degree, got married and had a child. I started a business, but then as a result of a family dispute where I threatened court action to maintain custody of my child, I became targeted for false complaints about to my parole officers. My parole was subsequently suspended and revoked on a number of occasions. I was later told by CSC and PBC officials that this should not have happened.

At one point, I was released on day parole and several months later I was again granted full parole. This is where my life experiences with Prime Minister Stephen Harper's policies crossed paths. During my parole hearing, I admitted that I smoked a joint to help with the stress of moving from a small town to a large city, leaving my family and friends behind, and starting all over again. I was given a "substance-abuse condition" even though the rules state that conditions could only be imposed if it was a "risk factor" that contributed to my offence, which it was not. I was told by an official that the imposition of this condition was a direct result of the federal government's 'tough' stance on marijuana.

While on full parole and issue free, I was suspended for an alleged assault and I was later revoked in February 2014 without a hearing. The charges were later dropped in court as the person whom claimed that I assaulted him admitted that the accusations were false and that he was the one whom had assaulted me. I had requested that my revocation hearing be postponed until after my court date because I knew that I was innocent. However, I was not granted this request. I was told that the federal government had put in place rules that if a prisoner is charged with a new offence that their parole is automatically suspended and revoked.

After returning to prison, I grappled with memories of childhood abuse I experienced. As I tried to access counselling, I was informed that because of CSC cutbacks mandated by the Harper government as part of their austerity plan there were no trained counsellors I could speak to. In 2014, I met with a contract psychologist for a risk assessment. She recommended that I be transferred to the minimum-security unit, attend church via Escorted Temporary Absences (ETAs) for three months and then be released. My faith was identified as an important factor in my being crime-free for over four decades. I filled-out the transfer paperwork and should have been transferred with a couple of months, yet the process took five months. During this period, I was given a new untrained parole officer who could not handle the work load and went back to being a correctional officer (COII). My files were a mess and within a half a year I had five parole officers.

In 2015, I was transferred to the Minimum-Security Unit (MSU) of Drumheller and my new parole officer applied for an ETA to church at per the recommendation of the psychological risk assessment. However, there was a new problem. The Conservative government imposed a new condition on people serving a life sentence, whereby the power to grant ETAs was taken away from the Institutional Warden. That power was transferred to PBC.

During a parole hearing held in 2015, the board members denied my case management team's request for faith-based ETAs to deal with issues I had experienced in my life. In their decision, PBC members noted:

> Your release plans for the proposed ETA's are aimed at assisting you in rebuilding your community supports through church activity. The Board notes these are similar to what you have done in the past and yet you have been suspended and revoked with these in place. The Board has concerns that this plan will not result in future success and also given your history that your involvement in these will not contribute to public safety at this time.

To support their decision, they made the following erroneous statements: that I was revoked in for being involved in a "hit and run accident"; and that I had a substance abuse condition, which I violated a year after it was imposed. After a file review by my case management team concluded that the information quoted by the PBC was erroneous and misleading. The Manager of Assessments and Interventions (MAI) instructed my parole officer to write to the PBC three times to correct the facts, which were refused. Finally, I was instructed to appeal the PBC decision, which turned out to be a waste of time. The Appeal Division – an in-house body – denied my request, sending me to the Access to Information and Privacy department, which in turn sent me to the Office of the Privacy Commissioner. They in turn instructed be to again contact the Access of Information and Privacy department of CSC looking to start the process to correct the erroneous file information. This process so far has taken more than a year and a half, and the erroneous issues have still not been resolved. I was told that because of Harper-era cutbacks, correcting erroneous file information, which likely needs to be remedied if I am ever to be released, can take forever. With a parole hearing scheduled with the support of my institutional case management team, the uncertainty I am living with is unjust.

ON PRISON LIFE

Beyond the issues with respect to conditional release noted above, my stay in Drumheller Institution has brought to light several dysfunctions in the federal penitentiary system that have emerged as a result of Harper-era laws, policies and practices.

One area of profound change is with respect to trades and education. During their time in office, the Conservative government created a false illusion to the public that you could get a trade while in prison. When I was first incarcerated you could access skills training in the following areas: auto body, auto mechanics, electrical, plumbing, sheet metal, machinist, cabinet making, welding and painting. Now, only a handful of prisoners can access welding and pre-carpentry. The biggest complaint that I hear amongst prisoners is that they cannot get a trade while in prison. Many leave this place almost as they have arrived, not able to get a job. The system no longer cares if you can get a trade while in prison as long as they can show that you have taken their psychological programs, which most prisoners see as a waste of time. At one time, you could get help taking university level courses like I did. Today, only GED is on offer. As a result, many just return to the penitentiary because of no jobs and/or a lack of education where they are just mandated to take another psychological program.

A related issue is the fact that the Harper government removed employment incentives in the penitentiary so that you could save money for when you got out. People are now leaving prison with only $80 to their name and no chance of getting a job. One person that I know asked the PBC to spend the last six months of his sentence at a halfway house so that he could save money, find employment and find a place to live, while under the supervision of CSC. The PBC refused and sent him into the community with no money, no job and no place to go. How many days do you think he lasted, just to return to prison at a cost of more than $100,000 a year to taxpayers? It is as if the system is just one big make work project for them where everyone else pays the bill.

Another area of change is drug urinalysis for marijuana. At one time in the penitentiary, guards were not concerned about someone smoking marijuana because it kept everyone calm. However, with the previous federal government's anti-marijuana agenda, the system has cracked down on the substance, causing prisoners to turn to harder drugs because they stay in your system for much less time. This, in turn, has created a new generation and class of drug addicts leaving the federal penitentiary system. This causes the spread of HIV/AIDS and Hepatitis-C to their families and communities.

There appears to be very little accountability toward inaction by staff members in the system. For example, every forty-five days the rules state that you are supposed to meet with your COII, to go over issues that are occurring your case. I have gone eighteen months without such a meeting. Under the Harper-mindset of getting 'tough' on prisoners, people are not doing their jobs and CSC management appears powerless to do anything about it.

I hope these observations assist others in understanding what happened at CSC and PBC during Prime Minister Stephen Harper's reign.

Having lived on this earth for more than a half-century, I have spent over two decades behind bars, despite being eligible for parole for more than 10 years. In my time in the federal penitentiary system, I have seen so many changes and most of them not for the good.

In recent years, we are now having to additional pay room and board, which is deducted from our institutional pay every two weeks. As well, we have lost our dollar a day work incentives through CORCAN. Our chances for a better education are almost non-existent in the Prairie Region, aside from being able to get a GED. Our health care is lacking and all the doctors seem willing to commit to in terms of care is prescribing an assortment of pills, including for mental health issues – simple zombification.

We need better support for our loved ones while we are incarcerated, such as family programs. We need better support for mothers and family that find themselves suddenly alone when we are incarcerated so that they do not have only welfare to get by.

Anything that we have to purchase through canteen or catalogue purchasing comes with a considerable mark-up, so unless you are wealthy on the street, you are a beggar behind bars. Even up at the minimum where I currently am and have been for the last number of months, we have to buy our groceries from a paltry weekly allowance with a mark-up from the wholesaler and supplier to the institution.

I hope you can use this information for the betterment of all concerned.

Dispatches from the Pacific Region

Mission Institution
Anonymous Prisoners

In speaking with key members of our resident population here at Mission Medium Institution, we hope our response provides relevant insight into just how severe the current 'correctional' system has deviated from how we believe real corrections, justice and true human rights interests fit with the 'Canadian values' identity of this country. As the Harper government gutted CSC, they in effect created a series of warehouses for the incarcerated and a set them up for failure model of release. Coming up with the first five of our top ten areas of reform that are needed was easier than the remainder. In fact, curbing it just to ten was more than difficult.

1. **Pay Structure**
   a. Per diem pay rates dating back to the 1980s – there has to be a way to implement an increasing pay structure based on job skill sets and accountability so that residents can again *save money* for eventual and successful release.
   b. The additional 22 percent deduction for room and board, along with the 8 percent deduction for phone system administration instituted in 2014 needs to be abolished.
   c. Ineffective employment programs and subsequent performance reviews need to be reviewed, along with the cash grab that ties a resident's pay scale (performance) as Commissioner's Directives 710-1 *Progress Against the Correctional Plan*[1] and 730 *Offender Program Assignments and Payments*[2] lack clarity.

2. **Food and Beverage Policies – "Cook Chill" Meal Plan**
   a. Current food and beverage policies, which were modified in the name of cost savings, do not meet Canada Food Guide criteria.
   b. The portions have been cut and served by stewards who openly speak about being disgruntled and underpaid, which makes food lines stressful.
   c. There is no training – vocational, safety or otherwise – in the kitchen as everything has been cut to the bare bones. A kitchen where actual skills are taught is needed.

3. **"Prototype Catalogue" – Sole-source Supplier Model**
   a. The new sole-source supplier model has resulted in price gouging, with significant mark-ups (e.g. a television at $215 in the catalogue

can be purchased at Walmart for $89 or running shoes at $118 that can be bought in any store outside for $49 – how is that fair market value?). In response to grievances on this matter, we have been receiving a form letter stating that prisoners "are receiving fair market value prices".

b.   We have access to poor, low-quality selections that ship inconsistently or not at all, increasing frustrations for us and our loved ones.

c.   Local businesses and community support has been cut-off, leaving us without a means to make contacts and offer support that are valued on paper in our various reintegration plans.

4.   Correctional Management Team (CMT) Process and Support Model

a.   There is little case management outside of timelines. Correctional Plans lack any reality and teeth in that they act more as a record of ineffective programs. We need tools to help us move forward into a more productive lifestyle as a contributing member of society, which requires updated programs with accurate facts.

b.   There are few opportunities to apply goal setting or model the behaviours using the very skills taught in our Integrated Correctional Program Model (ICPM) programs.

5.   Vocational, Educational and Employment Models

Simply, the model is broken. A limited number of prisoners get basic vocational skill 'workshops' (e.g. first aid, landscaping theory, core construction basics, etc.). There seems to be *no* real integrative plan of action. Rather, like so much of what we see now, it is all just shoot from the hip, and repeat the failing programs and policies so someone, somewhere can show they have done something. Educational programs are thin at best. This is such a major component of life success and is most likely a major reason for a vast majority of the incarcerated populations backstory (how and why we have arrived in prison), yet it is always cut (sometimes first) with *no* real plan of action. Why? We need to begin focusing on skills for release in this new job market. Educational programs and training that reflect the society we will be returned into need to be implemented. Otherwise, what is the option (recidivism usually with escalation)? There could be more real opportunities inside

these walls through employment that will build skill sets necessary for
success outside. Instead, with most jobs CSC chooses to placate the
residents with meaningless opportunities. We fully understand routine
and basic work ethic is important. We get these types of lower skilled
opportunities may be a starting point, but what about an action plan that
a resident can see movement forward and work toward achievement as
opposed to simply existing throughout their sentence with no real plan?
Where does the term 'Correctional Plan' come into play? Is it just to
"maintain employment", nothing more, nothing less? How does this
really help? Putting a plan together with the prisoner would require
not only regular meetings with them, but also breaking down the silos
and communicating with CSC colleagues and coordinating between
departments.

6. **Healthcare Model (Overall)**
   a. There is little tangible mental health and addictions support.
   b. Eye care has been cut to the point of real concern.
   c. Basic dental care and costs post-release must be increasing, because
      the 'care' offered inside is pathetic.
   d. The failed mental health and addictions policies lead the individuals
      with immediate needs to monopolize healthcare time, leaving the
      vast majority of other residents with limited or no time. When care
      is available, the medical staff are highly suspicious of prisoners or
      turned off to any listening or offering real compassion – few get
      served.
   e. Make no mistake, healthcare is horrendous today. Men with cancer,
      blood in their urine and stools (for months at a time), diabetics and
      other health based / nutritional diets are ignored, and we could go on.

7. **Ineffective and Inconsistent Policies, with a Lack of Timely
   Consultation with Prisoner Representations / the Inmate Wellness
   Committee – Commissioner's Directives, Standing Orders,
   Security Bulletins, and Guidelines**
   a. The approach to policy changes involves little consultation with
      prisoners.
   b. Policies are constantly changing with everything seemingly *very*
      off-balance (e.g. just think about NHQ policy being constantly

modified by RHQ and/or the individual institution), which increases tension and confusion at the institutional level. We live in a world of "alternative facts" within CSC institutions.

c. Old and new changes often contradict each other.

d. Attempts to deal with small portions of the penitentiary population through policy changes impact the whole, leaving no room for individualized planning and support.

8. Integrated Correctional Program Model (ICPM)

"Integrated" programming is premised on the idea of combining participants based on need. However, more often than not you have residents put together for personalities (i.e. tolerance), which obviously needs to be considered, but specific program needs must be paramount. This is a modular program and as such facilitators should be able to build productive groups with very specific program needs (e.g. addictions) using the modules.

9. Visits & Correspondence (V&C) and Private Family Visits (PFV)

a. Both of these areas are considered key components of the rehabilitation and reintegration process, yet because of the historical contraband issues tied to this entry point into federal institutions, the resulting policies and Standard Operating Procedures continue to restrict (for *all*) and now new restrictions are bordering on illegally infringing on the rights of the incarcerated, *but also* the families and friends who visit (e.g. CPIC and criminal record checks, and forced visitor applications to verify relationships).

b. There is *no* budget to support the maintenance of institutional PFV houses as this is left to the Inmate Welfare Committee. Given the constantly decreasing earning potential and ability to save these dollars, PFV visit opportunities are also decreasing. This very important component of our rehabilitation and reintegration plan is being slowly made smaller and smaller, thereby decreasing the incarcerated person's ability to repair, maintain and build upon key inner circle relationships for their eventual release. There must come a point where CSC does their job as opposed to continually muddying the waters of policy and staying the course of becoming a simple warehouse where the incarcerated just 'do time'.

10. Lifers' Programming

a.   A large portion of the incarcerated population are Lifers (the majority of prisoners at Mission Medium Institution) and many others are doing long-term sentences of ten years or more. Lifers programs need to be reinstated (e.g. Life Line) and their initiatives need to be adequately supported. There is a Lifer's Resource Strategy (a four-module program), but CSC does not recognize, nor provide any resources for its proper implementation (budget again), even though they produced the program in collaboration with the community agencies supporting the penitentiaries across Canada.

b.   Establishing Lifers living units where prisoners have the ability to manage their own meals, budgets and the like should exist when someone enters medium-security, which would go a long way in building institutional adjustment and quality of life.

c.   Like most of the institutions across the country, *every* institution should have a specific space for Lifers. Here at Mission, for example, we have *nothing* that is Lifer specific. The men here have very unique needs and these are not being addressed. Even the Lifers group is hindered on a daily basis to build positive directions at this institution for the more than 180 men that live within these fences.

In closing, we want to address that there is a serious split in the staff and management when it comes to how to deliver the mission and values that reside in Commissioner's Directive 001. There are still a serious number of staff that privilege 'coercive corrections' (punishment) that adopt the "take, take, take" model. The other side of their teams believe in more of a serve your time and build new skills to reduce recidivism model. This latter group of employees believe in a more conversational approach, while ensuring basic security and rules are followed, and they should be empowered as public safety and prisoner reintegration are better served.

Currently, we are still experiencing the tail end of the Harper government's agenda characterized by *cost-reduction driven 'corrections' as opposed to a focus on reducing recidivism rates*. This just seems wrong on so many levels. We would love to be a part of any focus group or planning opportunity to build a more collaborative and productive approach to corrections in Canada. There are many examples from our past that will show some of the best practices and many that we can rule out as not workable solutions. The bottom line is that the incarcerated human beings living with federal penitentiaries today are some of the best voices when it comes to reality and what works versus what does not.

ENDNOTES

[1] Please see: Correctional Service Canada (2017a) *Commissioners Directive 710-1 Progress Against the Correctional Plan*, Ottawa. Retrieved from http://www.csc-scc.gc.ca/lois-et-reglements/710-1-cd-eng.shtml

[2] Please see: Correctional Service Canada (2017b) *Commissioners Directive 730 Offender Program Assignments and Inmate Payments*, Ottawa. Retrieved from http://www.csc-scc.gc.ca/acts-and-regulations/730-cd-eng.shtml

Mission Institution
Trevor D. Bell

I wanted to take this opportunity to express some long-running concerns that I have in regard to the current status of the Canadian criminal justice system. More specifically, I wanted to bring direct light to the dilution of the trial hearing process, the desecration of Correctional Service Canada (CSC), the partisan behaviour within Parole Board Canada (PBC), and the imminent peril to society that is resultant from the draconian actions of former Prime Minister Stephen Harper and his Conservative colleagues.

First and foremost, I feel it necessary to disclose my personal history by way of background to contextualize my arguments. I am a federal prisoner currently housed at Mission Institution serving a Life sentence for second degree murder with parole eligibility set at fifteen years. Prior to this offence, I did not have a conviction for any criminal offences within Canada. However, I did incur one conviction in the United States of America in 1998 when I was 23 years old for possession of narcotics. I subsequently served three years and three months within the U.S. federal prison system prior to receiving a Treaty Transfer back to Canada in 2001.

I am a well-educated, articulate and affable individual who was raised in a pro-social family environment. I have two loving parents and one brother who steadfastly support me in my endeavours with respect to my rehabilitation and future reintegration into society as a law-abiding citizen. Furthermore, my family support network approves of my advocacy work on behalf of all prisoners wherein identified deficiencies within the criminal justice system need addressing.

It is as a result of my rather unique personal history with respect to my incarceration within both the United States and the Canadian correctional systems that I have a defined perspective on the current status of the environment upon which I currently reside. I have both witnessed and experienced first-hand the United States system of incarceration wherein the primary goal is retribution and retaliation, where the guiding principle is punitive in nature. This is not a system upon which Canada should be modelling itself. Unfortunately, Prime Minister Harper and his colleagues have demonstrated through their actions over the past number of years that their ideology is sadly in line with that of the United States. Mass incarceration, lengthy sentences and punitive policies do not make for a safer society. In fact, they produce exactly the opposite results.

Within the last couple of years, the failure of such a system has been recognized by factions within the American penal system. The State of California almost went bankrupt trying to maintain the overflowing capacity of such a flawed system. Several individual states, along with the U.S. federal government under former President Obama, were in fact moving away from such a defective penal system. In defiance of a substantive amount of empirical data, common sense, as well as the recent actions of the various U.S. penal jurisdictions, Prime Minister Harper continued to sail this country head long into a storm upon which the entire country may sink and never recover in the long-term should the current government not take the necessary measures to change course.

I am cognizant along with all prisoners of the concerns within society, amongst victims and their rights within the context of the penal system. Victim empathy, remorse, restorative justice, and risk management are all factors that guide me throughout the trials and tribulations of daily life within the federal penitentiary system. However, if the paramount consideration within our criminal justice system is the safety and security of citizens, then the very system we are currently operating under is among the greatest threats to the very citizens it was designed to protect. Simply put, you cannot lock a human being away for months, years, or decades while repeatedly abusing them and expect the end result to be anything but negative. The Harper government continuously espoused rhetoric with respect to "standing up for victims". The sad fact is that through their actions they will undoubtedly be the cause of future victims. All individual prisoners must ultimately be held accountable for their personal actions, however, releasing individuals into society after years of abuse with no realistic skills for employability, a complete absence of technological aptitude, as well as absolutely no social acumen whatsoever is most assuredly a recipe for disaster.

The precipice for the creation of this letter was initiated through countless hours of discussion with my fellow residents. Contrary to the rhetoric that has emanated from the Conservative Party of Canada over the years, there is a large portion of the prisoner population that is highly articulate, educated and has considerable insight into the modifications required to affect positive change within the Canadian criminal justice system. Simply put, we are not three toed, one-eyed monsters that live under the bridge. It is my submission that any government would be remiss in failing to access the plethora of knowledge held by the very residents contained within our correctional facilities. I am aware that it is a political 'hot potato' whereby engaging in a consultation process with the criminalized can be misinterpreted by other political parties as being 'soft on crime', which most assuredly no governing party wants. With that being said, it is my submission that heading into a comprehensive review of the criminal justice system with itemized and specific information directly from the incarcerated will undoubtedly avail you with an identified advantage in this area of social policy.

In light of the forthcoming review and study into *human rights* within our criminal justice system, I felt it was my duty to systematically address both the positives, as well as the frailties within the current structure of the Canadian penal system. In order to ensure that each topic receives the thorough attention it so justly deserves I will proffer the information in the following four parts: Trial Process/Sentencing, Correctional Service Canada, Parole Board Canada and Legislative Acts-Repeal.

PART I: TRIAL PROCESS AND SENTENCING

Mandatory Minimums
The immediate cessation of any and all mandatory minimums within the Criminal Code of Canada is necessary. Empirical data shows that longer sentences do not make the public safer and only serve to make harder criminals who will eventually be released into society.

Life Sentences
The immediate cessation/commutation of mandatory Life Sentences for individuals convicted of second degree murder is needed. This section within the Criminal Code of Canada should be changed to reflect a fixed term with a maximum sentence not exceeding 12 years of custodial time followed by a period of supervised release in the community to be affixed by the courts. This model is highly successful within several Scandinavian countries and surely has led to are far lower rate of recidivism. It is extremely rare for Lifers on parole to ever commit another indictable offence. Simply put, the Canadian taxpayers spend millions of dollars supervising individuals for the rest of their lives who statistically will never commit another offence. Statistics have shown that the vast majority of the criminalized convicted of second degree murder were crimes of passion or situational circumstances; there was absolutely no pre-meditation, hence a decreased risk to the community.

Legal Aid

Although I recognize that this issue is within provincial jurisdiction, it greatly affects individual's access to justice. Funding for legal aid needs to be vastly increased to reflect the current need within the judicial system. The federal and provincial governments need to partner on a funding model that ensures all accused have a reasonable opportunity to an adequate defence and appeals.

Automatic Appeals

Upon the imposition of a Life sentence there should be a provision within the Criminal Code of Canada that the convicted person be granted an automatic appeal funded by either Legal Aid or the Attorney General, similar to section 684 of the Criminal Code. After all, the loss of a life via sentencing merits maximum protections to prevent injustices.

Elimination of Deals

The practice of Crown counsel and/or the Attorney General providing financial remuneration and/or a reduction in sentence in exchange for testimony must be abolished. The incentive to put forth false testimony at trials is far too great and has led to countless wrongful convictions and serves to undermine the principles of fundamental justice.

Crown Interviews

A provision is required within the Criminal Code of Canada that directs Crown counsel to digitally/video record all pre-trial interviews with witnesses and submit those recordings to the defence counsel no later than 72 hours before the start of the trial. This action is to ensure transparency within the process and to uphold the principles of fundamental justice. This provision would eliminate the coaching of witnesses to put forth false testimony resulting in wrongful convictions.

Marijuana

The legalization and taxation of marijuana should occur immediately. This fact is supported by the recent actions within some jurisdictions in the United States of America wherein they have moved to a regulatory system that benefits the tax-paying citizen. The continued practice of incarcerating Canadians for marijuana-related offences, while spending millions of dollars in the pursuit of maintaining a flawed process is the very definition of insanity.

PART II: CORRECTIONAL SERVICE CANADA

Correctional Investigator

A complete overhaul of the operations, mandate and powers of the Correctional Investigator needs to be immediately enacted. The current structure has proven to be fruitless. Without the ability to enforce any of the recommendations identified to correct the deficiencies within the operations of CSC, the Office of the Correctional Investigator will continue to be nothing more than an irritant, a simple fly buzzing around the room annoying everyone, but causing no real threat. It is my submission that the Correctional Investigator needs to operate under a system wherein mediation and/or binding arbitration is within their powers to force the immediate enactment of corrective measures to alleviate any identified deficiencies.

Prisoner Grievance Process

The current structure of the Grievance Process is a colossal failure and an unmitigated disaster that recklessly wastes millions of taxpayer dollars every year. The fundamental structure of the Grievance Process wherein co-workers investigate fellow co-workers at both the Complaint and Institutional Level is simply asinine. Grievances are consistently denied at the first two levels only to be upheld at the final National Level more than a year (or two) later. This has become so common place that all prisoners openly state that it will take at least a year (or two) to solve any issue. Correctional staff are aware of the systemic failure within the Grievance Process and regularly laugh at prisoners when making an unlawful decision and dare them to file a complaint, knowing full well it will take a year or more to resolve. Many prisoners have been released or transferred prior to ever receiving a response to a complaint. The most disturbing part is that every issue must be argued as if it is the first time it has happened. Millions of dollars are wasted each year with staff investigating the very same issue over and over again. It is my submission that the entire Grievance Process requires a complete overhaul wherein it becomes a 'case law' style system. The logging of each upheld decision would go into a national database accessible by both prisoners and staff, thereby negating the need to re-argue identical issues over and over again, thus saving the taxpayers millions of dollars in correctional staff hours, as well as alleviating countless incidents of violence within each facility in the country due to frustration over the

Grievance Process. Submissions within the aforementioned case law system would be voluntary on behalf of each prisoner, could be redacted to ensure compliance with the *Privacy Act* and would be available within the library at each institution.

Accountability

At this current juncture, there is simply no level of accountability within CSC. The malaise within staff morale and complete lack of professionalism has reached epic proportions. Staff regularly make decisions or take actions which they know to be in direct breach of the Canadian *Charter of Rights and Freedoms*, the *Canadian Human Rights Act*, correctional policy, legislative acts and Commissioner's Directives. Their response upon being questioned is inevitably, "Go ahead and sue us!" I have even had senior managers tell me, "It doesn't come out of my pocket". Such wanton disregard for adherence to policy or simple respect for the law is nothing short of atrocious. The very fact that some CSC employees think that the Canadian taxpayers are their personal ATM machine to pay lawsuits as a result of their negligent conduct is abhorrent and unconscionable. They truly believe that they are above the law and without repercussions for their behaviours. It is my submission that the only way to address this conduct is through the implementation of a "Performance Standards Policy", wherein defined punitive actions will be levied against each individual staff member for repeated failure to adhere to the law. The aforementioned policy must be made public and shared with all prisoners. The Treasury Board guidelines currently in place are wholly and completely ineffective.

Mental Health

The current state of mental health treatment within CSC is virtually non-existent. Unless an individual is suicidal or engaging in acts of self-harm, they are likely to receive absolutely no treatment whatsoever. The Harper government repeatedly cut funding to the correctional system, allocating little to mental health in general, yet the presence of those living with mental health issues within penitentiaries is a pressing issue. The correctional system has become for all intents and purposes nothing more than a mental hospital without the requisite level of care or any treatment whatsoever. It is my submission that there needs to be an immediate influx of funding to provide for on-site mental health treatment to any prisoner who requests it. This program should be voluntary. The basis of the program should also be anonymous in nature, assuring that doctor patient confidentiality is maintained commensurate with community standards wherein disclosure would only occur if evidence of harm was imminent. Many prisoners with identified mental health issues would fear attending regular counselling sessions due to the fact that under the current CSC system any information disclosed by the prisoner can be used against them by their assigned case management team. I am not talking about psychiatric assessments; I am talking about regular counselling to address a prisoner's ongoing mental health needs. A vast majority of the criminalized within the correctional system have suffered mental, physical, sexual or emotional abuse as children. Until such time as they address the underlying mental health issues that reside deep within them, they will never truly be able to move forward in a productive manner and be a contributing member of society.

Psychiatric / Psychological Assessments
Once again, as a result of funding cuts by the Harper government it is virtually impossible to attain a psychiatric/psychological assessment within a reasonable time frame. The waiting list for prisoners to receive a requisite assessment prior to a transfer decision for lower security, escorted temporary absences or release decisions pertaining to parole into the community can take several months, and in some cases more than a year. Some institutions have backlogs as long as three years. Recent information came to light wherein there was one doctor for over a thousand prisoners in the Pacific Region for the express purpose of psychiatric assessments. This asinine ratio was as a direct result of funding cuts by the Harper government. This exorbitant delay is costing the Canadian taxpayers millions of dollars in increased housing costs. It is far cheaper to house a criminalized person in minimum-security than in a medium-level facility and it is considerably more cost effective to supervise them within the community on day parole.

Health Care
Once again, as a result of funding cuts by the Harper government, there is practically a non-existent health care system inside of federal corrections. Aside from medical emergencies wherein an ambulance is called, it takes weeks to even get an appointment with a doctor. Upon finally seeing the doctor they tell you that there is nothing they can do and/or you are told

to take an anti-inflammatory. It most assuredly does not meet community standards or comply with the *Charter*. If you did not know better you would think you were in a third world country. I have watched countless individuals die from cancer or suffer debilitating long-term ailments that could have been prevented, while it took months or years of arguing with health care to get any semblance of treatment, and by that time it was too late. The status of health care in corrections is a modern-day atrocity.

Dental Care
Once again, as a result of funding cuts by the Harper government, there is practically a non-existent dental care system inside of federal corrections. Aside from dental emergencies wherein you are writhing in pain, your mouth is bleeding or half a tooth has fallen out, it takes weeks or months to even get an appointment with the dentist. Upon finally seeing the dentist they tell you that there is nothing they can do and/or they pull the tooth. It most assuredly does not meet community standards or comply with the *Charter*. There are absolutely no preventative check-ups, nor is there an annual cleaning as required by the Canadian Dental Association. Again, if you did not know better you would think you were in a third world country. I have watched countless individuals have all of their teeth slowly deteriorate to the point where they eventually had them all pulled over a number of years. All of the associated pain that accompanied the aforementioned deterioration of the prisoner's teeth could have been prevented. The status of dental care in corrections is also a modem-day atrocity.

Case Management
This area is by far the most deliberated daily subject within the penitentiary population in every facility across this great country. There is absolutely no continuity within the management of federal prisoner cases across Canada. Once again, due to a lack of funding by the Harper government, there is an identified deficiency in the number of contracted parole officers at each facility. The effect is that CSC management continuously shuffles parole officers around within the facility and from site to site in an attempt to alleviate excessively overdue case management decisions. I have had as many as four different parole officers within a twelve-month period. How is a prisoner supposed to build a working relationship, address their dynamic risk factors and move forward within the system when they are seeing a

new face every other week? This revolving carousel is costing the Canadian taxpayers millions of dollars a year in increased housing costs by keeping prisoners in higher level security facilities than they are required to be in. If there were continuity in case management, decisions would be made in a timely manner and prisoners would move to a lower security and/or be released on parole into the community.

Programs
CSC continually espouses rhetoric to the Canadian public about the plethora of behavioural programming offered to prisoners within federal penitentiaries. Within the Pacific Region there is only one program offered called the "Integrated Correctional Program Modules" (ICPM) that is offered in either a moderate- or high-intensity version. The program is viewed as a nonsensical annoyance by many within the penitentiary population as its contents serve no logical purpose, with a composition and structure that are counterintuitive to the actual needs of prisoners. Asking grown men what their emotional colour is (green, yellow or red) and what their frustration number is (1 through 10), only wastes millions of dollars of taxpayers' money. Prisoners are threatened to take the program by their case management team and suffer dire consequences if they refuse. Trying to obtain a transfer to lower security or parole without jumping through this hoop virtually guarantees a negative decision. The fundamental deficiency with the current structure of the program is the lack of qualified and available facilitators. Many of the facilitators do not have a bachelor's degree and simply took a training module offered thereby enabling them to teach the program. Countless correctional officers and stewards from the kitchen have become program facilitators. How is it possible that a course rooted in Cognitive Behavioural Therapy (CBT) that has built-in psychometric measures that will ultimately determine someone's liberty is being handled by someone who used to turn keys every day or flip eggs in the kitchen? The most distressing aspect is that prisoners are prohibited from discussing any concerns they have about CSC employees while in the program; facilitators call it "CSC bashing". Prisoners are being taught to suppress the very emotions that they are supposed to be learning how to deal with. Some prisoners wait for years to get into the program in the hopes of obtaining a transfer to lower security or obtaining parole, but unfortunately there are often no available facilitators or spaces in the program due to funding

cuts by the Harper government. This problem was recently highlighted in a recent Auditor General's report pertaining to the inefficiency of program delivery within CSC. The effect of prisoners' waiting years to obtain a program is that they are forced to reside in a facility of higher security than they would otherwise require. Many could be in the community on parole being effectively supervised. The savings to taxpayers whereby having the prisoners in lower security or on parole would be considerable. It is my submission that the fundamental principle and purpose behind the delivery of programs within the correctional system needs to be completely overhauled. There need to be highly qualified professionals with either a bachelor's or master's degree that are independently contracted from outside of the correctional system who are there to deliver the programs moving forward. The impartiality of the professionals coming into the system is essential to ensure credibility among prisoners, which would translate into more voluntary and active participation. If you have to threaten or force someone to take a program, the results are clearly going to reflect that mindset. We need to make the program something that individuals will feel comfortable taking that will actually address their current cognitive concerns.

CORCAN Industries
The current configuration of the CORCAN industries within this facility is nothing short of a complete boondoggle. It serves little to no purpose and most assuredly offers no practical industry training whatsoever. It is virtually impossible to acquire certification for trades within the industries area, thus causing a malaise among prisoner workers. The problem was further compounded by the Harper government instituting the elimination of incentive pay for workers, while also putting in place additional room and board charges to all prisoners. Now there is simply no motivation whatsoever for the average prisoner to put forth any effort whatsoever towards employment within the CORCAN industries area of the facility. Simply put, these regressive reforms need to be overturned or these shops should be closed down and the area re-assigned for the implementation of an actual trades certification program that would truly benefit all prisoners.

Trades Certification
There are currently no trade certification programs at this facility. The number one identified risk factor for the vast majority of prisoners is

employability and job skills. The majority of prisoners become recidivist's due to a lack of career opportunities upon release or defined skills training. There needs to be the immediate implementation of a federal-provincial partnership for qualified trades certification programs within all federal penitentiaries in Canada. The facilities already exist within the nearly defunct CORCAN industries. Practical on-going trades programs should be contracted out with the help of each province, whereby prisoners could obtain journeyman certification in welding, electrical, plumbing and carpentry. In-class training, along with practical hands-on skills application, can be achieved within the facility, thereby ensuring prisoners a logical and sustainable career choice upon release into the community. The investment in such a program would save the taxpayers millions of dollars through the long-term reduction in the rate of recidivism and the decrease in the prison population. The most beneficial factor would be the elimination of any new victims being created; something that everyone can agree upon as serving the best interests of society.

Computers
The current status of computer access and education within the Canadian correctional system is laughable at best. There are no computer education classes or technology training whatsoever at Mission Institution even though the education department has computers in the classroom to help facilitate prisoners obtaining their GED or Grade 12 equivalency. Prisoners not enrolled in basic education training only have access to a single computer on their living units that must be shared with up to 60 prisoners. The most distressing problem is that these computers would best be described as archaic. They are so outdated that the very composition of their design no longer exists within society! Until recently they operated on Windows 98 or XP, which are so old that Microsoft recently discontinued any tech support for them! The fix orchestrated by CSC was to install Windows 7, which is nearly a decade old already! The computers have so many administrative blocks that it is little more than a glorified typewriter. When typing a letter, we have to use 3.5 inch diskettes to save the information. The company that manufactured these disks went out of business more than a decade ago. You cannot even buy a computer today that accepts these obsolete storage devices. The vast majority of prisoners within this facility have absolutely no idea how to use a computer; one recently asked me how to turn it on so

he could type a letter to PBC. Prior to 2001, all prisoners within the federal correctional system could purchase a personal computer for their cells. In an ever-evolving world wherein knowledge of computers is an essential element of daily life, CSC eliminated prisoners' ownership of personal computers. How is an individual supposed to succeed in society upon release without any reasonable level of technical ability? The entire operational basis of our society now stems from computer technology. If corrections are supposedly preparing us for release into the community, why are we not receiving training in the most critical area that will help us to succeed? It is my submission that immediate funding and direction is required to mandate the provision of computer technology to all federal prisoners by CSC. A voluntary program wherein prisoners can achieve certification in programs such as Word, Excel, AutoCAD and Photoshop would be fundamental to achieving substantive rehabilitative goals. A further directive should be enacted to once again allow for the ownership of personal computers in prisoner cells. Until such time as we address such a critical area within the rehabilitation process, the incarcerated will continue to become recidivist's due to their inability to mesh with the technology-based society that they are going to be released into.

Dietary Nutrition
The current status of the dietary food delivery program within the Pacific Region is a monumental waste of taxpayers' money. The switch to a chill and serve program was nothing more than a punitive action by the former Conservative government wishing to inflict pain upon the penitentiary population. The quality of food has decreased to such a level that serious health concerns have arisen throughout the federal prison population. The vast majority of the meals are not in any way edible. Many correctional staff have commented how they would not feed that 'slop' to their dogs! It is truly unconscionable in this day and age that we have reverted back to a time where prisoners are provided with only enough food to barely keep them alive – not healthy, just alive. The most disturbing fact is that this was imposed by the Harper government as another cost-cutting measure. However, upon examination there is no substantial financial savings to taxpayers. The chill and serve program costs an exorbitant amount of money to implement and when factoring in the compensatory buyouts to senior level kitchen stewards. Moreover, the implementation of the chill

and serve process caused the cancellation of the Culinary Arts Program wherein prisoners attained certification within the food service industry, thereby enabling employment within the community upon release. The aforementioned Culinary Arts Program was one of the longest running and successful programs at this facility, and was truly revered as extremely beneficial by all staff and prisoners. The short-sighted actions of the former Harper government wherein they eliminated another successful rehabilitative program only to institute a punitive measure against all prisoners demonstrates a severe lack of insight into the management of the correctional system and a complete disregard for the safety of everyday citizens in society. Of more immediate concern is the massive increase in violent incidents within the facility. It is common knowledge within the correctional system that one of the most contentious issues is the delivery and quality of the food. One only has to examine the history of penitentiary riots and incidents in this country to ascertain that there is a direct link between the lower quality of food and the increase of violence. Another troubling concern with respect to the chill and serve program is the dramatic increase in environmental pollution. With the implementation of this program, CSC trucks are driving all over the region in commercial vehicles delivering food to the penitentiaries. These trips would not have occurred prior to the implementation of this program. I fail to see how this meets CSC's commitment to green initiatives or minding the environment. It is my submission that an immediate review of this entire program needs to be undertaken with a projected cancellation and reversion to the prior model of individual institutional food provision.

Visitation

One of the foundational components to a successful rehabilitation and reintegration into society is having a strong community support network. The aforementioned network is generally comprised of family members, extended relatives, friends, as well as community contacts. Regular contact visits with these individuals are critical to the on-going mental health and well-being of all prisoners. Unfortunately, as a result of the former Harper government's policy decisions, the environment and the overall process for visitation within federal penitentiaries has deteriorated to the point that many visitors now refuse to attend due to the abuse they undergo while attempting to attain entry into the facility. The paranoid and neurotic ideology with respect to security screening has gotten to the point that visitors are regularly treated like common criminals for attempting to show love and support for an incarcerated family member or friend. I am aware of the concerns with respect to halting the entry of drugs into the institution, but the current legislative provisions and correctional policies in force far exceed any rational operational process and only serve to alienate those community support members who are so vital to successful reintegration. The primary source of the alienation is the use of ion scanner devices at the principle entrances of each facility. The technology is highly controversial and is consistently misused, causing undue hardship and embarrassment to those visitors. There are currently over 1,100 items that test as a 'false positive' for registered narcotics on the ion scanner device. When a 'false positive' happens, correctional staff treat this as proof positive and refuse visitor access in the majority of cases. The frailty of this device is evidenced by the fact that its application is not used on correctional staff upon their entrance into the facility, yet they are caught every year introducing narcotics into federal penitentiaries. Why are they not subjected to the same entry process as our visitors? If the threat of narcotics is so severe as to alienate our visitors and treat them like criminals, then why are all correctional staff not enduring all of the same procedures to ensure continuity in the process? The answer is quite simple – the various unions representing all correctional staff have steadfastly refused to allow their members to be submitted to any such process for fear of negative ramifications upon a positive reading. Simply put, they are fully and completely aware of the inconsistencies in the technology and therefore have refused to engage in such a process. If safety and security of penitentiaries were actually the primary objective, then every single person would be subjected to the same entry procedures, regardless of who you are. It is my submission that if you enacted a policy whereby all staff had to submit to the same entry procedures, they would immediately call for the discontinuance of ion scanner technology. An exhaustive review is required into the visitation process within all federal penitentiaries in this country with an eye on improving and supporting access for all visitors. Improved access for visitors will only enhance community support networks and enable greater opportunities for successful reintegration. With the aforementioned successful reintegration, there will most assuredly be a decrease in the rate of recidivism, which will save the Canadian taxpayers considerable expense through the decrease in prisoners.

The most significant benefit will be the fact that another victim will not be created; something that everyone can agree is of utmost importance.

Recreation
Within the confines of Canadian federal correctional institutions, the recreation areas are by far the most accessed by prisoners on a daily basis. Empirical data[1] has shown that a consistent physical fitness routine releases positive endorphins helping to ward-off depression, increasing overall health and wellness, as well as helping to instil a solid foundational base for a healthy lifestyle moving forward. With a plethora of evidence available with regards to the positive short-term and long-term benefits of a consistent physical fitness routine, it simply belies any rational thought process as to why the former Conservative government has done everything in their power to eliminate prisoner access to such facilities. The former Harper government cut correctional funding so drastically that there are few to no resources allocated for recreation whatsoever. A considerable amount of the recreation equipment and weight training apparatus at this facility are nearly three decades old, purchased when the institution first opened. The budget was cut so deeply that a vast majority of the equipment is in a state of disrepair. When something breaks, it just gets thrown in the garbage as there is no money to have it repaired. The vast majority of prisoners enter the correctional system with a history of drug abuse and unhealthy lifestyles. It defies logic as to why the encouragement of a positive fitness lifestyle is not part of the mandate within CSC. In fact, this facility has done everything in their power to limit access to the recreation area. Until several years ago, prisoners not at their work assignment could access the recreation area, outside yard or gymnasium morning, afternoon or evening. This was when our daily population numbered around 250 prisoners. Morning access was soon eliminated and afternoon access was severely restricted shortly thereafter as our population grew to over 350 prisoners with the addition of a new living unit that was placed where our baseball field once existed. The effect has been an increase in tension, anxiety and overall violence within the facility. The former Conservative government's ideology concerning the safe management of penitentiaries is to drastically increase the number of prisoners, while removing access to the activities that help alleviate stress and violence. It is no wonder the rate of violent incidents across the country increased. It is my submission that a review of the annual funding allocation

towards recreation facilities and activities is required. Investment in health and wellness is critical and can be immediately implemented, providing substantive short-term and long-term benefits towards overall wellness, while decreasing violence within the federal penitentiary system. Instilling a positive and healthy lifestyle while incarcerated will most assuredly enable an increased opportunity for successful reintegration within the community upon release into society by all federal prisoners. The first step is to debunk the myth that prisoners are simply laying around lifting weights all day. Instilling a healthy lifestyle is an important step in rehabilitation.

Library
As a result of funding cuts by the former Harper government, the condition of our library services is in a state of utter disrepair. For many years, the configuration and structure of our library facilities, programs and the overall operation were the envy of many countries around the world. The ability of a library program to provide literary access, as well as educational support and general information is a key component within a prison system. For decades, the library at this facility was open and accessible for prisoners during the morning, afternoon and evening. This was a key linchpin to ensuring the maximum opportunity for intellectual stimulation within the banality that is the penitentiary environment. Unfortunately, over the last couple of years I have witnessed the desecration of a once great library program. Presently, our library is unable to sustain itself. There was no discernable money for new books this year and next year's budget is projected to decrease. Our hours of access have been reduced dramatically, with both morning and afternoon access removed within months of each other. Now 350 prisoners have to cram into one small library space for approximately two hours each evening; this is simply a recipe for disaster. Last year, the position of our librarian was cut from full-time to part-time. The librarian at this facility is a true professional who works diligently on a daily basis ensuring all prisoners acquire the requested information to enable their continued forward progress with regards to their individual learning needs. The reduction of the librarian position is simply ludicrous. Many prisoners are unable reference or locate the material they require without the help of a librarian to assist and encourage their continued learning and literary expansion. This funding cut is another hare-brained example of the legacy of the former Harper government's complete lack of insight into

what is required to operate a federal penitentiary. Education is the key to rehabilitation and removing a key component of the education process puts prisoners at a disadvantage when released into the community. The cost of that increase will go far beyond simple dollars and cents. It will be the cost of harm to society by way of a new victim created at the hands of the former Harper government through their near-sighted, draconian policies.

Prisoner Pay

The prisoner pay program, wherein the incarcerated receive compensatory remuneration for work performed or program assignment attended during the daily course of incarceration, was first instituted in 1981. There has not been a review of prisoner pay or an identified measurable increase in more than three decades. Unfortunately, the cost of living has increased, while the value obtained for each dollar has been drastically reduced in over three decades. Prisoners are no longer able to attain the basic necessities with their meagre institutional pay. Compounding the problem is the abhorrent actions under the former Harper government, whereby CSC instituted an additional 30% deduction of a prisoner's gross pay for room and board, as well as telephone system management. This action is arguably unlawful in its very nature and is currently being challenged in the courts by a consortium of prisoners from across the country. The contextual basis of the argument is that the process of deducting money from prisoners' pay is in direct contravention of both the purpose and principles contained within *the Corrections and Conditional Release Act*. CSC's mandate is to support our rehabilitation and reintegration into the community. That is simply not possible when an individual now has to choose between calling his community support network, buying deodorant, sending a card to his daughter or going hungry in the evening hours for two weeks. The aforementioned choices are not something any human being in this country should have to make. Yet, as a result of Harper's draconian policies, that is exactly the choice many prisoners have to make on a daily basis. We have already established that the current dietary menu is not sufficient, nor does the level of hygiene provided for prisoners meet acceptable standards. Prisoners having to supplement these depleted areas most assuredly causes an identified reduction in their ability to engage their community support network. It has been clearly identified that the primary source of successful reintegration is through the establishment of a solid foundational community support network. The former Harper government's response to this knowledge was to all but eliminate a prisoner's ability to regularly maintain positive interactions with people in the community. Such actions are near-sighted, reckless and mean spirited. It is my submission that an immediate review of the policy whereby the charging of additional room and board deductions against federal prisoners shall no longer be permitted. A comprehensive review of the federal penitentiary system pay scale needs to be undertaken with an eye on affecting an increase to the overall remuneration offered to prisoners. This increase should take into account the rates were created in the 1980s, while also factoring-in the standard cost of living and increase in general consumable goods. I understand the concern that providing prisoners with increased remuneration does not seem like a good investment, but if you facilitate the creation of a positive living environment where rehabilitation truly occurs, the result will be the release of prisoners into the community that will be successful and not return to prison. The reduction in the overall rate of recidivism will offset any perceived financial expenditures incurred by Canadian taxpayers. Many jurisdictions around the world (e.g. Germany, Finland, Norway)[2] pay a fair rate to those incarcerated and help them save and prepare for release into society. Currently, prisoners in this country are only guaranteed $80 upon their release into the community. I fail to see how that is supposed to ensure their success. Simply put, you need to invest for success.

Double Bunking
Where institutional crowding is an issue, the current practice within CSC is to place two prisoners in the same cell for cohabitation against their will. This practice is commonly referred to as 'double bunking'. CSC repeatedly espouses the rhetoric that this practice is temporary and that all prisoners have the opportunity to attain a cell with single occupation. During the Harper years, this was a complete misnomer as many waiting lists were years long for some prisoners who were released before they ever got a 'single cell'. The practice of placing two prisoners in a space designed for one is in breach of the minimum standards for the ethical treatment of prisoners as established by the United Nations. Moreover, the practice of double bunking causes a significant strain on the correctional system. As a direct result of double bunking there is an increased rate of general violence within the facility, a lack of available programs due to crowding, as well as an increase in bullying between cellmates. Such an environment most assuredly does not enable an appropriate atmosphere for a prisoner

to address their dynamic risk factors; they are more likely to be focussing on survival. The damaging effect and subsequent cost to the Canadian taxpayer by way of elevated rates of recidivism is simply unfathomable. It is my submission that new victims are being created in society as a direct result of the current practice to openly breach of international standards via 'double bunking'. While rates of this practice have declined in recent years, more is needed (i.e. an immediate cessation to this practice at all federal penitentiaries within this country).

Tattoo Program

The current stance by CSC is to prohibit the practice of tattooing within all federal penitentiaries. The aforementioned 'ostrich approach' adopted by the former Conservative government and CSC, whereby sticking your head in the sand and hoping the problem will go away, is just plain bad social policy. Several years ago, there was a progressive pilot-program where CSC permitted tattooing to occur in federal penitentiaries in a safe and sterile environment, thereby preventing the spread of communicable diseases. This program was truly a ground-breaking endeavour that helped to reduce the spread of Hepatitis, HIV and AIDS. Unfortunately, for whatever reason the program was cancelled. It is my submission that such actions are irrational, negligent and not in the best interest of the public. Infections rates among prisoners for blood borne illnesses are higher than the general population. These individuals will be returning to society as infectious carriers and spreading preventable diseases. It is simply poor social and health policy to ignore something that you can easily prevent.

Needle Exchange

It is common knowledge that some prisoners are using intravenous drugs within the federal penitentiary system. It is also common knowledge that those prisoners are engaging in extremely high-risk behaviour wherein they share the same syringe. This risky and sometimes deadly behaviour is a main cause for the spread of blood borne infections that explode within carceral settings devoid of harm reduction. Failing to address such an epidemic is not only bad social policy, it is negligent and bordering on criminal behaviour. Many of the prisoners in this facility come from Vancouver's downtown Eastside where they have the "INSITE" safe injection site, as well as various facilities that offer needle exchange programs to ensure relatively safe and healthy practices, as well as harm reduction. It is my submission that CSC should immediately enact a needle exchange program with a harm reduction component.

PART III: PAROLE BOARD CANADA

Partisanship
There needs to be a review of the partisan appointments within the current structure of PBC. During the Harper years, the conduct, behaviour and decision-making process amongst the membership of PBC became rather suspect to say the least. Based on the tenor of our parole hearings, many prisoners came to the conclusion that Prime Minister Harper and his government appointed individuals who espoused their ideological beliefs. Recently, as the new Liberal government entered office, the behaviour of PBC members appears to have stabilized. However, a statistical review of all decisions made before and after the Harper government is needed to ascertain any anomalous patterns.

Parole Hearings
Flowing from Harper's political agenda were several procedural changes to how parole hearings are allocated and performed.[3] Some of such changes include extending the legislated parole review period to at least two years following a waiver or denial of parole for those serving time for violent offences, as well as, among others, entrenching victim-centered principles. These amendments have served to do nothing but deny basic procedural fairness to all prisoners, as well as increase the danger to society as a whole. The resultant effect of the aforementioned amendments is to deny individuals parole and keep them behind bars longer. The recent report put forth by the Auditor General clearly shows the link between gradual release and the rate of recidivism. The sooner you return an individual to the community under supervision, the greater their chance of success. Keeping people incarcerated longer does not make for a safer society; in fact, it impacts exactly the opposite effect.

PART IV: LEGISLATION TO REPEAL

Bill C-10
This bill was coined the *Safe Streets and Communities Act* by a majority Harper Conservative government and received Royal Assent in 2012. There

are countless sections within this bill that are simply bad policy and need to be repealed, while others, like mandatory minimum sentencing and truth in sentencing have been ruled as unconstitutional by the Supreme Court of Canada.[4] One of the primary changes was to institute more mandatory minimum sentences, which is an approach that has failed in the United States instituted over the past 30 years. Longer sentences do not make a society safer, rather they simply make for hardening the criminalized. The discretion of matters pertaining to sentencing must remain with the judges that have been tasked with overseeing the independence of our judicial system. While the courts have begun to rule some of the recently enacted mandatory minimum sentences to not be in keeping with principles of fundamental justice and the *Charter*, there is a need to repeal those that remain. A second major series of changes contained within Bill C-10 was to radically alter the very fundamental mandate of the Canadian correctional system. Within the bill, direct and specific amendments were made to the *Corrections and Conditional Release Act* (CCRA) that altered both its "Purpose" and "Principles". The aforementioned changes shifted the central focus of the Canadian correctional system from rehabilitative to punitive, with less emphasis on preparation for release. How much punishment can be inflicted upon each prisoner prior to the expiration of their sentences arguably became CSC's *raison d'être*. In its current state, CSC requires a name change to accurately reflect the mandate it carries out. There is nothing 'correctional' about the system and there is definitely no 'service'. It is my submission that either the mandate and direction of the entire system should be changed or the new name should be the "Canadian Penal System" so as to accurately reflect its purpose. If we are truly a progressive country then the *Act* requires drastic review with an eye on repealing a majority of Prime Minister Harper's amendments, thereby ensuring a system based on rehabilitation and hope, not one of punishment and despair. The third change contained within C-10 was for the radical transformation of PBC. With an altered mandate, purpose and principles, the new format no longer holds accountable the Institutional Parole Officer or those within the correctional system for the work they perform. The prisoner bears the brunt of any errors on behalf of correctional service employees. Accountability within the system is now solely for the prisoner and nobody else as CSC employees are above the law. The fourth change contained within the bill amended the *Criminal Records*

Act making it more difficult to receive a 'pardon' for some and impossible for others. Now called a 'record suspension', the process has become far more arduous and long, with a cost that is nearly unattainable for many citizens. This reform was simply spiteful and does not reflect Canadian values. As a Canadian it is incumbent to believe in the redemption of your fellow citizens, and support their efforts to change and become a productive member of their communities. There are various other changes that are too numerous to list and require a thorough analysis to ensure that the values Canadians hold dearly are not destroyed.

Bill C-14

This bill was coined the *Not Criminally Responsible Reform Act* by the former Harper Conservative government received Royal Assent in 2014. This bill amended the Criminal Code and *National Defence Act* pertaining to mental disorder. The basis for this bill was another prime example of Conservative pandering to their Reform Party roots. There was simply no need to create the special designation of a "High-Risk Accused" within the structure of a "mentally ill offender" who has been found not criminally responsible. The courts and the Honourable Justices already had the latitude under the old system to maintain an individual in custody indefinitely wherein they felt he/she posed a threat to themselves or society in general. This bill was nothing more than politicking at the expense of those living with mental health issues, who are only further alienated and stigmatized.

Bill C-479

This bill was coined *An Act to Bring Fairness for the Victims of Violent Offenders* via a Conservative MP's private members bill and received Royal Assent in 2015. While I am cognizant of the rights and concerns of victims, care and concern must be taken when enacting any legislation to ensure that it meets the test as set out in the *Charter*, and is in keeping with the goals of good public policy and appropriate fiscal management. This bill does not meet any of the aforementioned objectives and was another example of Conservative politicking to their right-wing base hoping to gather more strategic votes. The provision wherein the increase of parole hearing application timelines increases from every two years up to every five years is most assuredly unconstitutional. This amendment represents a *post facto* increases of a person's sentence who received final adjudication prior to 23 April 2015 on a charge involving violence. It is arguably a direct breach of the *Charter* to affect any increase to a criminalized person's sentence following the conclusion of the judicial process. Parole eligibility hearing dates would have been one of the factors considered by a judge when determining the length of a sentence. Moreover, this amendment disproportionately impacts those convicted of second degree murder seeing as the judge's factor in the duration of time to be served prior to one's initial parole eligibility for a Life sentence and forthcoming subsequent applications. It is my submission that this amendment will not withstand a judicial review within the courts. Moreover, this single amendment will cost the Canadian taxpayers millions of dollars in additional housing costs maintaining incarceration of prisoners that are ready for release, but unable to obtain a parole hearing due to the statutory regulation. This is not sound public policy.

Bill C-483

This bill amends the *Corrections and Conditional Release Act* in relation to escorted temporary absences (ETAs) of prisoners and received Royal Assent in 2014. This entire amendment was politically motivated and increases the overall risk to society. The previous version that was in effect gave the Institutional Head the authority to issue ETAs, which has been demonstrated over a lengthy period of time to be. The use of ETAs leading up to day parole hearings was an invaluable tool for PBC to assess a prisoner's suitability for obtaining day parole. With the implementation of this amendment, day parole for prisoners serving a life sentence has been effectively eliminated at their eligibility date. This action means that a minimum of three years can be added to all affected prisoner's time behind bars due to the fact that PBC has consistently maintained the position that they require several successful ETAs prior to the granting of any form of day parole, an action than can cost Canadian taxpayers between $300,000 to $500,000 dollars per prisoner in increased housing costs. The vast majority of those prisoners could be housed in the community at a fraction of the cost. This was simply bad policy that pandered to Prime Minister Harper's electoral base and it should be immediately repealed in the interest of proper fiscal responsibility, social policy, and public safety. Moreover, this amendment created an undue backlog of paperwork of the entire system for no other reason than ideology.

Bill C-12

This bill was coined the *Drug-Free Prisons Act* by the Harper Conservative government and received Royal Assent on the 18 June 2015. This bill amended the *Corrections and Conditional Release Act*, but has not stopped the flow and use of narcotics within the federal penitentiary system. Moreover, there is no treatment or harm reduction component attached. Instead, it enables the denial and/or cancellation of a prisoner's parole for a positive urine test prior to their release. It also permits the cancellation of parole for a prisoner who is simply unable to provide a sample within the two-hour time limit. Speaking from personal experience, it is very hard to consistently provide a sample upon demand within this timeframe due to various external factors such as summer dehydration, spoiling activity, illness or the time of day. To cancel an individual's parole on this basis is unfair and unjust.

CONCLUSION

Throughout this piece, I have attempted to put forth a thoughtful analysis of the deficiencies within the Canadian criminal justice system through the viewpoint of a prisoner. It is my submission that my perspective and that of my fellow residents are of value. If the goal of the federal government is to put in place policies that are in the best interest of the entire country and the safety of its citizens, then the measures enacted under the former Harper government's reign have not met the threshold for responsible governance. It is my sincere desire through the creation of this document to elicit a meaningful discussion with members of both the academic and political community. Now that there has been a change in government, it is my hope that an extensive review will be undertaken to investigate the rather dilapidated state of the Canadian penal system and more specifically, our federal penitentiary system. Former President of the United States Barack Obama toured a federal prison in his country therein becoming the first sitting President to do so. There, he openly acknowledged the failure of his country's mandatory minimum sentencing policy, while noting that longer, harsher prison sentences do not make society safer. Such actions by the former American President took true courage and intestinal fortitude. To those who have instituted policies that impact prisoners without ever listening to what they need to have access to in order to become productive members of society, I would like to formally invite any citizen, community volunteer or member of any political party to attend Mission Institution for a roundtable on the state of the Canadian penitentiary system. The meeting can be a one-on-one or with a select group of a few residents or a gymnasium full of prisoners. I am amenable to either an on the record interview with media in tow or an off the record informal discussion wherein you simply tour the facility and hear the concerns of prisoners like myself, not those cherry picked by institutional officials to convey a CSC-friendly version. I am more than willing to assemble a small group of appropriate candidates for a concise, diligent and articulate discussion that I truly believe you will find eye opening.

This year will be the twenty-fifth anniversary of the implementation of the *Corrections and Conditional Release Act* in 1992. That particular legislative act is the foundational document that governs everyday life for all incarcerated federal prisoners in this country. Former Prime Minister Stephen Harper and his team enacted countless amendments that have altered the very structure and operations of the Canadian penitentiary system, the vast majority of which will most assuredly endanger society in the long run. As a review of Canada's criminal justice system moves forward, I encourage those involved to come to Mission Institution so that legislation can be developed to address the current deficiencies, including those that are at work inside CSC facilities.

ENDNOTES

[1]   Please see Dunn, A. L. and J. S. Jewell (2010) "The Effect of Exercise on Mental Health", *Current Sports Medicine Reports*, 9(4): 202-207.

[2]   In the Scandinavian countries: "Though worse for wear, rooms feature flat-screen TVs, sound systems, and mini-refrigerators for the prisoners who can afford to rent them for prison-labor wages of 4.10 to 7.3 Euros per hour ($5.30 to $9.50)" (Larson, 2013).

[3]   *According to the Parole Board Policy Manual Annex D:* Second Edition – no. 03 (2015-04-24) The passage of Bill C-479 - *An Act to amend the Corrections and Conditional Release Act* (fairness for victims) has resulted in amendments to the *Corrections and Conditional Release Act* (CCRA) which came into force on April 23, 2015" (Parole Board of Canada, 2017).

[4]   Please see Hopper (2015).

REFERENCES

Hopper, Tristin (2015) "A scorecard of the Harper government's wins and losses at the Supreme Court of Canada", *National Post.* Retrieved from http://nationalpost.com/news/canada/scoc-harper-gov-scorecard-741324

Larson, Doran (2013) "Why Scandinavian Prisons are Superior", *The Atlantic* – September 24. Retrieved from https://www.theatlantic.com/international/archive/2013/09/why-scandinavian-prisons-are-superior/279949/

Parole Board of Canada (2017) *Decision Making Manual for Board Members.* Retrieved from https://www.canada.ca/content/dam/canada/parole-board/migration/008/093/dpm-mpd.pdf

Mission Institution
Anonymous Prisoner 20

B ased on my experience as a Canadian federal prisoner since the early-
2000s, this paper explores the changes that have negatively impacted
penitentiary life from the time the Harper Conservative government was
elected to power. My experience within the federal penitentiary system is
one of despair as I have watched it spiral closer and closer to the failed prison
models used in the United States. In particular, I have seen a significant
negative shift in Correctional Service Canada (CSC) staff culture over
the past decade, which I attribute to the Conservative Party of Canada's
punishment agenda and their use of fear mongering when it came to selling
it. This agenda has infiltrated the core and culture of CSC, and is a significant
driver behind issues such as the significant number of prisoners being
released from medium- and maximum-security penitentiaries on statutory
release, along with their warehousing in these higher security institutions
when many affected prisoners do not require this level of intervention.

In 2016, an Auditor General report noted these issues and attributed
them to a lack of objective evaluation tools and training. However, as true
as these findings are, they do not tell the whole story. The present culture
fuelled by punitive attitudes has seen the privileging of 'public safety'
premised on incapacitation, rather than reintegration and rehabilitation in
CSC's policies and practices. The individuals working within this cultural
context are resistant to the use of objective evaluation tools because the use
of more subjective evaluation allows them to apply their bias. Thus, in my
opinion, it is a much deeper problem than what the Auditor General noted.
This is one legacy of the Harper government's influence on CSC that every
federal prisoner must face.

As is documented in my psychological report and other documents
written by CSC staff prior to the Harper government, I was diagnosed
as suffering from Post-Traumatic Stress Disorder (PTSD) and "battered
spouse syndrome" as a result of my relationship with my deceased wife,
who was violent and abusive towards our children and myself. As my
doctor noted at the time, my only risk scenario for violence is in the event
that I perceive an imminent deadly threat to the life of someone I love
and that I believe I have exhausted all avenues to protect them. Within a
culture of rehabilitation and reintegration, the recognition of addressing
this and acknowledging my lack of propensity for violence would be
significant. However, within the present culture, I received no support

in terms of dealing with this diagnosis. Further, my attempts to seek help and have this help noted on my file have been circumvented by actions driven by the punishment agenda and the subjective bias associated with it. For instance, in 2013 my Institutional Parole Officer (IPO) denied me the opportunity to consult an outside therapist who had worked in CSC facilities to receive therapy. Nine months later, I discovered through another prisoner that the therapist was already providing therapy to a prisoner at this institution and I was able to get her contact information. Within ten days of sending my letter to the therapist, I started my sessions. Despite having taken the initiative to work through my issues, my therapy did not make its way into my Correctional Plan Update by my IPO, which stated that I had made next to no improvement in my two risk areas even though I had successfully completed my correctional plan as well.

Considering that my only risk areas are personal/emotional and marital/family, and that I was receiving therapy for PTSD that stemmed from being in a relationship with a violent and abusive individual, it would seem that talking to the therapist would have provided significant input regarding these risk areas. Had my IPO met my therapist as I requested, the subjectively biased opinions included in my file would have been challenged and the tenor of their report would have required significant adjustment.

Towards the end of 2015, I was assigned a different IPO who initially appeared less prone to abide by the punishment agenda that had come to characterize life and work in the federal penitentiary system. However, within a few months it became apparent that the same bias was present as a 2016 Assessment for Decision questioned if I was ever actually diagnosed even though the judge in my case acknowledged this a decade earlier. The IPO also made the false statement that I demonstrated a desire for control with respect to my daughter even though she made it clear, through communication with my IPO and the warden that I have never acted in this manner since our reconnecting in 2013. Numerous other unsubstantiated opinions, which were contradicted by notarized affidavits on file (e.g. statements made to the police and testimonies of individuals that resided in my home) were also part of this report. As this was the last assessment written prior to an independent assessment being submitted for my judicial review, I have fought the contents of this document for almost a whole year and at present it is still 'open'. I have received little to no support from those involved in getting this document corrected, which has stalled the independent review and thus the decision of the Chief Justice in regard to my receiving a judicial review hearing. In fact, I wrote a letter to Justice Minister Jody Wilson-Raybould outlining dozens of violations of the *Standards of Professional Conduct in the Correctional Service of Canada* by my IPO.

The last incident that demonstrates the permeation of the punishment agenda throughout CSC is the reaction of my most recent IPO, who stated that "I haven't done enough time" when I tried to make a plan to cascade down to a minimum-security institution as I have now entered my seventeenth year of my sentence with a good possibility of my receiving a judicial review hearing and thus a possible reduction on my parole eligibility date(s). The idea of moving forward makes sense to me as I need to prepare for a safe and productive transition into the community.

I see the need for those serving extended sentences to have a significant portion of their time, prior to possible parole, being served in a minimum-security setting to help off-set the effects of long term incarceration. To me the idea of a prisoner spending a minimum of 20% to 25% of their overall time in minimum-security, prior to parole eligibility dates, would help in the reintegration and acclimation of these individuals. However, within the present setting I have noted the tendency to hold many individuals, who do not require higher levels of intervention, until they are much closer to their eligibility dates than needed. This, in turn, results in the individual not being prepared to move forward by their day parole eligibility dates. This phenomenon is directly related to the punishment agenda and the attitude it has instilled amongst CSC staff whereby prisoners that pose a minimum risk to public safety are being held at higher levels of security than necessary for no other reason than punishment. In my case, the effects of this are amplified. As a person suffering from PTSD, I am forced to engage in an environment that is significantly more prone to aggression and violence to the detriment of my emotional well-being, with the potential of undermining the efforts made in this area. In closing here are my top ten issues I would like to see the present Government of Canada resolve:

1. *CSC's mission statement* needs to place greater emphasis on the 'rehabilitation' and 'reintegration' process as a means of shifting staff culture.
2. *The warehousing of prisoners* at higher levels of security than necessary in the name of public safety needs to stop.

3. *The lack of accountability amongst CSC staff*, particularly amongst IPOs, as well as those responsible for managing assessments and interventions, needs to be addressed. Reports are constantly being used to falsely characterize prisoners as not holding themselves accountable to stall their movement through the system. There is a consistent failure to observe the Commissioner's Directives, in particular Commissioners Directive 700 *Correctional Interventions*[1] and Commissioners Directive 701 *Information Sharing*,[2] which govern CSC practice on correctional interventions and information sharing respectively. Current practices are tantamount to violations of the *Standards of Professional Conduct in the Correctional Service of Canada*.

4. *The lack of authority of the Correctional Investigator*, along with the ineffectiveness of the grievance process and alternate dispute resolution process to provide oversight and serve as remedial mechanisms, needs to be given the authority to correct unjust actions within the system. Prisoners should not have to turn to the courts and use legal documents, such as the *Standards of Professional Conduct in the Correctional Service of Canada*, to remedy issues. Taking up court time and resources would not be necessary if there was real accountability through the above-mentioned avenues. Moreover, very few prisoners are capable of effectively using legal means to address these unjust actions and are being victimized by the system.

5. *A lack of funding for prison advocate organizations* has effectively created a situation where individuals are leaving prison with minimal support available to them. Due to budgetary constraints, numerous organizations have reduced or cut from their budgets activities inside penitentiaries. In other instances, the federal government shut down support services such as Life Line. For the wrongfully convicted, there is really no avenue to have their cases properly evaluated by organizations as so few dedicated to such injustices exist and there is no public funding of them, resulting in many viable cases not being pursued due to a lack of resources. Prisoner support and wrongful convicted organizations ought to be better supported by the federal government.

6. *The double taxing of prisoners* for room and board, along with telephone access, for the purposes of enhancing public perceptions

of accountability ought to end. This matter is presently in front of the courts, however, the government ought to acknowledge that room and board was always part of the evaluation when prisoner pay was first initiated in the 1980s. The equation that determined the pay scale was based on the Canadian average for minimum wage minus this sum for welfare recipients. As to the additional charge for phone administration costs, it is my understanding that within the 11 cents per minute that prisoners pay for long distance calls a portion of this was already allocated for administration overhead. Simply put, CSC is double dipping and these two taxes are nothing more than a money grab. These actions have had significant impact on the penitentiary population as a whole. Even for those able to budget themselves and use self-control, it has still undermined their ability to maintain family and outside support. I have had to cut back on my phone calls to family simply because of the loss of funds to cover these costs. Where I once consistently spoke to siblings and friends, I have now cut back my calls to my daughter and step-mother once a week. All my other calls have to be made collect because I do not have the funds to cover them and thus I have drastically reduced my outside contact. In fact, I now have to ask my family to occasionally send in money so that I can maintain some semblance of outside contact through the phone or private family visits. Prior to these policy changes, I was able to cover all these costs. Was it the intent of the Harper government to make the families of prisoners 'accountable' also? For those with addiction issues and/or lack of self-control the problem is compounded. In these instances, not only has it removed their ability to maintain family and outside support, it has also created an environment where violence is more prevalent in the form of muscling, assaults and the like. This increases the number of incidents leading to segregation, increased involuntary transfers and results greater instability within the institutions. Lastly, these measures have virtually removed a prisoner's ability to save money for their release, which means more and more are returning to the streets – especially those coming from medium- and maximum-security – with only the mandatory $80 in their pockets. This is just an accident waiting to happen.

7. *The loss of incentive pay at CORCAN industries and other work-for-pay programs* needs to be reversed as they have compounded the problems noted above. When I worked at CORCAN, I was actually able to send money out to help my family with costs incurred travelling to see me and for such things as presents for my children. Now I have to have my family send money to me and I have watched my prisoner account consistently dwindle from the $2,000 I had saved to now just over $400. What money I had saved and was able to send out to invest in GICs is now being cashed out on a regular basis to help my children. At this rate, I will leave the penitentiary in my sixties with no funds to help in my reintegration into Canadian society.

8. *Mandatory minimums and the overall shift towards the failed U.S. prison system models* needs to be abandoned. There are way too many individuals presently in federal penitentiaries who do not require this form of institutionalization. Just being in this environment is making a situation worse, not better. Also, it would behoove the Government of Canada to acknowledge that the system that was in place prior to the Harper administration better dealt with the issue of criminality. A new direction is needed whereby evidence based policy making and lessons learned from the American failed prison experiment inform practice; efforts to educate the Canadian public to prepare for this change should be the priority. Why does the federal government continue to bang its head against a brick wall expecting something to change without making a fundamental shift in its approach to the problem? I hope Prime Minister Trudeau recognizes this and will bring us in a new direction.

9. *Subjective evaluations impacting prisoner pay* should be constrained by clear guidelines. At present, CSC evaluates a prisoner's pay level by supposedly tying accountability and motivation to the equation. Prior to this move, the system attempted to reduce its overall prisoner pay budget by informing work supervisors that they were to stop evaluating prisoners as excellent on work performance evaluations. This was not successful because most supervisors chose to continue to evaluate based on the worker performance, especially considering existing room and board/

telephone reductions factored into our pay levels. In response, the system changed the evaluation process and added the subjective evaluation by IPOs in the areas of accountability and motivation. The end result at this institution was that the number of prisoners receiving Level A pay dropped from more than 250 to six within one pay evaluation period. Only those that were designated as moving to minimum retained their Level A pay and only those who move into this category are given Level A pay. Meaning this institution only has to pay the individual top-level wages for the short duration the prisoner remains here. This is nothing more than another money grab. Putting it into financial terms, when I worked at CORCAN, before the removal of incentive, my average take home every two week was $110 to $120. This allowed me to cover all my phone calls costs, have funds to pay for private family visits, cover my canteen purchases including stamps and envelopes, and have money to send out to support my family. After the incentives were taken away, my take home dropped to roughly $54. This eliminated my ability to send money out, while reducing my ability to maintain contact with extended family and friends. My parents not only have to cover their travel costs, but also had to help to pay for the food purchases for private family visits, which resulted in a reduction in my ability to stay in contact via letters as my ability to buy postage was reduced. With the double taxing my take home pay on a full two-week pay dropped to roughly $38 and with the new evaluation system this has dropped to $34. I do not think I have to list how this has continued to negatively impact the penitentiary population on the whole. Where else in Canada would these types of measures ever be considered just especially when considering that prisoners have never received a pay increase since the pay scale was introduced in the 1980s?

10. There is a *lack of educational upgrade opportunities beyond high school equivalence*, which makes little sense when education is one of the key factors in reducing recidivism. Avenues to higher levels of studies have been virtually cut off given the financial situation that prisoners presently face. However, even before the Harper government and their financial measures were initiated, access to higher education courses were thwarted by CSC who feared public

perception of prisoners getting cheap higher education. Rather than educating the public on the benefits of affordable higher education provided by institutions willing to offer courses, CSC institutions withdrew their support.

To conclude, there are many measures that have constituted the downward cycle of CSC to the detriment of Canadian society. I have included a couple in the hopes of stimulating further discussion on how things could be changed to benefit all.

ENDNOTES

[1]   CD 700 Correctional Interventions, in effect 2017-05-15: To ensure correctional interventions contribute to the rehabilitation of offenders and their successful reintegration into the community (Correctional Service Canada, 2017a). Correctional Service Canada (2017a) *Commissioners Directive 700 Correctional Interventions*, Ottawa. Retrieved from http://www.csc-scc.gc.ca/lois-et-reglements/700-cd-eng. shtml

[2]   CD 701 Information Sharing, in effect 2016-06-01: To ensure information is received and shared with the appropriate individuals and/or groups pursuant to legal requirements and protocols (Correctional Service Canada, 2017b). Correctional Service Canada (2017b) *Commissioners Directive 701 Information Sharing*, Ottawa. Retrieved from http://www.csc-scc.gc.ca/politiques-et-lois/701-cd-eng.shtml

Mission Institution
Simon Chow / Inmate Welfare Committee Chairman

My name is Simon Chow, and presently, I am the Inmate Wellness Committee Chairman of Mission Minimum Institution. I am a Lifer who has spent over 17 years in many federal penitentiaries, which include Kent Institution, Edmonton Institution, Grande Cache Institution, Matsqui Institution, Mission Medium Institution and Mission Minimum Institution. I have the first-hand experience with respect to the effects of the Harper government's punishment agenda.

I started serving my federal time in 2000 under the Liberal government's policies and mandates, which at the time focussed on rehabilitation and harm reduction. Then in 2006, we were under the Conservative government's 'tough on crime' policies and mandates, which focus on punishing and keeping prisoners behind bars longer. I do not think I need to tell you the distinctions between the two sets of policies and mandates. However, I would like to mention one thing that is quite distinctive. We all know that tattooing in prison is forbidden, but is unstoppable. Prisoners infected with Sexual Transmitted Diseases (STDs) is quite common within the penitentiary population. Under a Liberal government harm reduction policy, institutions could create a tattoo artist job position and provide a safe environment for tattooing. When Conservative government took power in 2006, they cancelled the tattooing program and the consequence was that the health care costs increased significantly. This example clearly differentiates the policies between the two past governments. The old program needs to return to save lives and taxpayer dollars spent on health care.

After receiving the invitation to participate in this *Dialogue*, I sent out a communiqué and asked the prison population for their comments. In addition, at the Restorative Justice weekly meeting, penitentiary reform was the topic for group discussion. The discussion for the evening was quite productive. We shared our experiences with the volunteers and came-up with some suggestions in improving the correctional system. In conclusion, we all agreed with the recommendations found in the *Out of Bounds* article and its demands for penal reform.[1]

After many discussions amongst the population here, not surprisingly, we all agreed that food is the highest priority on the top ten list. Previously, under the Liberal government, every medium- and maximum-security institution prepared prisoners' meals in their own kitchens. Presently, all regions are serviced by central feeding, in which every region designates one or more institutions to prepare all prisoners' meals in its region.

232

Meals, prepared days ahead and frozen, are put inside hot meal carts and delivered to the institutions. Both the quality and quantity of the food are insufficient. Moreover, prisoners housed at all different security levels used to be confined in penitentiaries that allowed food drives, with the funds raised for local initiatives, as well as opportunities for prisoners to order food from local restaurants. In maximum-security institutions, the food drives were not only used to support local businesses, but also served as a tool to encourage prisoners to maintain good behaviour. For example, in 2005 at Kent Institution, when the living unit maintained charge free and incident free for two months, prisoners were allowed to have a food drive. Prisoners who want to have access to good food outside would try their best to keep their living units in good order. At Mission medium, where food drives were permitted, prisoners could order outside food for special social family events. At Mission minimum, prisoners could order food delivery from local restaurants and consumed it with their family during the visiting hours. Unfortunately, under the Harper government's punishment agenda all the food drives and food orders were suspended.

In addition to the food issue, I would like to point out another issue that should be looked at, which is better access to education on technology. We used to have access to computers for personal use. In 2000, because of security concerns with respect to an Internet access breach, CSC ceased to allow personal computer for prisoner use. The rationale was that a prisoner could have access to Internet with a cell phone, which was frequently found in prisoners' possession against institutional rules. Computers and computer-related gadgets have become one of the most essential tools in daily life outside. It would be greatly beneficial for prisoners to be able to learn or improve their computer skills. Moreover, all night schools were suspended due to the budget cut from the Conservative government. Everyone agrees that education is one of the most important programs for prisoners' rehabilitation.

Most, if not all, issues need time to amend and reinstate except for those noted above, which would only require amendments to Commissioner Directives. Therefore, I believe these issues should take priority to get them fixed first.

ENDNOTES

[1] Demand Prisons Change (2015) *Dear Liberal Government*. Retrieved from https://demandprisonschange.wordpress.com

ECONOMIC IMPROVEMENT FOR PRISONERS

When the Conservative government made all prisoners pay additional fees for room and board, pay administrative fees for things like servicing the telephone lines, and took away CORCAN incentive pay, they created undue hardship on prisoners and their families. It is more difficult for prisoners to pay for phone calls, pay for food for Private Family Visits and to buy anything that they may need that health care does not provide. A lot of prisoners used to send money home to their families when they were being paid their full pay before all the deductions were imposed. Now the amount they can send home is greatly reduced or non-existent.

Another issue that needs to be addressed is when prisoners are released from the penitentiary they have very little money, if any, to help them readjust to life in the community. This only adds to the possibility that a prisoner may commit a crime to support themselves.

To remedy both issues, I propose bringing back the CORCAN incentive pay, not making us pay room and board, and abolishing administrative fees. These measures would go a long way to alleviate the stress and hardships placed on all prisoners and their families under the previous, short-sighted government.

HONOURING PRISONER PAROLE
ELIGIBILITY DATES AND TRANSFORMING
THE CULTURE OF CONDITIONAL RELEASE

My personal experience relating to this subject has been echoed by many other prisoners while I have served my sentence. I have found that most of the Institutional Parole Officers (IPOs) who I have dealt with have very similar beliefs and attitudes when it comes to honouring parole eligibility dates. It seems that for a majority of them our parole eligibility dates do not really matter or that we are not ready, in their opinion, even after we have completed our Correctional Plan. I have found that in my case, and in most of the prisoners that talk to me about their case, we are being persuaded and pushed to waive our right to apply for parole when we are eligible. I have been told things by IPOs such as "I will not support you for parole unless you wait it out", "I am 99.9% sure that you will not get parole if you do not waive or postpone your application for parole", and "why are you in such a rush to get out of prison?", at which point I had been in prison for over half of my sentence.

With respect to Parole Board Canada, I have not been in front of them for almost a decade when I was serving a previous sentence. However, I have observed that more prisoners are getting day parole over the last couple years both in Mountain Institution and Mission Minimum Institution since the new Liberal government took office. This has been a positive development for prisoners looking for more reintegration opportunities to ensure their success in the long-term. Work in this direction should continue in order to enhance correctional outcomes and public safety.

VOCATIONAL TRAINING, PROGRAMS
AND JOB OPPORTUNITIES

The conservative 'tough on crime' approach trickled throughout Correctional Service Canada (CSC), negatively impacting both staff and prisoners. As a result, the foundations of belonging and rehabilitation were eroded, while opportunities to attempt to better oneself and morph from a nuisance to a contributing member of a growing society were stripped away in an attempt to appear pro-public safety. In the process, vast sums of taxpayer dollars were wasted.

Basic vocational training opportunities such as first-aid, WHMIS, H2S alive, forklift training to name a few are still offered, albeit very sparingly and with unrealistic criteria to qualify to get access to them imposed. Waitlists and general transparency regarding programs required to address dynamic risk factors are challenging and almost non-existent. The ability to learn about oneself and one's criminal past, coupled with a chance to replace harmful thinking and pro-crime attitudes, hinges on CSC and their officers' willingness to deliver programming opportunities. Some prisoners wait twelve to twenty-four months to receive programs they are mandated to take as per correctional plans.

So-called employment opportunities within the institutions have been clawed back, withdrawn, or split in half, creating conflict among prisoners, a poor work ethic, and hampering the ability to develop life skills such as motivation, continuity, and attention to detail. There are very few educational avenues available. Even the attempts at self-education through prisoner paid for correspondence courses are met with extreme administrative red tape and an all-around lack of support. There are limited opportunities to pursue some recognized trades, however course material, and access to write exams is outdated, and generally denied.

On paper, it may seem as if the penitentiary system is geared towards accountability, restoration, and rehabilitation, but in fact the system is broken beneath the surface, morale amongst staff is low as most feel handcuffed by unrealistic and uneducated political bureaucracy focused on punishment to win votes, as well as support from the lay public. The criminalized feel uncared for, which in turn lowers esteem and creates explosive environments where people, both prisoners and staff, experience physical and mental trauma.

The idea of using one's prison sentence to reflect, rebuild, renew, and attempt to return to society seems a thing of years gone by, a relic of history, much like most of the education and opportunities offered to federal prisoners at present.

Mission Institution
Ronald Small

Thank you for giving me the opportunity to share my thoughts and experiences while being incarcerated in the Canadian federal penitentiary system and declared as a 'dangerous offender'. I served a lot of years at Mountain Institution and finally I earned my way to Ferndale Minimum Institution. I was at Ferndale Minimum for nearly five years, until 1 May 2008. I was shipped to a higher security – Mission Medium – when all 'dangerous offenders' who were in minimums across Canada to be placed in higher security. Staff used creative writing to justify this and as a result there was ten of us from Ferndale that were removed. The only problem I had at Ferndale was that I tested positive on a urinalysis test, which was the result of my taking a dentist prescribed Tylenol 3. I served several days in segregation for that and became the victim of creative writing so this punishment could be justified. The fact is, I was punished for something I should not have been punished for.

While I was at Mission Institution from 2008 to 2015 *life* became pure *hell*. In a span of two years, I had approximately eighteen institutional parole officers (IPO). Some were correctional officers in acting positions as parole officers. I even had a clerk acting as one. In 2015, the Parole Board granted me day parole. Unfortunately, I breached my conditions in 2016 and was placed at Mountain Institution. In this document, I make reference to *The Standards of Professional Conduct in the Correctional Service of Canada Declaration*, hereafter referred to as *the Declaration*. Enclosed you will find ten items I believe should seriously be looked into.

INSTITUTIONAL PAROLE OFFICERS

IPOs must be held accountable for their actions and inactions. These people signed *the Declaration* agreeing to undertake and maintain, in the course of their employment, the standards of professionalism and integrity that are therein set forth. The last IPO I had at Mission Medium Institution routinely put false and misleading entries in my file. I told him several times this was illegal. His response was that he was exempt from the law and could do whatever he wanted, and there was nothing I could do about that. On one occasion, he laughed at me and told me to file a complaint. I obliged and became a victim of abuse from upper management. I also confronted him in early 2015, telling him he was in breach of many of the conditions in *the Declaration* and also that I felt that he was 'sluffing' me off. He looked at me, laughed and agreed to what I said, then stated, "so why don't you take me to court?" This is just a sample of what I had to deal with on the caseload of one IPO. Had this person been working in the private sector he would have been fired. I believe a study of IPOs should be looked into as I have witnessed many problems they have caused me and many of my fellow prisoners. These people are supposed to be role models for us. If we followed their current lead Canadian society would be worse off.

ACCOUNTABILITY

I believe case management should be held accountable for their actions and inactions. Upper management is also included in this to the extent that these people go through the process of covering up for themselves and their co-workers, which is getting really bad. Saying, "Sorry, I made a mistake and I will correct it", is non-existent. The amount of time and taxpayer money that wasted on cover-ups is ridiculous. If a lot of these people were held accountable to *the Declaration*, they would be unemployed.

FOOD

The quality of the food we are given has really gone downhill. This budget saving project has turned out to be a failure. I have witnessed the kitchen staff hanging their heads in shame because of what they are forced to serve us. You will find that the waste of food being thrown out is extremely high, which converts to wasted taxpayer money.

PRISONER PAY

Our pay, along with the implications of paying additional room and board, has had a very dangerous and negative effect. Most prisoners do not have any money for themselves and with what little money we do get, it has forced an increase in sub-culture activities and also a financial burden on prisoners' families. What I see happening now is prisoners' planning their next score because they have no money upon release. I would suggest that Prime Minister Harper's punishment agenda, which still has effects today, is putting public safety more at risk by putting so many prisoners in a situation where they are forced to fall back on their bad behaviours.

CORCAN INCENTIVE PAY

When CORCAN incentive pay was taken away, I think it was a big mistake. This not only taught good work habits, but in many cases prisoners were able to financially help their families and loved ones. Why take this away from us if our families and the communities we return to are the primary beneficiaries?

TELEPHONE SYSTEM

This telephone system is a very expensive necessity, which a lot of prisoners cannot afford. Considering the little we get after additional room and board is deducted, we have very little left to cover the costs of communicating with our families and loved ones, especially if long distance phone calls are required. This has only limited communication with family, loved ones and support people, causing a financial burden on all.

PRISONER PURCHASING

Restricting prisoner purchases to a centralized catalogue system run by one company is a monopoly that few 'free market' proponents would ever tolerate. After additional room and board is deducted from our pay, we have very little money left to purchase items with. With what little money we make, we are now forced to buy products with inflated prices, price gouging, from a monopoly that is allowed to function without any real oversight. For example, London Drugs sells RCA 19-inch television for around $120 or less. We are forced to buy the same television from the CSC contracted vendor/catalogue /warehouse for well over $200. This is just one problematic example of many.

GRIEVANCES

This grievance and complaint system is completely broken, which the Correctional Investigator and the courts have routinely observed. This is demonstrated in the *Spiedel versus CSC* case. In this case, a self-represented prisoner who was serving a life-sentence in British Columbia challenged the efficacy of CSC's internal grievance procedure and was able to establish that the organization "failed to provide a substantive response to his grievances in a number of cases". One such grievance took 242 days to even receive a single response from CSC, who are legislatively obligated to respond within 15 working days.[1] This system has been purposely abused by CSC, which also solidifies the many breaches of *the Declaration* by so many CSC personnel. *The Declaration* states that CSC staff are supposed to be role models for us. I think you would have to agree, CSC has really failed in this department.

WAREHOUSING

Warehousing prisoners at higher security is now common, particularly for those with lengthy sentences. I am a prime example of this practice. I was at Ferndale Minimum for about nearly five years, and then was shipped to higher security and punished for something I did not do. I was warehoused at Mission Medium Institution for eight years. In August 2015, the parole board told my IPO that he had failed to do his job and I was granted day parole. On many occasions, myself and many fellow prisoners have been told we "haven't done enough time yet". I have asked for the policy on this issue and got nothing but anger and abuse as a response.

HEALTH CARE

I have been victimized by the health care department like so many other prisoners. They are accountable to no one. I arrived here at Mountain Institution in 2016. I have arthritis and was given medication for that until it was cut down by a third by some doctor I did not know. It took about 45 days to see a doctor and get my medication back. It was the same doctor who took my medication away previously. While I was on parole, a street-doctor had me x-rayed and informed me I had advanced deterioration of my left hip. I put in to see the doctor here for help with the pain I have. This doctor looked at me, re-diagnosed me and gave me a needle in my left hip. I asked if this would help and he said probably not. Later that year, I asked to see the optometrist to get prescription glasses I needed. It took ten months for this to happen. I have filed a complaint with the College of Physicians and Surgeons, but I do not expect much help. I have found, like many other fellow prisoners, that to receive help we need to take it outside of the institution. I personally feel the abuse we get from health care should be exposed and those people involved should be held accountable, even if just to the letter of *the Declaration*.

CONCLUSION

I could write more, but I believe I have contributed enough to help inform future reforms to CSC. I am writing this document knowing that I have a parole hearing coming soon. I have been advised my freedom could be jeopardized by my writing this document to you. I am an elderly man and will not be victimized by fear and intimidation, and bullying that is commonly used by CSC personnel. I really hope what I have written will be useful in helping to shape the future of federal imprisonment in Canada.

ENDNOTES

[1]   Spidel v. Canada (Attorney General). 2012 FC 140.

The following includes a number of concerns raised by prisoners at Mountain Institution with respect to past penal reforms in Canada and what could be done going forward.

1. During the ten-year period that Prime Minister Stephen Harper's regime was in power they implemented a number of changes that have had a disastrous effect upon the lives that they touched. These most significantly affected 'dangerous offenders' and Lifers. Many of these individuals were on the verge of earning various forms of release, either to minimum-security facilities or day/full parole. Their release plans interrupted and put on hold until the government completed the review process prior to the implementation of many of the changes to Correctional Service Canada (CSC). In most cases here at Mountain, these individuals are now being subjected to serving many additional years before they will even be considered for any form of release. The likelihood of Lifers or 'dangerous offenders' attaining a release is now greatly diminished after the Conservatives very public tirade in which they employed their favourite tactic of scaring the hell out of the population with fictions, denying the fact that Canadian society had become safer before they came into office. There is a very clear pattern in which they artificially heightened public awareness and then refuse to release individuals' due to having a high profile in the community.

2. There is also a very real concern with regard to the fact that many of the people appointed by the Conservatives to key positions within CSC and related departments such as Justice Canada have not been replaced by the new federal government. The frightening thing for many prisoners is that these individuals appear to be leaving key aspects of the Conservative agenda of being 'tough on crime' in place, retaining prisoners in custody beyond what is necessary. There are a great number of on-going *Charter* abuses associated with the warehousing scheme. It is hoped that the new federal government will either replace these people or put in place a truly independent oversight mechanism, such as a balanced group of Senators or a similar model, in which said group would actually have the power to make decisions and impose sanctions. Such

extremes may be the only way to ensure fair practices and to take the strain off of the court system that will inevitably face more *Charter* challenges should necessary reforms to observe human rights behind bars not take place.

3. At least at this facility, there is a common practice in which Institutional Parole Officers are making promises and then failing to honour them when it comes time to act on them. It becomes a scenario involving the prisoner's word against that of the recognised government official. Prisoners tend to lose these arguments simply because they are incarcerated. We as a population would like to see a standardization of a practice where all agreements are provided in writing so the prisoner may have a written record as evidence that an agreement was made.

4. On a similar note as the third item, at one point in time there was a procedure brought about as a result of grieving unfair practices in which the officers would sign a section of a prisoner's request form and return one of the pages as a receipt for the prisoner to demonstrate that they filed for interventions or remedy within a particular time frame. The problem now is that most staff members have begun to refuse to sign these request forms and their immediate superiors are refusing to police them when this occurs. This is another example of why truly independent oversight is required.

5. As noted in a recent Auditor General's report, parole officers are intentionally taking away pay levels from prisoners in an effort to recover from overspending on the part of CSC elsewhere. Never mind the fact that they are heaping the accountability for their management on the backs of prisoners, a more serious problem that has arisen is that they are using the categories of 'motivation' and 'accountability' as reasons to justify taking away pay levels from prisoners. The real issue arising here is that the two categories have a direct and significant impact upon parole eligibility, while prisoners are also being denied support on the basis of alleged low motivation and low accountability. Further, the individuals who are assessing and grading these traits have no medical credentials to produce any meaningful or ethical decisions about these subjects. The people who are typically conducting these assessments hold the job title of CXII (Correctional Officer 2) or Institutional Parole

Officer. The practice results in gross abuses of power that must be addressed and curtailed. It should be a relatively simple matter to correlate the timing in which CSC began a widespread program of financial cutbacks, along with the significant rise in the practice of utilising motivation and accountability to deny pay levels.

6. There is a general consensus amongst prisoners, at least at this facility, that CSC seems to be reverting back to a system of punitive measures, rather than actually encouraging meaningful rehabilitation. One product is that many staff express views on a daily basis that are either demeaning or completely dismissive of pain and suffering. Many of these individuals simply ignore the directions provided by the courts and when prisoners complain to the upper echelon within CSC it appears that their complaints fall on deaf ears. Why do we even have a *Charter*? Again, there is a significant need for independent oversight to ensure compliance with the law. It is possible that the solution lay in the appointment of a true ombudsman only answerable directly to Parliament and not to the government of the day via the Minister of Public Safety.

7. There is another disturbing trend of using the maintenance program excessively to delay receiving support for any form of release, nor transfers to the minimum-security setting. It is logical to conclude that there will be the occasional prisoner that would benefit from an additional eleven-week maintenance course, but at some point it becomes an abuse of process. It is as though the maintenance program has been subverted for another purpose beyond what it was originally intended to serve. It is currently being applied in such a manner as to assess a prisoner's 'motivation' based upon whether he will comply with being told to repeat the course of maintenance or suffer the consequences. This process has been applied to some prisoners repeatedly and this practice seems to be spreading to become the standard practice.

8. There is an issue with the privatization of health care in that prisoners are getting substandard treatment and care. Prisoners are left in pain and denied the necessary treatment such as surgery or pain management programs available to persons out in the community. We are supposed to be receiving health care on par with citizens out in the community, but this is a fallacy. It has been

shared with the prison population that the person that holds the contract to provide health care had limited the amount and kind of medication a prisoner may receive based upon standards, rather than the actual needs of the patient. These policies were created in two main health care policies:

a.   The essential medical services handbook; and
b.   The national drug formulary.

The continued use of denied medical treatments are a direct violation of the Istanbul protocols of the World Medical Association and the United Nations' declaration of what constitutes torture.

9.   Within corrections the free and fair market economy of purchasing has been compromised insofar as it has recently been privatized to an American company out of Texas, which hurts local business that historically benefitted from prisoners' purchases. While they were still in power, the Conservatives privatized the prisoner purchasing process, resulting in exaggerated mark-ups with items being as much as 200% to 300% greater than we were paying for the same items prior to the changes. When coupled with the additional 30% deduction for room and board implemented at roughly the same time, virtually every prisoner experiences financial hardships and those with families out in the community find themselves unable to provide financial assistance to them. How is it ethical for these new suppliers to get rich off of impoverished prisoners?

10. The present Correctional Investigator left his employment with CSC and stepped directly into a position of the Executive Director prior to assuming his current role, becoming what is portrayed as being an independent ombudsman. The position of the OCI has never been an ombudsperson and nowhere in the *CCRA* sections 159-196 does it use the terminology ombudsman. This is a misnomer used for a whitewash effect. There is a concern that there has not been any kind of cooling off period before taking this position and a greater concern arising from the fact that he is known to be a stalwart and advocate of CSC policy, including the denial of some of the harms of solitary confinement. CSC not only needs real oversight, but also a body whose recommendations are bidding.

Mountain Institution
Joe Convict

There are a lot of prisoners who are terrified to speak out – even through written words that will be read by parliamentarians – for fear of retaliation from staff. There is so much wrong with the system, but I will try to keep my points brief.

"CSC BASHING" AND
PUNISHMENT FOR PROTEST

There is now a mantra being pushed by all levels of Correctional Service Canada (CSC), including as a requirement for all participation in programs: there is a zero tolerance for "CSC Bashing", which means you are forbidden to complain about their abuse. You can be expelled from a program if you raise too many abuse concerns in a session. They are even placing it in writing in the form of behaviour contracts, which prisoners are forced to sign. This agenda is also being pushed by every department within CSC: prison and parole officials, prison chaplains, Indigenous elder's, psychology and health care, where psychologists and psychiatrists tell you out-right that they do not want to hear any "CSC Bashing" or they will terminate your interview if you continue. I believe this new brainwashing mantra is in response to CSC's utterly corrupt and broken grievance system.

Further, there is a very real consequence of institutional charges, segregation, and even being sent to the max if a prisoner persists in naming an abusive staff member or accusing them of a crime. I have personally been told I may no longer use the word torture in anything that I write, in either a grievance or request, and if I do, I will incur the previous consequences. When I continued to demand a torture investigation be conducted by the Royal Canadian Mounted Police (RCMP), which to date has been refused, and to speak out about being medically tortured by doctors and nurses, refused the necessaries of life, criminally neglected, criminally harassed, and criminally intimidated by staff to silence me and the like, I was charged repeatedly. When the institutional charges were heard, and I demanded a copy of the damning recordings of their criminal threats and harassment, institutional management destroyed the tapes.

I find it puzzling why little is being said in the public domain about CSC's culture of extreme secrecy. Throughout the country, the greater majority of staff refuse to wear their name tags or identify themselves, which they are required to do by law. If a prisoner actually dares to ask a guard for their name, it will result in a ballistic confrontation. I have been repeatedly charged institutionally and found guilty of being disrespectful for simply asking for a staff member's name. I have also been jumped by guards, handcuffed and thrown into the hole for asking to speak to the supervisor of guards who would not give me their name. All grievances and complaints about this are denied, including at the national level. Can you say: "Secret Police"?

DETERIORATING JUSTICE: THE CCRA, THE OCI AND THE POLITICS OF PUNISHMENT

That being said, I think your current study should move beyond the reforms that were enacted while the Conservatives were in federal power to look at our deteriorating justice system even before they came to office. I believe there should be a real review of the penitentiary system since the inception of the *Correctional and Conditional Release Act* (CCRA) and *Correctional and Conditional Release Regulations* (CCRR), which was made law in 1992 by a Progressive Conservative Government. The Conservatives of the day began with a broken model, knowing it would fail to meet reasonable or modern standards of justice. They created a penitentiary model that would allow them to continue to tinker with it for years, all in the name of perfecting their "tough on crime" credentials to which, previous Liberal governments, also jumped on board on occasion. Conservatives and the Liberals knew it would be a reservoir of political capital which they could mine for decades, until inevitably, a new system of laws would have to be created.

I have been in prison for the last twenty years straight and I can tell you the rot started long before the last Conservative government came to power. Remember it was the Liberals who took away personal computers, cooking pots and coffee makers from cell use. They have done away with advanced education subsidies and true rehabilitation training in the trades to name just a few.

There is a very systematic agenda of removing all correctional staff's accountability, through a mastery of propaganda campaigns and distractions such as all Office of the Correctional Investigator (OCI) reports. To explain, the OCI has not now nor have they ever been an Ombudsman. They are a part of the *CCRA*, which is the same act that governs the penitentiary system. Nowhere in the *CCRA* does it use the word Ombudsman to refer to them. An Ombudsman is answerable to Parliament, which they are not. They are answerable to the federal Minister of Public Safety and whichever party happens to be in power. All of their reports give the illusion of accountability without there being any changes to policy because there is no teeth to their recommendations.

There is a flourishing culture of brainwashing, harassment and torture that the OCI has become a very real part of. Their omissions, refusals to investigate torture complaints and their determination to protect individuals guilty of blatant acts of torture, and criminal-level abuses, has become ethically and morally repugnant. If a prisoner complains of a serious crime or abuse being perpetrated against them by a CSC staff member, in their written responses, the OCI often sides with them based on the version of events the institution decides to put forward, despite all evidence to the contrary that indicates a crime being perpetrated against a prisoner.

This entrenched culture of corruption is meant to protect CSC against any allegations that would lead to a civil suit or undermine their appearance of legitimacy. Given the nature of the OCI's public mask of being above reproach in their findings, if they would more frequently find, in writing, to be in favour of the prisoner, it would give great weight to a prisoner's allegations in any court room. This would lead to more civil actions being filed and won against CSC. Ultimately, this would undermine Canada's propaganda of having a system where the rule of law and the human rights of its citizens are respected.

If you need further proof of the OCI's culture of corruption just look to their historic unethical hiring practices. They routinely hire staff right out of police forces and CSC, who obviously carry their previous loyalties with them. Further, an OCI official can find themselves investigating an institutional complaint, with the full knowledge they will be gainfully employed by CSC in near future.

If you think the abuse is just happening to prisoners, I have witnessed CSC and OCI staff victimizing each other. The RCMP has just begun to expose their harassment culture and I can tell you, CSC is far more corrupt than the RCMP, and more secretive to boot. A staff member who speaks out about abuse, either against one of their own, or on behalf of a prisoner, will be fired or driven out.

The *CCRR/CCRA* was supposedly meant to improve conditions and create an environment of prisoner accountability and rehabilitation. However, since its inception there has been a very systematic dismantling of its claimed purpose through more and more arbitrary interpretations of the Commissioner's Directives (CD) and institutional standing orders.

If the Liberals really wanted to be bold in this new world of incarceration, which borders on mass imprisonment for some populations like Indigenous peoples, they need to create a new justice model based on what works. Just think, a new model, using the dynamics of other countries' successes and Canada's own Indigenous justice concepts. They have a real opportunity to mold modern justice methods that would truly surpass the *CCRA/CCRR*, as one of rehabilitation, accountability, and true restorative justice. Bringing such a bold plan forward, would of course, be a boon for the narrative the Liberals are pushing that they are the progressive choice of the future. It would be difficult endeavour, but one I feel is worthy in the minds of many.

How long has it been since Prisoners' Justice Day began? More than four decades after its inception, prisoners are still being murdered and tortured to death by guards. Just look at the recent torture and outright murder of prisoner Hines in Dorchester Pen as recent proof. Prison guards brutally beat him as he was heard to scream: "please help me they're killing me, please don't let them kill me!" At the time of his death, his parents and the public were told he died of another cause. Evidence as to the cause of death shows his lungs were full of water. They literally water boarded him to death. They claim, however, that his lungs spontaneously filled with water because of pepper spray. CSC forgot to disclose to the public that he was found after death in the shower with his soaking wet t-shirt wrapped around his head and arms. This story is the epitome of oppression against the very vulnerable Canadian prisoner. This behaviour has become normalized inside prison walls.

Out of sheer boredom staff routinely look for a reason to brutalize, and if they cannot find one, they incite one. CSC guards see how the American Justice System turns a blind eye on cops and prison guards, who kill with impunity, and seemingly wish to emulate them. From my perspective, the current treatment of prisoners in Canada must be called what it is, a "national disgrace".

PRIVATIZATION OF PRISON ADMINISTRATION

Why is nothing being said about the Conservatives' privatization of several aspects of CSC administration and legislated responsibilities? Below are a few examples.

Prisoner Purchasing

All prisoner purchasing of allowable property, health supplements and the like is now done through a National Centralized catalogue. The supplier is out of Texas and has marked up products prisoners can buy locally by up to 300% to 400% percent. They have cut out local Canadian suppliers and retailers altogether. When you compound this with the abolition of food drives (i.e. prisoner's occasional group purchases of fresh foods from grocery stores and restaurants), there is a real multimillion dollar economic price being paid by local Canadian businesses in the form of lost revenues. Not to mention the fact that this is not in keeping with Canadian laws pertaining to a free and fair-market economy. This new privatized purchasing system is based on sheer greed and price gouging of one of the poorest demographic in Canadian society.

Health Care

One of the most life-threatening decisions was to privatise the provision of health care to federal prisoners. All CSC doctors are now contracted by a private corporate carrier, who holds the contract to provide doctors to a penitentiary. CSC has ceded its legislated responsibilities (CCRA, 85 to 87) to a private contractor, who will obediently carry out any CSC or state agenda. By law, CSC is responsible for the hiring of individual doctors and to ensure they meet provincially regulated standards. Currently, there is no federal oversight body who licenses doctors. There are also no federal laws to protect the prisoner from extreme medical neglect or abuse, and yes even medical torture is now routine. I speak about torture as defined by the *Istanbul Protocols* (I.P.) and the internationally accepted ethical standards of doctor's para. 51-73 of the World Medical Association (WMA). These protocols, among others were created for the UN to assist the world courts in determining what constituted torture. The above-mentioned paragraphs, define the ethical responsibilities of doctors who work for the state.

HEALTH PROFESSIONALS WITH DUAL OBLIGATIONS

The privatized medical contractors who work for CSC are placing their lucrative contracts above the health of their incarcerated patients.

> Health professionals have dual obligations, in that they owe a primary duty to the patient to promote that person's best interests and a general duty to society to ensure that justice is done and violations of human rights prevented. Dilemmas arising from these dual obligations are particularly acute for health professionals working with the police, military, other security services or in the prison system. The interests of their employer and their non-medical colleagues may be in conflict with the best interests of the detainee patients. Whatever the circumstances of their employment, all health professionals owe a fundamental duty to care for the people they are asked to examine or treat. They cannot be obliged by contractual or other considerations to compromise their professional independence. They must make an unbiased assessment of the patient's health interests and act accordingly (United Nations, 1999).

Contrary to the above, CSC contract doctors, as a matter of continued employment, place the wants of CSC above the medical needs of the prisoner. Presently, CSC doctors can get away with refusing us proper medical treatment equal to that of community standards of professionalism (CCRA 86, 2) through serious jurisdictional loop-holes. For example, the provincial legislative body who created the "provincial by-laws" that enable doctors and other health care professionals to be licensed under a college of their peers, have absolutely no jurisdiction over a federally contracted doctor's behaviour. The reason for this is that these doctors are acting under the direction and pay of the private contractor who is beholden to the federal government, an institutional management for which a contract is held.

These doctors are not under the provincial healthcare system and blatantly refuse to give their full names or private practice addresses when requested by prisoners, interfering with formal complaints to provincial colleges. Doctors are given their legally binding marching orders because of their private contractor agreements to abide by CSC's determination of what medications and medical treatments should be available to prisoners. These unlegislated and unregulated, CSC-created, medical delivery protocols, are known as "the national drug formulary" and "the essential medical services handbook". This includes an unwritten (or written in contract agreements) rule that allows for the suffering of prisoners by refusing or severely restricting pain medications and other treatments as a matter of course.

Medications and medical treatments are being cut off as forms of punishment if you are accused – even without a shred of proof – of non-compliance with a doctor's prescription parameters. In some instances, unsound medical demands ensue (e.g. I was told I would be cut off essential pain medication "as a punishment' if I did not take an unnecessary anti-psychotic drug, Stemetil, that I did not need or want). One month later a doctor at Mountain Institution carried out their threat and cut me off. Now as a matter of a directive from CSC national headquarters, I may not receive any form of pain therapy medication, see any pain specialist, or doctors who are not under the control of the contracted health care provider who would inevitably contradict the current "medical torture" agenda of Mountain institutional management and doctors. I have the above in writing.

Further, "suspicion" of the diversion of a medication by any staff member, even non-medical personnel, will result in being cut-off of all essential medications and medical treatments, including anti-psychotic and schizophrenic medications. Also, if staff want to target a prisoner with serious psychiatric disorders, doctors are ordered to cut the prisoner off of their necessary medications, so staff will then have a reason to go after that prisoner. These prisoners will inevitably have a psychotic or schizoid episode (i.e. a mental break from reality). These prisoners often become violent, begin to self-harm, and/or become the target of prisoner abuse because of bizarre and irrational behaviours. This leads to long terms spent in segregation where they are then seriously abused by guards in a secretive environment.

As sad and horrifying as these realities are, they say nothing about the fact that many prisoners are being routinely given unnecessary psychiatric drugs by unscrupulous psychiatrists and doctors as a form of power and control over prisoners (i.e. babysitter drugs or 'bug juice'). These drugs are still being inappropriately prescribed.

The use of unnecessary drugs such as Seroquel have a cumulative effect on the brain and probably causes a deterioration in one's ability to cope. This inevitably leads to behaviour problems which guarantee longer stays in the penitentiary, more time in segregation, more institutional charges and security incident reports, as well as escalations in security classifications and placement into higher security facilities, and reoffending upon release.

Why, you may ask, would CSC employ these repugnant, immoral and unethical practices? It all boils down to job security and guarantees more income for federal government employees. The higher the security level, including segregation at any level, the higher the costs, not to mention what has become a grotesque waste of hundreds of millions of tax-payer dollars being unnecessarily paid in "over-time" for CSC guards. Remember, the prison industrial complex generates billions towards Canada's GDP. The Canadian government, whether Conservative or Liberal, do not want to see this end, because the end of the criminalization of the poor, minorities, the uneducated, and the mentally ill would cost jobs. Alternatively, the reality is, more jobs would be created by a healthy populous ability to be gainfully employed, but it is more expedient in the short-term to lock people up, rather than better their plight.

Intentional medical neglect and the withholding of emergency medical and dental services, along with the use of a prisoner's medical treatment needs as opportunities for abusive guards, are just some of the daily practices we endure. These practices have become so normalized that they can only be described as what they are, a government initiated "program".

NEAR DEATH EXPERIENCES

My life has almost been repeatedly cut short by CSC's agenda of medical torture and intentional neglect. Most terrifying is that this is a provable ongoing campaign to end my life in the most horrific and painful way possible. I have zero protection from this horror of an existence, as there are no mechanisms in place in Canada to protect me from my torturers. I am refused legal-aid and not a single organization or lawyer, from the hundreds I have contacted over the years, will help me. I cannot afford the $70,000 to $100,000 up-front costs to retain a lawyer for a medical malpractice and torture suit against CSC and their doctors.

What is most insidious about this form of torture is that government officials of all levels, including CSC staff and medical personnel, get to use my own body and medical needs as a weapon to cause me pain, suffering and my inevitable death. CSC gets to use my disease as their favourite point of contention and a convenient vehicle for the constant harassment and torment I receive for complaining.

For example, when I am listed for an outside healthcare appointment, escort guards will routinely subject me to humiliation sessions that can sometimes last for hours. This behaviour includes screaming profanities at me, name calling, refusing to feed me or give me water, degrading me by forced strip searches where females and other staff are walking around, mocking my body, making sexual comments, and in some instances I am even forced to use secure, but public toilets in the hospital with the door wide open while members of the public and hospital staff have a clear view of me. When I vigorously complained to Mountain Institution management, I was told that guards are allowed to exercise their absolute discretion in how they wish to treat a prisoner while on escort. Now because I refuse to be escorted by these abusive guards, I am refused all medical escorts.

Of note, not all guards engage in these practices and those who do are the minority. For me, however, because I have named the abusers, as part of CSC's harassment campaign to silence me by any means possible, I may have no other escorting guards except those who terrorize me. The reason for this is so when I die as a result of medical neglect they get to blame me, stating that I refused to be escorted to medical appointments. These tyrants get to sit back, watching me suffer a horrible preventable death, without raising a finger to help. In the end, they will be able to say I died of natural causes, when in fact they will be 100% responsible for causing my death. From my perspective here, living in this daily hell, this is the epitome of diabolical, premeditated murder through medical torture and neglect. This is also a clear example of the Canadian government's total loss of all human decency or respect for the rule of law.

If you think I am being too over-dramatic, I will relay just a few examples of what I am enduring and I will let you draw your own conclusions. For many months now I may no longer see any doctors except for corporately controlled doctors who are beholden only to the medical contract holder of Mountain Institution. If I refuse to see a doctor who has been abusive, negligent and torturing me, I am refused all medical treatment. In other words, these doctors can neglect and abuse me to death without fear of consequences, and I have zero protection or recourse left. I have even told these four doctors to their face that I do not want to be treated by them and want to see another doctor. Their responses (in writing) are that they do not care whether I consent to be seen by them or not. According to them and CSC, I have no choice – it is them or they will leave me to suffer and die.

I have been repeatedly hospitalized near death with blood pouring out of me, after what is now, more than a decade of neglect. I have been begging for years for help from every conceivable avenue. And I am always given the same responses, "It's not my job", "let me suggest so and so organization", and so on. Everyone passes the buck or ignores me outright, refusing to respond in any way. The present Minister of Justice Jody Wilson-Raybould and the Minister of Public Safety Ralph Goodale are cases in point. After more than a year of begging and pleading for my life, and for them to help me to end the medical torture and neglect that I am enduring, both cabinet ministers, not to mention my own local MP, all refused to help me in any way or put a stop to my horror of an existence. Once again, I now face hospitalization and I am rushing to finish this letter before I am incapacitated for months. I am in a full blown ulcerative colitis flare-up, I am in crippling pain, bleeding internally, and have chronic bowel movements. The institutional management and medical staff have made it clear their agenda is to neglect me to death.

In 2015, after enduring more than ten years of neglect for internal bleeding due to CSC's refusal to band two internal hemorrhoids which led to the complication of developing ulcerative colitis I was hospitalized. For approximately eight weeks, I was in an isolation cell in Kent Institution suffering from a full blown attack and was refused all forms of medical attention. The attending physician of Kent Institution refused to even examine me. Management isolated me in basically a deserted part of the institution to hide me from too many witnesses. Without a doubt, I was left to die. I was using the toilet about 70 to 80 times a day around the clock discharging bloody diarrhea. During the last few weeks there, I was literally screaming in agony every-time I used the toilet. Sometimes I would find myself on the floor after I had passed out from the pain. Over the last month prior to hospitalization, I developed more than six hemorrhoid thrombosis, both internal and external (which are basically massive blood blisters that swell from the size of a golf ball to a grapefruit and then burst causing hemorrhaging). Hemorrhoid Thrombosis usually form when the ulcerative colitis has reached the last stages of a flare up and it is the number one cause of death from those who die from an attack of this kind.

The day I was finally taken to hospital, I had one of these internal thrombosis, which was the size of a grapefruit burst and I began to hemorrhage in earnest. The problem was that the thrombosis had caused a blockage in my bowels and was preventing me from having any bowel movements. After almost two days, my abdomen was massively swollen and distended, and my body took over as I sat on the toilet. My body, in an uncontrollable strain pushed until I literally heard and felt a pop inside of me as diarrhea and blood began gushing out. By the time I was done, I had filled the toilet to the top of the bowl. I began screaming for help and pushing my emergency medical button. The guard who responded refused to look at all the blood and finally called health care after I begged all day.

When two nurses showed up, I told them I was dying and needed to be taken to hospital immediately. At first, they began mocking me and said I was going nowhere, nor would they help in any way. It was then that I told them if they thought they would get away with murdering me through neglect they were wrong. I listed the many witnesses I had both inside and outside, including MPs and the media, that they were neglecting me to death. They then became obviously frightened and asked what I wanted them to do. I told them to send me to the hospital right now, because I was dying.

The receiving doctors in Chilliwack General Hospital told me when I finally arrived, I was suffering from extreme dysentery and was less than 24 hours from death, as I had already lost much of the blood of my body. They also said that mine was the worst case of neglect they had ever seen. I ended up receiving four blood transfusions and spending six weeks in hospital.

In 2016, after complaining of deteriorating health for ten weeks, I began begging for my life as a massive hemorrhoid thrombosis had formed in my bowels and was blocking my ability to use the toilet. This was the kind of ulcerative colitis attack which usually causes hemorrhaging and death, to which Mountain Institution doctors and nurses refused to send me to hospital. I also begged the OCI to help me and they refused to help. Three days before the thrombosis burst, while at health care, a nurse began throwing diapers at me while laughing, saying they were to soak up the blood with when I started to hemorrhage. I actually offered to beg on my knees to go to the hospital. This made them very angry and they ordered me to leave health care because according to them my behaviour was threatening and erratic.

That same month, the internal thrombosis burst and I began hemorrhaging. I began begging a guard to take me to the emergency room and was refused. Further, the Correctional Manager in charge of such decisions refused to see me. The message I was given by the guard was that "you should fuck off and die." It would take me more than ten hours to be seen by medical staff and taken to hospital as they refused to assist me in any way. I had to deal with guards, for hours, telling me I was faking it and if I was not that I deserved to die because they were sick of listening to me complain.

Over a period of almost two weeks that followed, a CSC contracted physician refused to stop the hemorrhaging for 9 days and had to be forced by a surgeon that my family had contacted. Over the first nine days I lost more than 15 liters of blood, requiring 8 blood transfusions. I know this because nurses collected and weighed each bleeding session in disposable bedpans every 30 minutes around the clock. On day two of my hospitalization while I was sitting on the toilet with blood spraying out of me, CSC's contracted doctor opened up the bathroom door and told me I would not be examined until a few days later. I showed the blood spraying out of me and asked, "are you going to let me hemorrhage here for two days with no treatment"? The first response was, "it will stop on its own". I said it will not stop on its own as I have already been bleeding for more than two full days. The doctor then became very aggressive and said, "you're lucky I'm seeing you at all. You were not scheduled to be seen for another month. So just be grateful I'm seeing you at all. Besides it's not two days". I again said, today is Monday and Wednesday is two full days away, what do you mean, it's not two days?" In response, I was told, "Today is almost over, so today doesn't count". The doctor then screamed at me, "you need to learn to keep your fucking mouth shut!" and slammed the bathroom door in my face.

I felt so helpless, humiliated and outraged. I could not even get up as blood was still spraying out of me. By the time I did manage to get up I was hysterical with absolute terror. I had the overwhelming feeling they were going to let me bleed out. I began screaming "Help me Dear God, Help me!" I told the guards I would not die without a fight and if they did not get me medical help right away I would force them to shoot me or I would dive out the window. At least this way I would leave this world fighting, on my terms by my own hands, and not tortured to death by sadistic doctors like many of my Jewish ancestors were.

Nursing staff came in, and between them and the two compassionate guards they finally managed to calm me down. Aside from occasional comfort, I endured abuse for 13 days at the hands of many nurses, doctors and guards. For 13 days, I was not allowed any form of entertainment. I was refused writing paper, magazines, books, a TV, and had to watch as guards played their DVD's and surfed the net. My only entertainment was to keep track of how much blood I was losing. During my whole stay, low ranking guards had absolutely no supervision by superiors. I was refused all access to management level staff and any complaints were turned against me by abusive guards in toxic reports.

When I returned to Mountain Institution, in an effort to silence me, staff began a harassment campaign against me. They demanded I stop using the word torture or accusing anyone of torture or they would segregate me, send me to Kent Max or start institutionally charging me. They did charge me repeatedly, then destroyed the minor court recordings to cover up their crimes of criminal harassment, neglect causing harm, assault with restraint equipment, attempted assault, torture, intimidation, and intimidation of a justice system participant not to mention a host of *Charter* violations. This harassment went on for months until they thought I had stopped complaining. What I did instead was to change tactics. I began to finish a manuscript I have been working on for years about the torture and brainwashing culture within CSC.

For the record, the Correctional Investigator's Office was and is an active participant in the abuse and cover up of the crimes being committed against me. I have been told by an official there, "You know that we will never help you in any way, so why do you keep calling and wasting our time". They told me they were sick of me calling and banned me from calling to complain. They have said I may only write, and they refuse to investigate any CSC staff wrongdoing against me, even those staff whose neglect has just about cost me my life repeatedly. They also say that they have no jurisdiction to investigate complaints of medical neglect or medical torture. They also side with all CSC decisions even if it could cost me my life. Being tortured is now the norm for me.

PATHS FORWARD

There needs to be a full Canadian Auditor General's audit of CSC's historic non-compliance with:

1. Their obligation to provide the necessaries of life to prisoners.
2. The Constitution and *Charter*.
3. All laws and acts of both provincial and federal parliaments.
4. Protecting prisoners against acts of torture and to provide a complaint process in which such criminal accusation is investigated.

> Further, if a person does complain of torture against state officials they should be protected against those they have accused of torture.

As it stands now there is no mechanism in Canada by which a Canadian prisoner can lodge a formal torture complaint. Remember, the Correctional Investigator is answerable to the government of the day. They are not now, nor have they ever been a separate entity from CSC as their mandate exists within the same Act of Parliament. They function hand in hand with CSC to protect the staff of CSC from accusations of torture. If this is not the case, then how would it have ever been possible that Ashley Smith and other prisoners like her died in the first place?

REFERENCES

United Nations (1999) *The Manual on Effective Investigation and Documentation of Torture and Other Cruel, Inhuman or Degrading Treatment or Punishment* (THE ISTANBUL PROTOCOL), Submitted to the United Nations Office of the High Commissioner for Human Rights – August 9.

Mountain Institution
R. Mark Simpson

To be very clear, my story is not about me decrying the fact I am in prison. I am very guilty and justifiably sentenced as a 'dangerous offender'. In my own opinion, I should be incarcerated for a very long time. My complaint is the state of incarceration with Correctional Service Canada (CSC) penitentiaries today.

I have been in for eleven years on this sentence and eight years on a previous one starting in the 1990s. The decline of the system could be seen in the late-1990s, even before the Conservatives took federal office in 2006. Yes, prison 'clientele' has changed over the years. There is way more of a gang mentality, coupled with way less respect and personal integrity. However, the system has not changed its policies and procedures accordingly or appropriately to address this 'new generation'. They have fought fire with fire only creating a much larger fire. There is also a change for the worse in attitudes of new and younger employees. New prisoners and new staff both seem to have an unhealthy sense of entitlement, disregarding the bigger common good, which necessarily takes some sacrificing of personal comfort. As for staff, in my opinion, the worst culprit in the 1990s was the guard's union playing games – directly and indirectly creating a more volatile environment – for bargaining chips at the contract negotiating table, which continues to this day. However, since the Harper administration things have gone drastically downhill with the management of cases and a continuing loss of privileges. It feels like the only freedom of choice is in how we choose to react to adversity, which is very disempowering.

Maybe I am getting old, but I see in the employees here a reflection of our socio-cultural decline in society – poor work ethic and everyone looking out for number one – which manifests itself in doing whatever is necessary to keep job security. Relations between prisoner and staff are worsening with things becoming more and more confrontational and adversarial. Even relations amongst staff are often tense, cold and uncooperative. Politics and media only fuel the drive for self-survival (CSC's that is) at the expense of humane, realistic, cost-effective and beneficial-to-public-safety practices in the system.

I think just about anyone with some insight into human nature and basic psychology would agree that what is behind nearly every criminal's anti-social behaviour is low or no self-worth. The current penitentiary environment only deepens and reinforces these negative deepest beliefs about ourselves. There is very little reward for sincere hard work and efforts towards change, and too much punishment for airing grievances, as well as issuing requests and making comments. Case Management Teams outright lie, exaggerate, and tailor documents to reflect the narrowest scope and most damning impression of the prisoner. They have become very skilled in creative writing and delaying tactics – "sluffing us off".

There have been outright threats, but much more implied threats to any prisoner who pursues their rightful parole eligibility to the Warden and at parole hearings if it interferes with the Institutional Parole Officer's (IPO) own plans/ulterior motives. The pen is truly mightier than the sword. There is no room for human expression of natural modest emotion. My IPO once wrote in an Assessment for Decision (A4D) that they felt I was engaging in my 'crime cycle' because I expressed my frustration with their delaying and avoiding my requests to meet and get working on applications. Trust me, it was a very mild expression – a staff member standing right next to us at the console did not notice anything other than regular conversation. You can imagine how that looked to the Warden at my hearing. And get this – I only received a copy of that A4D a minute before going into the hearing with no time to read over it to see what he had read already. It was not until after the hearing, in my cell, that I read it and almost choked at how overblown some comments were. My IPO rarely met with me, and only briefly, so how could they have any read on who I am? This is only one example of many and of what many others have experienced.

Today I am gun-shy. I am scared, at times filled with anxiety when I have to deal with them. It reminds me of being a kid when my dad would blow up on me and I had no idea what for. I cannot just be myself in any interaction with them. Therefore, they may be getting an inaccurate impression of me and our encounter. The most accurate of my many assessments over the years was by a psychologist here who spent a whole five hours in total interviewing me. It was not glowing or supportive, but it was accurate – my warts and all. This I respect and can work with. Sadly, this more detailed and rigorous report was not referred to by any other writers (i.e. my IPOs). How convenient.

I am sorry I cannot articulate better a more specific list of ten things I see requiring systemic change, but I am sure you can extrapolate a few from what I have written. All I can state is the Case Management Team hierarchy, the 'intervention' line of people, are all scared to risk their job security, do not want their wrists slapped or hurt their chances promotion by supporting someone. We had one program facilitator who eventually quit their job because they had integrity and because their superiors kept returning his final reports after being quality controlled saying they were too supportive (i.e. not critical enough). At each level, under the previous administration the writer's afraid of their superior's reprimand all the way up to the Prime Minister. Most importantly, I strongly believe the training is all misdirected, inadequate and unrealistic.

To be fair, I have faith in the goodwill and natural wisdom of people when allowed to be expressed freely, without repercussion. Therefore, here are a few recommendations for positive change:

1. I personally believe the IPOs are overworked, leaving them unable to commit much attention to any one case. They need to spend more time with each prisoner, so hire more of them.
2. Free the reins of the IPOs, removing any threat to reporting their own true assessment to their superiors.
3. Provide much more initial training and on-going training to all staff for all positions and at all levels. They constantly need reminding we are human beings and not just a commodity that serves their job security – psychology, social work, sociology, compassionate training and the like, coupled with a hard look at the deeper needs, fears and pain of prisoners. To me, this simply translates into realistic common-sense. I cannot say enough about appropriate training and maybe better screening processes in hiring. Hire those with a bigger, or higher, or more long-term and more inclusive view of justice. Whatever happened to the restorative justice movement that CSC itself claimed to be a part of? Lip service again?
4. Offer much more, and always available, trauma counselling for staff members themselves. They require individual and group therapy for some of the things they encounter at work.
5. I am not really sure how realistic this one is, but what about separating prisoners who clearly prove they want to help themselves from the 'other' ones. Set up tiered programs and environments where the individual is enabled to continue growing and changing, developing self-respect, self-worth and a sense of purpose. Offering practical and effective job skills would go a long way.

6. Here at Mountain our access to the Chapel and social events have been drastically reduced. There is nothing to do. This, in turn, has diminished the 'life' of the joint, reducing outlets for positive interaction and things to look forward to. Of four hundred prisoners, we have a hard time finding enough guys to put a team sports together. The enthusiasm or spirit has been lost. The Security and Programs departments need to loosen the reins to realistic and productive levels on reasons to deny events. The Lifers' Group is barely functioning without a common lounge/office with the ability to only meet every two weeks in Visits & Correspondence. Of approximately one hundred and thirty eligible members, there are maybe twelve or less regulars. Incentives have been removed, such as better fundraising options and connections to community organizations. This brings me to the next suggestion.

7. Again, the Security and Programs departments need to loosen the reins on the ability of visitors and volunteers to enter the prison and interact with us. The ion scanners are unrealistically hypersensitive, hence unreliable. Family and loved ones are turned away after travelling hours and spending so much money. Volunteers have admitted to me personally they feel like they are treated as the criminal when trying to come in. CSC gives lip service of gratitude to volunteers, but in reality over-scrutiny and suspicion is overbearing and discouraging. The risk to benefit ratio is totally unbalanced in favour of oppression and counter-productivity.

8. Perhaps most important of all is, a piercing probing look has to be taken into consultants, policy makers and bureaucrats at the highest levels. All must be held accountable for legislated budget spending and their own personal motives. It only takes a few bad apples, with a lot of authority, to corrupt the whole bushel. We all know 'shit rolls downhill'. Maybe hiring a Correctional Investigator with the ear and sympathy of MPs and Senators would be a good start.

I am a huge advocate of the benefits of good human relations. Anything that cultivates and nurtures good relations can only translate into real rehabilitation and a safer society. Invest the extra funds today for the long-term savings. Who does the risk and cost-benefit analyses anyway? The media who conveniently profit from sensational headlines and extremely unrealistic catchphrases like 'one victim is one too many' and 'zero tolerance'? Or is it politicians and their big business buddies pursuing their power-lust and greed? It sure is not common-sense folk with society's best interest in mind.

Change comes slowly – one heavy ball rolling will take time to stop and the next one needs to build momentum. Change, however, is a constant – it will happen. Let us just hope it is for the better. I for one appreciate any and all efforts for progressive penitentiary reform. A Russian author once said, "A society can be judged by the way it treats its prisoners". Does our great Canadian society, taxpaying voting electorate, have the will to look at itself, as a whole, and ask itself this question: How do we treat our prisoners (and their loved ones and those who would help)? And would they like the answer... if they knew the truth and what that reveals about all of us?

Kent Institution
Anonymous Prisoners

During the era of Harper, which started in 2006, nothing but a string of negative policies and procedures were implemented time after time. This has caused us to feel more isolated, depressed and demoralised. The policies that have been implemented have served to strip us of our identities and to embarrass us continually. The reason for this sentiment will be outlined below.

The food quality has significantly diminished. Previously, we were offered a healthier selection of food that was for the most part cooked fresh on-site. When the cooking was done on-site we had input into the specifics of the diet, as well as the means of the preparation of the food we were consuming. Now that the process is centralized, it is impossible for us to have any input into quality concerns. The diet that is forced upon us consist of items that are classified as scoop-ables, that is they are served out as slop. All of the meals are smothered in sauces that give no nutritional value, and are loaded with artificial thickeners colors and preservatives. The food appearance is grotesque, consistent with vomit. The taste is often worse than the appearance. Approximately 20% of the penitentiary population here suffers severe digestive problems due to the food forced upon us. These range from bloody anal discharge, bloody stool, lower intestinal cramping and bloating, constipation and diarrhea, as well as stomach pains. Prisoners have described the feeling of digesting crushed glass, coupled with acid reflux and heartburn. Two of the three writers are currently suffering several of these symptoms. We feel this is tantamount to torture as we are forced to experience physical pain just to receive the sustenance to maintain life. Most seek help from outside health care staff hoping to receive food that does not hurt us and instead they receive medication that, at best, reduces the problems minimally. We also do not believe that the diet is balanced. We receive way too many calories from simple carbohydrates. Hearing our complaints, the penitentiary pastor chose to subject himself to a week of our meals to see it from our perspective. He came away from the experience concluding that the meals being served here were inedible.

We would like to bring to light the problems caused by the additional 30% room and board pay deduction. This is an absolute ridiculous policy that was implemented despite the fact that we have not had a pay raise since the 1980s. At that time, our pay checks were based off 15% of the federal minimum wage, which had already factored in the cost of room and board. We are being double charged room and board. If you factor in today's rate of minimum wage in British Columbia of $10.85 we should be making more than two and a half times what we were being paid back in the 1980s. Instead, we are being paid $30 less than the 1980s wages per pay period. The most one earns at Kent is Level C pay, which is $5.80 per day, minus the deductions, which never reaches $30 per ten-day pay period. Due to the fact that most institutions are in rural locations and calls to family are long distance, these funds do not go very far to help us keep strong contacts with family and the positive supports that we have in the community. Due to the dietary issues already mentioned, it is necessary to supplement our daily diet with canteen items to meet our daily needs.

Purchase orders through our new catalogue is being monopolised by one provider who is not even Canadian. We are subject to inflated prices, low quality goods and a limited selection overall. The *Competition Act* of Canada clearly states that we have a right to the best possible price for items available to us. This Act is clearly being violated behind the walls of federal penitentiaries. For example, items such as a 19-inch RCA television, before the catalogue was introduced, cost $99 plus tax. When the new catalogue was introduced the exact same television was listed for well over $350. After a swarm of complaints, it was lowered to $225 plus tax. How is this justifiable in any way? Having to purchase our clothing and accessories from one supplier with a limited selection also restricts our individuality and diminishes our sense of self.

In years gone by, prisoners had access to post-secondary education. Prisoners were encouraged to better themselves and acquire skills that could assist them in becoming productive members of society upon release. Now access to post-secondary education is virtually non-existent. Prisoners have to fight tooth and nail to purchase what courses are available to them through the mail as CSC is not affording the opportunity to access schooling via the web. Obviously, this is an archaic policy as it is 2017 and paper is obsolete. In the recent past, prisoners had access to any high school level program that they wished to participate in. Now, if you have a GED you are not allowed to participate in any pre-graduate course and you cannot obtain your diploma. If you wish to upgrade to post-secondary education you are made to pay for it yourself and most prisoners cannot afford this as it is at least $600 per course, and we do not have any adequate source of income here. It would appear from any outside observer that CSC is in fact trying to inhibit our ability to rehabilitate ourselves, instead of promoting the stated goals of corrections.

Access to trades and vocational training has been significantly reduced nationally and is non-existent here at Kent Institution. Again, this does not meet the stated purpose of corrections. Prisoners are not better able to support themselves legally and productively than when they began their sentences. It is a widely shared desire among the population to participate in programs that would result in a successful trade or career, which would translate into their successful reintegration into the community. Why CSC removed training programs involving carpentry, electrician, auto body and plumbing mechanics when the infrastructure is already in place is inexplicable.

It is also important to mention the removal of what was called incentive pay, where prisoners could make extra money for working overtime more than eight hours a day. Some prisoners used to work over 50 hours Monday to Friday just to make $150 with the hope of saving a small amount of money for their release. This was facilitated in penitentiaries that have a CORCAN factory where prisoners are the sole workers producing items that prisoners use such as blankets pillows, mattresses, winter spring jackets and nearly every prison issued clothing that prisoners wear, which the penitentiary makes mandatory to wear during work hours. It taught prisoners the value of hard work for the pay check and also helped them plan for their futures. CORCAN continues to sell various items to other facilities and programs across Canada for a ridiculous profit, yet very little is shared with the prisoners who labour in their factories.

Limits to the amount we can spend in our own money, be it the pen pack limit of $1,500 with the extra allotment of $300 for jewellery or the cap that is in place at $750 regarding how much we may spend of our own money on personal property canteen and hygiene. These numbers were put in place in the 1980s, and along with the pay policy has likewise not received a raise to these limits since that time. With inflation, we are crippled by the fact that a t-shirt today may cost $50 when in the 1980s it would have been $5 to $10 on average. We are given a list of items that we may have sent in during the initial 30-day window for our pen packs, but once the items get here, the staff in admissions and discharge routinely mark down the items for ludicrous amounts, stopping us from getting anywhere close to what they say we may have. It is an unfair practice. If you take into consideration it has been 31 years since our last update where monetary values are concerned, our limits should be almost 100% higher just to keep up with rising inflation.

In conclusion, we understand that we are not perfect people, we have made mistakes, but how can we change and each become a better person when we are not even given a chance?

RESPONSE

More Stormy Weather or Sunny Ways?
A Forecast for Change by Prisoners of the Canadian
Carceral State
Jarrod Shook and Bridget McInnis

INTRODUCTION

Upon being elected, Prime Minister Justin Trudeau (2015) mandated the Minister of Justice and Attorney General of Canada Jody Wilson-Raybould to review criminal justice laws, policies, and practices enacted during the 2006-2015 period where successive Conservative federal governments were in power. With the change in government there has been some initial, albeit cautious, optimism that Prime Minister Trudeau will follow through on his professed commitment to "sunny ways" (e.g. O'Connor, 2015; Doob and Webster, 2016). This optimism is not unfounded. Anecdotally, editorial staff from the *Journal of Prisoners on Prisons* (JPP) are hearing that parole grant rates have improved. The newly appointed Correctional Investigator Ivan Zinger has also recently reported a "sharp decline" in the use of solitary confinement (Harris, 2017). Nevertheless, as this special issue of the *JPP* demonstrates, a storm rages on in Canadian federal penitentiaries and the prisoners who have been weathering it have a forecast for change.

As a prisoner-written, academically-oriented, and peer-reviewed non-profit journal based upon the tradition of the penal press, the *JPP* brings the knowledge produced by prison writers together with academic arguments to enlighten public discourse about the current state of carceral institutions. As such, the editors of this special issue are of the belief that part of the Government of Canada's promised review of criminal justice laws, policies, and practices should involve direct input from prisoners who, having experienced recent penal reforms first-hand, are well-positioned to assess their impact upon their lives and what changes are needed moving forward.

To this end, the *JPP* undertook a Canada-wide consultation of its own to request that Canadian federal prisoners provide their observations regarding what has changed in the penitentiaries where they have served time during the last decade in relation to the Harper government's punishment agenda. We asked them not just what they think about those changes and how they have impacted their lives, but also what prisoners would like to see moving forward in terms of their main priorities for change and the types of social action those outside of prison walls could engage in to help address the challenges that presently characterize life in a federal penitentiary (see *Appendix*).

We mailed out sixty-nine letters to every federal penitentiary in Canada, accounting for the fact that many institutions confine prisoners at maximum-, medium-, and minimum-security levels all within the same compound. Moreover, we had to consider the fact that CSC now classifies prisoners into sub-groups and also incarcerates those deemed to be living with mental illness in their regional treatment centres. We also sent letters to 'healing lodges', which are classified as minimum-security penitentiaries.

The response to our callout was overwhelming. The breadth and depth of the response letters we received back from prisoners covering all of CSC's five regions, spoke prominently and thoughtfully to the many challenges that currently characterize life inside a federal penitentiary. What these letters convey to us is that imprisonment, independent of the Harper-era punishment agenda, is damaging, yet the laws, policies and practices instituted under the last three Conservative federal governments have impacted prisoners in all the more cruel ways – ways that both undermine honest attempts by prisoners to better themselves and ultimately put at risk their chances for successful re-integration into the community if given the chance. If the current government is serious about "rehabilitation and public safety" they would be wise to heed prisoner's reasonable calls for an opportunity to better themselves in spite of a system which, whether intended or not, works against their attempts to do so in many instances.

Taken on the whole, the letters we received from prisoners, which are included in the pages of this issue, comprise a comprehensive account of the impacts of the punishment agenda, along with pragmatic recommendations for change to immediately improve life inside federal penitentiaries. Despite a fairly wide range in the scope and interpretation of these impacts, along with the type of changes that prisoners would like to see moving forward, the ten most prevalent areas of concern and reform that emerged are as follows: sentencing, mental health, health care, food, prisoner pay, old age security, education and vocational training, case management and staff culture, parole and conditional release conditions, and pardons.

There were also several other issues identified by sub-groups of prisoners, which we address immediately following our overview of the Conservative punishment agenda that offers a snapshot of the context where an intensification in the pains of imprisonment was endured by the contributors in this volume.

AN OVERVIEW OF THE
CONSERVATIVE PUNISHMENT AGENDA

The scholarly literature and government reports engaged with below provide us with an overview of what has been said by experts about reforms to laws, policies, and practices related to the federal penitentiary system under the previous government. While the body of work tended towards organizing this information chronologically and in relationship to the distinct electoral cycles in, which former Prime Minister Stephen Harper and his Conservative government were in a position to roll out their 'tough on crime' agenda (minority: 2006-2008, 2008-2011 and majority: 2011-2015), we have chosen to organize this information thematically.

Laws

In the legislative realm, we found that the academic community was particularly concerned with changes to the Criminal Code (Cook and Roesch, 2012), including the introduction of mandatory minimum sentences (Fournier-Ruggles, 2011), alterations to the criteria for an accused to access bail (Doob and Webster, 2015), a widening in the scope for 'dangerous offender' designations (Cook and Roesch, 2012), the creation of new offences for driving while impaired (Doob and Webster, 2016), and restrictions on the court's discretion to utilize alternatives to incarceration (Zinger, 2016). We also found concern on the part of the academic community regarding the elimination of additional credit that remanded prisoners received for time spent in pretrial custody (Doob and Webster, 2016), restrictions that were introduced on access to parole and statutory release such as the elimination of accelerated parole reviews (APR) (Parkes, 2014; Zinger, 2016), legislation that brings victims closer to the judicial and correctional decision making process (Cook and Roesch, 2012), and sweeping changes to the pardon system in Canada, now known as "record suspensions" (Doob and Webster, 2016). We further found that even though Canadian sentencing policy has historically been interpreted as one which valued "restraint", this fundamental principle went to the wayside under the Conservatives as evidence-based penal policy-making was dismissed and harsher punitive responses became the norm when new legislation was introduced (Doob and Webster, 2016).

On the whole, there seemed to be a consensus amongst those in the academic community that the legislative direction of the three Harper governments was one that would lead to a long-term overall increase in the penitentiary population who would now serve more time under harsher conditions, thus putting additional pressure on a system already strained to deliver on its mandate for public safety and rehabilitation. The pessimism expressed by academics regarding the Conservative legislative agenda concerning punishment was further enflamed by the fact that there was little by way of empirical support for their measures (Webster and Doob, 2015), as it was predicted that prisoners entering the system would ultimately come out the other side even less prepared for life in the community.

Policies

On the policy side, we found that one of the best sources regarding changes introduced as part of the previous government's punishment agenda were CSC's own departmental performance reports, which are a rich source of information regarding the implementation of laws, policies, and practices in the context of federal corrections. CSC highlights these as "achievements" and reports them as performance indicators. Significant policy changes related to this *Dialogue* can be organized according to three distinct themes: institutional security, cost-saving measures and accountability.

Institutional Security

During the Harper-era, CSC attempted to ramp-up its efforts to strengthen institutional security in a number of ways with new policies dedicated towards drug interdiction (Zinger, 2016), along with the alleged threat of "radicalized" prisoners (Monaghan, 2014) and other "security threat groups" (CSC, 2012, 2013, 2014, 2015, 2016). These included an expansion of the drug detector dog program (CSC, 2012), new search technologies (CSC, 2013), an increase in the frequency of searches (ibid), restrictions on access to "authorized items" (CSC, 2012; also see Parkes, 2014), increases in random urinalysis testing of prisoners (CSC, 2013), as well as the dedication of new resources towards securing perimeters, ION scan technology, and X-ray technology (CSC, 2015). Moreover, CSC developed new strategies in a stated effort to enhance the management of gangs, drugs and prisoners deemed to have been radicalized, including a National Radicalized Offender Threat Assessment in partnership with the Canadian Security Intelligence Services (CSIS), the Federal Bureau of Investigations (FBI), and the Federal Bureau of Prisons (FBOP) (CSC, 2012; also see Monaghan, 2014). As part of its focus on drug interdiction measures, along with alleged security threat groups and radicalized prisoners, CSC also made extensive revisions to its Commissioner's Directives to bolster the organization's power and authority to search prisoners, visitors, cells and vehicles, as well as intercept materials coming into institutions (CSC, 2013; also see Parkes, 2014).

The academic community anticipated that the increase in penitentiary population and length of time prisoners served before being released would necessarily bring about a strain on institutional resources, yet as Zinger (2016, p. 621) notes, "there always seems to be resources for more security measures and technologies" even in so-called times of fiscal austerity. This was a sentiment expressed frequently by scholars who seemed concerned that these additional security expenditures would take much needed resources away from rehabilitative programs and supports for prisoners (Cook and Roesch, 2012; Ricciardelli *et al.*, 2014).

Accountability
As part of a wider agenda which emanated out of the Conservative government's partisan *Roadmap to Strengthening Public Safety* (Sampson *et al.*, 2007; also see Jackson and Stewart, 2009), CSC also began placing a particular emphasis upon the subjective notion of "accountability" (CSC, 2012; also see Zinger, 2016). This entailed, as a matter of policy, bringing victims closer to the correctional decision-making process (CSC, 2012; Cook and Roesch, 2012), providing them with notifications, sending them information about prisoners and taking into consideration their concerns when making important decisions (CSC, 2015). CSC also began assessing accountability in the context of the 'correctional plan' (CSC, 2012), adding new procedures and methods touted as helping prisoners accept responsibility for their current behaviour and rehabilitation (CSC, 2013). This necessitated wide-reaching revisions to the case management policy framework that tied these factors to important decision-making processes like transfers to lower security institutions and access to parole (CSC, 2013).

Interestingly, even front-line workers have problematized the accountability measures and have questioned not just the logic of this approach to case management, but also the degree to which it has strained relations with prisoners (Comack *et al.*, 2015). Moreover, it was not lost on the academic community that measures of accountability, which "became a signature piece of the governments tough on crime message", were really just semantic justifications for austerity measures (Zinger, 2016, p. 216), many of which will be discussed below, and political maneuvering tactics and stratagems that the government relied upon to appeal to its base of support (Doob and Webster, 2015; Piché, 2015).

Deficit-Reduction Measures

CSC also introduced a number of cost-saving measures that resulted in drastic changes to a number of institutional policies related to services and programs designed to meet the needs of prisoners (CSC, 2012). These can be traced back to a $295 million reduction in CSC's operating budget as part of the previous government's Deficit Reduction Action Plan (DRAP) (CSC, 2012). These policy-related changes included a significant modification to the policies and procedures in the management of food and "accommodation services" (CSC, 2014, 2015) and a substantial revision to its Commissioner's Directive on prisoner accommodations. As will be discussed below, for a time, this had resulted in an increase of the practice of double-bunking and what CSC termed "modernizing" of its food services department by introducing regional meal production centres that utilize "cook chill" technology (CSC, 2015). Moreover, CSC made significant changes to the way that spiritual services are delivered in institutions, including cut-backs and the enhanced privatization of chaplaincy services (CSC, 2013). Significantly, on the case management side, they also streamlined services that modified the way that parole officers conduct casework, thus reducing the number of face-to-face contacts they have with prisoners, which lengthened the wait times for correctional plan reviews (CSC, 2014).

These measures came to be among the "perverse effects of a tough on crime agenda on the lives or prisoners" (Zinger, 2016, p. 621; also see McElligott, 2009). The Office of the Correctional Investigator (OCI), in fact, has made these issues a centrepiece of its reporting annually and problematized them as conditions of confinement issues in serious need of redress (OCI, 2012; OCI, 2013; OCI, 2014; OCI, 2015).

Practices

The above-mentioned changes to both legislation and CSC policies have had an impact on the everyday practices and culture within federal penitentiaries across Canada. Among these practices were a heightened use of segregation, double-bunking and the use of force. There were also practical changes more clearly associated with the pursuit of deficit-reduction.

Segregation

Though the length of time spent in segregation has been decreasing in recent years, the number of admissions per year had, up until recently, been increasing (OCI, 2015). This increasing number of admissions affects various sub-groups (i.e. Indigenous and Black prisoners), but not white prisoners (ibid). In the 2014-2015 fiscal year, there were 8,300 admissions to segregation (ibid). This practice continues to be used to handle what CSC would describe as 'difficult-to-manage' populations, including those who are deemed to be mentally ill, suicidal or engaging in self-injurious behaviours (ibid). Segregation has many consequences on prisoners. Prisoners with a history of segregation are more likely to be labeled as high-risk and high-needs, and are more likely to be identified as having low-motivation, low reintegration potential, and low accountability (ibid). Finally, administrative segregation has been and continues to be used to circumvent the limits of disciplinary segregation where prisoners can only be held for up to thirty days (ibid).

While it is recognized that there is a current trend towards reduced use of segregation (Harris, 2016), the academic community has long been concerned about this aspect of the "human cost" of the Conservative punishment agenda (Parkes, 2015; Piché and Major, 2015; Jackson, 2015; Kerr, 2015; Arbel, 2015). With an increased reliance upon punitive approaches, it was anticipated that the 'tough on crime' approach would result in an upsurge in such practices as segregation (Cook and Roesch, 2012). These concerns around segregation were tied in with legitimate fears about how this practice would affect the most vulnerable prisoners, those with "mental and physical health concerns", concerns which have become the impetus for the recent trend of a degree of restraint in the use of segregation as an administrative tool at the disposal of institutional authorities and now the subject of a class action lawsuit on the part of federal prisoners (Fine, 2016).

Crowding and Double-Bunking

Canada's rate of imprisonment, in contrast with trends seen in many other jurisdictions (for example the United States) had remained relatively stable from about 1960 until 2006 where it sat at approximately 103 people per 100,000 (Doob and Webster, 2006, p. 331; Piché, 2015). Under successive Harper governments, however, imprisonment trended upwards and the Canadian prison population steadily increased at both the provincial and federal level, rising by 20 percent and 14 percent respectively (Comack et al., 2015, p. 3). This significant increase in prisoners was particularly borne by certain segments of the population, with a 77 percent increase in incarcerated women, 52 percent increase in the Indigenous prison population, and a 78 percent upsurge in the Black prison population (ibid).

While there was an uptick over the course of the decade, more recently the Canadian penitentiary population has been showing some signs of decreasing in recent years as the federal incarceration rates decreased by four percent between 2014-2015 and 2015-2016 (Reitano, 2016). In fact, the overall prison population decreased from 14,983 in 2011-2012 to 14,742 in 2015-2016 (OCI, 2012; Reitano, 2016). Despite this recent slight decrease in the prison population, however, problems with crowding remain. One example of the problematic effects of crowding in penitentiary, both past and present is the practice of double-bunking, which continues to be used as a population management strategy.

As of 2014, the national double-bunking rate stood at 20 percent, with the highest rates in the Prairies (OCI, 2014). While some observed tensions arising between double-bunked prisoners (see Shook, 2013), there has been increase in the number of assaults, lockdowns, searches, and use of force incidents (OCI, 2012, 2013). It should be noted, however, that as of 2016 the national double-bunking rate had been cut in half (CSC, 2016). Nevertheless, during the period of penal intensification under discussion here, substantial amendments were made to CSC's policy on double bunking. Formerly, CSC had endorsed the principle that "single occupancy accommodation is the most desirable and correctionally appropriate method of housing offenders" (as cited by Shook, 2013, p. 44). This principle belief, however, was struck from Commissioners Directive 550 *Inmate Accommodation* as the federal penitentiary population grew (CSC, 2013b).

Research produced by CSC looking at the literature on crowding and double-bunking has suggested that the overall negative effect on prisoners and the institutional climate is negligble (Paquin-Marseille *et al.*, 2012). Despite these state-produced findings, qualitative research with prisoners (Shook, 2013) and front-line workers (UCCO, 2011; Comack *et al.*, 2015) suggests otherwise. Others have problematized this practice by drawing attention to the negative effects that it has upon an individual's "human spirit and human dignity" (Jackson and Stewart, 2009, p. 65). One need only look as far as any one of the annual reports of the OCI produced between 2006 to 2015 to find that the practice of double-bunking has been identified as a persistent problematic practice engaged in by CSC during the Harper-era.

Use of Force

In 2013-2014, the OCI investigated the largest number of use of force incidents in their history with the completion of 1,740 reviews (OCI, 2014). The evidence would suggest that there has been a heightened reliance on force to handle incidents, including those involving self-harm and suicidal behaviour (OCI, 2013, 2014). There has also been an increase in the use of inflammatory agents during these use of force incidents (OCI, 2014). Since 2010, correctional officers have been able to wear pepper spray around their belts, making it readily accessible during these use of force incidents (OCI, 2014). In 2013-2014, pepper spray was used in 60% of these cases (OCI, 2014). Research conducted by Chricton and Ricciardelli (2016, p. 428) suggests that corrections under Harper has reshaped "the obligations of prison managers and in response the occupational role of CO's". The prison officers they interviewed acknowledged the fact that "punitive disciplinary methods" are "increasingly used in non-violent situations" even though they apparently "felt less harsh measures, such as verbal techniques of de-escalation, would suffice" (ibid, p. 435). This qualitative research runs parallel with the quantitative findings noted above as there has been an increased reliance upon security measures.

Deficit-Reduction Measures Revisited

As indicated above, in an effort to reduce spending, there have been budget cuts throughout federal penitentiaries that have impacted the day-to-day lives of prisoners. Prisoners are being charged more for phone calls and more deductions are being taken from their pay to finance their "food and accommodations" (OCI, 2013; also see Shook, 2015). Despite these new deductions, there has not been an increase in prisoner pay since the 1980s (OCI, 2015). There have been cuts to social events and to library services, and prison farms were also being eliminated (OCI, 2013). Non-essential dental care was also removed, meaning that prisoners are only able to see a dentist in the case of an emergency (OCI, 2013). Finally, a new industrial food system has been introduced (the 'cook-chill system'), which has significantly impacted the diet and nutrition of prisoners (OCI, 2015).

McElligott (2009) and others predicted that such "no frills" measures would come to light as part of the implementation of the *Roadmap to Strengthening Public Safety*. Some questioned the fact that these cuts to programs, resources, and supports for prisoners ran parallel with an "overall increase in the Correctional Service of Canada's staff complement", which rose from 16,000 in 2006-2007 to 18,721 in 2014-2015 (Zinger, 2016). Also problematized was the fact that these changes coincided with heavy investments in both static and dynamic security measures, which the evidence has suggested do not yield commesurable additional public safety benefits, but may in fact serve to undermine them (ibid).

AN OVERVIEW OF DAMAGING PENAL POLICIES AND PRACTICES UNDER THE HARPER GOVERNMENT FROM THE PERSPECTIVES OF PRISONERS

Issues for Prisoners Pushed to the Margins

In his classic sociological study of a New Jersey state prison, Sykes (2007, p. 110) noted that "it might be argued that in reality there are as many prisons as there are prisoners—that each [prisoner] brings to the custodial institution [their] own needs and [their] own background and each [prisoner] takes away from the prison [their] own interpretation of life within the walls". Accepting Sykes claim that not all aspects of the experience of incarceration are universal, we recognized the importance of moving beyond issues that were widely cited by Canadian federal prisoners to also consider problems that appeared to disproportionately impact minorities incarcerated by CSC. Not wanting to overlook the latter, below we account for some of these concerns as issues of those pushed to the margins before addressing the most frequently cited themes.

Indigenous Peoples

Over the ten-year period under review here there was a dramatic increase in both the Black and Indigenous federal penitentiary population (Zinger, 2016). The Black penitentiary population has increased by 78 percent and the Aboriginal prison population has seen an increase of 52 percent (Comack et al., 2015 p.3). This increase for both groups occurred in spite of longstanding criticisms regarding their mass incarceration as compared to the population of white federal prisoners, whose incarceration rates have been on the decline (OCI, 2013).

Prisoners themselves problematized these trends. For instance, a group of Anonymous Prisoners held in Fraser Valley Institution indicated to us that in addition to the population "fast becoming increasingly Indigenous" that "The ladies that remain in max now feel they are not having their spiritual needs met by the Elder that is in the position to assist them". They further described a process that seems to be related to a high turnover rate for Elders in the system. While not identifying themselves as Indigenous in their paper, Rachel Fayter and Sherry Payne of Grand Valley Institution also brought to our attention the fact cultural events, like the Annual Pow Wow, that are prescribed for Indigenous peoples to maintain linkages with their cultures have been "cancelled without reason and without any communication to prisoners". Anonymous Prisoner 15, who is Indigenous and held at Saskatchewan Penitentiary, has spent two decades in the penitentiary system and recently underwent major surgery to remove a tumour after being diagnosed with cancer described to us a similar difficulty in staying connected to his culture. After being approved for "cultural escorted passes" and completing several successful ETAs, he indicated how the Harper government brought about policy changes requiring prisoners serving a life sentence to appear before the PBC to apply for and obtain passes. He described having "dealt with my childhood trauma, my residential school abuse issues", while "waiting for almost two years for approval to go on passes" to continue his cultural ETAs.

Another prisoner held in Bath Institution indicated to us that *Gladue* sentencing principles, which are legally required to be considered in correctional decision-making processes that have a bearing on an individual's liberty are not being followed. This prisoner asks that the current government "review all policies that the previous government installed that had an effect on and consequently engulfed First Nations people".

We received only a single response from an Inuit prisoner who described to us feelings of dislocation and the difficulty of maintaining family ties while incarcerated and the undue hardship brought upon family members who wish to maintain contact with their loved ones while incarcerated so far away from home. While we problematize his recommendation that "the federal government start considering to build a federal penitentiary" in Nunavut as its implementation would perpetuate the mass incarceration of Indigenous peoples, we appreciate why this prisoner would see this as a solution at a moment when the federal government has failed to deal with past and on-going destructive colonial relations (Monchalin, 2016; also see Martel *et al.*, 2011).

Black Prisoners

We received one piece from a prisoner who identified themselves as being Black. Michael Leblanc at Dorchester Penitentiary provided a lengthy and thoughtful submission which spoke with a great deal of clarity to the problem of systemic racism. His analysis suggested that "Many minority prisoners are warehoused in our Canadian penitentiaries" receiving "harsher sentences" due to discrimination experienced when trying to obtain and maintain parole. He further described to us, as did others who touched upon issues related to Indigenous prisoners, "the importance for a minority to stay connected to one's culture and customs". As "there are cultural needs and traditions that are not being observed" he calls for a "cultural liaison to represent these ongoing human rights abuses", while also recommending that an ethno-cultural advisory representative be the liaison between racialized prisoners and government.

Criminalized and Incarcerated Women

We were grateful to be in receipt of several responses from women across the country who spoke eloquently and passionately to issues that are unique to them. The content of their contributions reveals shocking and appalling conditions of confinement for federally sentenced women. For instance, Rachel Fayter and Sherry Payne of Grand Valley Institution describe a culture of debasement towards women on the part of the guards where:

> It is rare that a guard treats us with respect or dignity. They demean us, lie, make accusations and assumptions, tease us, restrict our choices, belittle

us, swear and call us names. For example, guards have made fun of what
clothing women wear, our make-up, our weight and how much junk food
we purchase at canteen.

Another criminalized woman, Stephanie Deschene, held in Fraser Valley
Institution described to us an experience of similarly poor treatment in the
hands of the state. She arrived at the facility in maximum-security thirty-
four weeks pregnant, describing that the decision making regarding her
institutional placement was, in part, paternalistic as she was accused of
continuing to remain "in an abusive relationship, of which my baby's father
was the aggressor" . She further described the insensitivity shown to her on
the part of the state following her giving birth to her son, when the very next
day she was "shackled and cuffed" and not allowed to "breastfeed, hold and
cuddle" her newborn son safely. This uncompassionate treatment continued
upon her return from the hospital where the institutional security climate
dictated that she would not be permitted to provide breast milk for her son
due to the potential for "contamination".

Given the unique circumstances of female prisoners who have become
pregnant before or during their incarceration, as well as those who have very
young children, CSC had set up a "Mother-Child Program". Rachel Fayter
and Sherry Payne described this as an initiative that "enabled women to live
with their young children, ages five and under in a cottage designated as the
mother-child unit located on the general compound". This program, which
served, in large to maintain the bond between mother and child was scaled-
back under the Conservative government. Thus, the visiting room became
the only place where some mothers could see their child. Rachel Fayter and
Sherry Payne argue "is not a conducive location for a mother to bond with
her child". Moreover, they note that in addition to the overarching security
atmosphere imposed upon prisoners and their loved ones, "women have been
denied the opportunity to hold their baby, breast feed and change diapers".

Another problem cited by the women who contributed to this project is
the lack of halfway houses for women. For instance, those incarcerated in
Ontario described women waiting months for a bed and being forced to live
"hours from their community when released on day-parole". Such neglectful
treatment shown towards women is an inequity that must be addressed.
Incarcerated women are entitled to an equal benefit of accessing conditional
release into a community of their choosing where they can remain close to

their family and support systems. To do otherwise is discriminatory and sets them up for failure.

LGBTQ Prisoners

We received one submission that spoke to issues that LGBTQ prisoners face while incarcerated and the impact that recent penal intensification has had upon their lives. Rachel Fayter and Sherry Payne observe that the "LGBTQ community at GVI feel they are not accepted as individuals and especially not as a community". They describe an atmosphere where there is a prohibition on same-sex relationships that are deemed unacceptable by the guards. Moreover, it was noted that "An individual's partner is often mentioned in paperwork" and "Women in relationships have not been supported for parole due to their relationship and their partner of choice. Same-sex couples are also not permitted to have Private Family Visits together". What is being described above are human rights violation in need of serious redress. Prisoners do not forfeit their human rights at the gate of the penitentairy and are entitled to being protected from discrimination on the grounds of their sexual orientation.

Elderly Prisoners

While there is not a standard definition of what it means to be "elderly", for the purposes of our analysis we have chosen to follow the guidance of the Office of the Correctional Investigator, which identifies those aged 50 and older as being elderly (OCI, 2015). This is to recognize also that men and women behind the walls may age physically faster than their chronological age due to a variety of factors up to, and including, substandard health care and poor diets in addition to the stress and the punishment of body and mind that comes with serving a prison sentence (OCI, 2015).

We received several responses from elderly prisoners who shared experiences of incarceration that highlight how penitentiaries are particularly punishing for the elderly. For instance, a groups of Anonymous Prisoners held in Fraser Valley Institution describe a "lack of approach towards dementia and elderly care", adding that "We have a number of older ladies and they are not respected in that manner". Moreover, Anonymous Prisoner 8 of Beaver Creek Institution discusses the circumstances of elderly prisoners who are unable to work for health reasons, infirmities, and the like. Thus, they find it difficult to meet financial demands and purchase "non-essential health care items". A number of prisoners who wrote to us expressed their frustration with the government's decision to remove access to old age pensions for prisoners aged sixty-five and over. In fact, this was a frequently cited theme, which will be discussed in greater detail below.

Despite the pessimism expressed on behalf of elderly prisoners, we recognize a certain resilience and courage on their part. For instance, one elderly prisoner who chose to remain anonymous stated in a letter to us: "I am writing this document knowing that I have a parole hearing coming soon. I have been advised my freedom could be jeopardized by my writing this document to you. I am an elderly man and will not be victimized by fear and intimidation, and bullying that is commonly used by CSC personnel".

Most Commonly Cited Issues
As we undertook an analysis of letters that we received from prisoners across the country describing the impact upon their lives of the Harper-era 'tough on crime' agenda, several recurring themes emerged from their responses. Below, is a summary of the most commonly cited issues that prisoners described to us and their reasonable forecast for change moving forward.

Sentencing
Under the Harper government, new mandatory minimum penalties (MMPs) were added to the Criminal Code. There are now over one hundred offences in the Criminal Code and the Controlled Drugs and Substances Act that carry MMPs (Eliot and Glynes, 2016). These MMPs can be applied in a variety of situations, including with drug offences and those who have been previously convicted (ibid). The use of MMPs, or sentencing in general, was mentioned throughout several letters from prisoners as an area requiring change.

According to Hyper A'Hern, MMPs take away judicial discretion by removing the judge's ability to choose a sentence that he or she deems fair and proportionate. This prisoner believes that this type of sentencing leaves judges with no other option but to impose a harsh sentence:

> We are sending a mixed message to the public by binding judges to these minimums. We are saying to trust the courts with applying the law, while at the same time undermining the judicial system by not allowing a judge to impose the sentence they deem adequate.

Many prisoners also mentioned that MMPs do not have a deterrent effect and that imposing harsher punishments does not reduce crime: "Empirical data shows that longer sentences do not make the public safer and only serve to make harder criminals who will eventually be released into society" (Trevor Bell held in Mission Institution). It was also noted by prisoners that there are many people in penitentiaries who do not need to be there and that serving time will likely make them more prone to commit new offences upon release. It was suggested that a review of current MMPs is needed and that alternatives, including restorative justice, should be more widely available to better promote rehabilitation and the repair of harm. Anonymous of Grand Valley Institution for Women concludes that a more compassionate approach is in order, one that includes "a close examination of the conditions that contributed their acts where relevant, including childhood abuse and suffering. These individuals need love, self-care and inner healing".

Another suggestion for change was to diver some people from the federal penitentiary system altogether: "Rather than mandatory minimum sentences, our justice system needs to consider alternative options. Persons who have not committed violent crime would be better off being referred to mental health, addiction or similar services as required" (1417 held in Riverbend Institution). It is evident when reading through prisoners' responses that they believe that the current sentencing system is broken and ineffective, and that far-reaching changes must be implemented.

Mental Health

Mental health care was identified as a central priority for federal prisoners. Stephanie Deschene held in Fraser Valley Institution noted that mental health personnel are understaffed, leading to long wait lists and a lack of timely access to necessary services: "Women who are trying to work past trauma and create healthy outlets are told they will be put on a waitlist. Should we not be *preventing* suicidal thoughts and actions not *treating* them once they happen?" Due to a lack of available staff, Trevor Bell held in Mission Institution argues that prisoners' mental health needs are only addressed in emergency situations:

> Unless an individual is suicidal or engaging in acts of self-harm, they are likely to receive absolutely no treatment whatsoever. The Harper

government repeatedly cut funding to the correctional system, allocating little to mental health in general, yet the presence of those living with mental health issues within penitentiaries is a pressing issue.

When individuals who are living with mental health issues while incarcerated are able to access psychological services, many prisoners who wrote to us described a scenario where rather than receiving therapeutic treatment they are simply medicated. This was described to us by both men and women. Michael Leblanc held in Dorchester Institution, referencing a study on the prevalence of psychotropic medications being offered to prisoners, states that "These medications are being prescribed to candy-coat the real issues of a prisoner's state of mind, rather than providing access to counselling and treatment". His position is that the "overmedication of federal prisoners must change, so that more resources can be dedicated to counselling". Yet even when prisoners are able to access such services, Rachel Fayter and Sherry Payne remind us that "since psychologists are employed CSC staff, women do not feel comfortable sharing their feelings and struggles based on the fear that what they say will end up in their paperwork", thus affecting "security ratings, temporary absences and parole". They recommend that "CSC return to hiring external social workers on contract to work with women in distress and those living with mental health issues, rather than CSC-employed psychologists".

Several prisoners also noted that prisons are not ideal environments for those suffering from mental illness and that being in prison can exacerbate their symptoms: "As a person suffering from PTSD, I am forced to engage in an environment that is significantly more prone to aggression and violence to the detriment of my emotional well-being, with the potential of undermining the efforts made in this area" (Anonymous Prisoner 20 held in Mission Institution).

It was also noted that prisoners may be required to participate in counselling sessions as part of their correctional plan, but they are unable to meet this requirement due to long wait periods and understaffing. For this reason, it was also suggested that more psychologists need to be hired to improve access to mental health services and to allow for more preventative and proactive care.

A final suggestion that was given related to mental health was to allow prisoners to have more contact with the outside world through volunteer programs. Such contact would be a way to improve mental health by decreasing feelings of isolation and solitude: "We can address this area [mental health] not by necessarily throwing more money at it, but by including our stakeholders – the community – through the promotion of outside volunteer participation, making our penitentiary walls more permeable" (Anonymous Prisoner 12 held in Beaver Creek Institution).

Health Care

The health of prisoners is not often considered a priority for the federal government despite high levels of chronic illnesses and infectious diseases amongst prisoners (OCI, 2016). For the prisoners who wrote to us, however, health care issues were a priority. Joe Convict held in Mission Institution draws our attention to the fact that the principle of equivalence is not being followed. He notes, "We are supposed to be receiving health care on par with citizens out in the community, but this is a fallacy". He further describes a situation where "there is an issue with the privatization of health care in that prisoners are getting substandard treatment and care. Prisoners are left in pain and denied the necessary treatment such as surgery or pain management programs available to persons out in the community". Other prisoners who wrote to us, including a group of Anonymous Prisoners at Kent Institution who drew a link between their physical health and the quality and portions of food that are provided to them, stating that "Approximately 20% of the penitentiary population here suffers severe digestive problems due to the food forced upon us, which has led to "bloody anal discharge, bloody stool, lower intestinal cramping and bloating, constipation and diarrhea, as well as stomach pains". Alarmingly, they describe prisoners seeking "help from outside health care staff hoping to receive food that does not hurt us and instead they receive medication that, at best, reduces the problems minimally".

Another issue described to us that has occurred with regards to health care is the removal of preventative dental treatment (ibid). Prisoners are only able to see a dentist in the case of an emergency. Preventative medical treatment in general is non-existent in penitentiaries, which, according to prisoners, is costing corrections more money in the long-run. Rachel Fayter and Sherry Payne of Grand Valley Institution state that "It can take weeks or months to see a doctor or dentist, even for antibiotics or a common cold or flu. The dentist at GVI specializes in extracting teeth and prefers pulling a tooth to providing a filling. There are no teeth cleaning or preventative care appointments available".

Prisoners are frustrated that they are not given the tools or opportunities to take their health into their own hands:

> Before prison, I was in great health and took care of myself, but how are we to take care of ourselves when we are not given the opportunities or resources? I have had a tooth ache for the last three months and I am told, once again, that I will have to wait due to the lack of funding. I have become a burden on society with my many ailments that continue to grow and get worse over time.
> — Anonymous Prisoner 3 held in Fraser Valley Institution.

Similar to the problems prisoners noted with respect to mental health care in penitentiaries, health care professionals are understaffed, leading to long wait-times and service provision largely limited to emergency situations. When treatment is given, in the domain of mental health, as is indicated above it is often limited to the prescription of medications as opposed to addressing the underlying causes of the illness: "and all the doctors seem willing to commit to in terms of care is prescribing an assortment of pills, including for mental health issues – simple zombification" (Anonymous Prisoner 19 held in Drumheller Institution). Exacerbating the situation is the fact that prisoners who speak out about their health concerns are treated with suspicion by healthcare staff, instead of compassion.

When discussing health care, most prisoners stated that better access to doctors is required, along with the hiring of more health professionals and enhanced provision of preventative services. It was also noted that prisoners often do not have a choice in their treatment plan (i.e. are simply prescribed a certain medication, which they are told to take regularly). Prisoners mentioned that it would be beneficial for them to be included in decisions about their health.

Food

As indicated in a previous section, one of the most common issues raised by prisoners was the poor quality of food. Anonymous Prisoner 12 held in Beaver Creek Institution described to us the new centralized food services model and "cook chill" technology: "The meal is prepared at a central site, packaged, frozen and shipped to the receiving institution. The institution then reheats the meal which is served to the prisoners". He goes on to state that under the old policy, "each institution had its own kitchen where staff and prisoners worked together" and "prisoners learned valuable skills that could easily be transferred to the community through the example set out by staff. They learned alternative ways of proper comportment".

This new policy, however, which was introduced as part of the previous government's cost-saving initiative, has been described as one where the quality and portions of food provided to prisoners has declined to such a degree that some prisoners have begun refusing to eat at all (CSC, 2015). Ronald Small held in Mission Institution describes having "witnessed the kitchen staff hanging their heads in shame because of what they are forced to serve us", he goes on to state that "you will find that the waste of food being thrown out is extremely high, which converts to wasted tax-payer's money". On a related noted, Anonymous Prisoner 17 held in Drumheller Institution states the following:

> I have heard many guys complaining about going to sleep hungry. Less money to spend in the canteen, along with the poor quality and quantity of food serviced in kitchen, has led to short tempers with violence erupting from individuals being hungry. This has increased the number of guys being muscled for their canteen or "taxed".

This analysis highlights the relationship between the quality and portions of food, and the institutional climate for violence and other incidents which rose sharply during the Harper-era (OCI, 2012, 2013). To Trevor Bell held in Mission Institution this is "It is truly unconscionable in this day and age that we have reverted back to a time where prisoners are provided with only enough food to barely keep them alive – not healthy, just alive". Hyper A'Hern described the current situation like this:

> I have also thrown up immediately after eating and as of now I eat almost exclusively bread, which consists of approximately 40% to 50% of our daily calorie intake. I do not need to express what this kind of malnutrition practice can do to a human body. We get fatter, while at the same time being malnourished. There are other animals in the animal kingdom that we do this to as well and their back fat makes a great burger taste better.

Given what has been described above, it should come as no surprise that for many prisoners there was widespread agreement that food in prison was among the "highest priority" (Simon Chow held in Mission Institution). The proposals that we received from prisoners with respect to food services are simple: "The central feeding system must stop. Prisoners are human beings and should be treated as such" (T.B. held in Port-Cartier Institution). Trevor Bell, held in Mission Institution, echoed this sentiment with his proposal for "an immediate review of this entire program needs to be undertaken with a projected cancellation and reversion to the prior model of individual institutional food provision".

Prisoner Pay and Purchasing

Another concern that was high on the list of priorities for prisoners was their pay for the work that they do in the institution that contributes to the operation and maintenance of the penitentiary. By charging prisoner's additional room and board, along with the cost of administering the telephone system, when they already have to pay for the calls themselves, prisoners have seen their meagre pay reduced by 30% in recent years. It should be noted that the most a prisoner can make in a single day is $6.90 and that the incentive payments that prisoners previously received for their productive labour at CORCAN have also been eliminated (Comack *et al.*, 2015; Shook, 2015).

It is important to consider the prisoner pay issue as it relates to their ability to maintain contact with their family members and also to take care of other basic needs that are not met by the institution, notwithstanding the supplementation of their diets due to the poor quality and quantity of food. Trevor Bell held in Mission Institution draws this connection by reminding readers of the following:

> CSC's mandate is to support our rehabilitation and reintegration into the community. That is simply not possible when an individual now has to choose between calling his community support network, buying deodorant, sending a card to his daughter or going hungry in the evening hours for two weeks.

Often times the public is misinformed of the degree to which prisoners are responsible for the costs of meeting their own needs in federal penitentiaries. In fact, their ability to make purchases for basic goods have been made all the more onerous with the introduction of a new purchasing policy brought about as another cost-saving measure (Comack *et al.*, 2015; Shook, 2015). Prisoners like Joe Convict held in Mountain Institution interpret the installation of a one company monopoly as an act of bad-faith on the part of the government, noting "This new privatized purchasing system is based on shear greed and price gouging of one of the poorest demographic in Canadian society".

As can be seen from the above, the pay issue cannot be interpreted as being independent from other issues that prisoners face while incarcerated such as interpersonal violence, thwarted reintegration efforts and barriers to family contact. It is for this reason, perhaps, that almost every response that we received from prisoners made reference to the pay issue either directly or indirectly by mentioning its impact on their lives. One prisoner who responded to our callout reminded us that "It will cost me five cents a page to print this letter and a dollar for the stamp" (Anonymous Prisoner 8 held in Beaver Creek Institution). With the new policy of charging prisoners additional room and board, even at the highest rate of pay available, after deductions, his ten page submission to us actually cost him two days pay for institutional work.

Once again prisoner's calls for change are reasonable: "restore prisoner work pay to where it was before" (Salomonie Jaw held in Beaver Creek Institution). Given that prisoners have not received an increase in wages since the 1980s and the cost of meeting their most basic needs have only ballooned, it would not be unfair for them to also ask for a wage increase (OCI, 2015). Yet the majority of prisoners who wrote to us were simply asking for enough to afford their necessities and maintain contact with their loved ones. The following proposal from Anonymous Prisoner 19 at Drumheller Institution is instructive: "We need better support for our loved ones while we are incarcerated, such as family programs. We need better support for mothers and family that find themselves suddenly alone when we are incarcerated so that they do not have only welfare to get by". Salomonie Jaw held in Beaver Creek Institution echoes this request by simply asking that CSC: "Assist our families and loved ones to visit us, providing an escort so that they will be safe and not get lost during travels".

Old Age Security

The federal penitentiary population is aging, with approximately one in four prisoners considered to be "seniors" aged 50 and older (OCI, 2015). This is in part due to the large number of prisoners – again, one in four – serving indeterminate or life sentences, as well as the increasing number of prisoners sentenced to MMPs that impact those entering the penal system later in life (OCI, 2015; Eliot and Glynes, 2016). This means that the removal of Old Age Security for prisoners by the Harper government has impacted a large proportion of the federal penitentiary population in a negative way:

> Even though a person may have been a Canadian born citizen who worked their entire life and paid their taxes, they are now denied the pension funds. I have seen many fellows, whose wives were dependent upon the income to maintain a roof over their head and food on their table, no longer being able to contribute to their family's well-being. They are also no longer able to afford their prescription drugs due to the high cost of same. They have, in some cases, lost their homes and ended-up either on welfare or eating at a soup kitchen post-release. With no funds to establish themselves properly into society, what are their prospects of success and what will be the impact upon their communities?
> – Anonymous Prisoner 9 held in Beaver Creek Institution.

There is a strong sense of injustice amongst prisoners who have been dependent upon the funds from Old Age Security to survive on the inside and to support loved ones on the outside. Without this source of income, it is difficult for prisoners to purchase necessities while imprisoned, particularly when they are unable to work institutional jobs. An example of a necessity, for some, would be adult diapers which are no longer provided free of cost, but are instead available for purchase in the catalogue (OCI, 2016). Responses from prisoners also mentioned that the idea of release back to the community scared them, as they no longer had access to funds from OAS to help with their reintegration: "They tell us that we can get our pension back when we get released, but that means those lucky enough to get released, get released with nothing. We have absolutely no way to save anything for anything, let alone release." (David Threinen held in Dorchester Institution). According to their responses, the solution to this problem is evident – reinstate OAS for prisoners.

Education and Vocational Training
The fact that education and vocational training can have a dramatic impact upon the lives of those who have been criminalized and now find

themselves within the confines of a penitentiary was also not lost on the prisoners who contacted us. As Anonymous Prisoner 12 held in Beaver Creek Institution notes, "Education and gaining marketable skills are the hallmarks of reduced recidivism". However, as his experience showed, "federal prisoners have little to no access to the Internet and as a result cannot access online post-secondary education programs". While CSC promotes its delivery of interventions that target dynamic risk factors in its stated pursuit of rehabilitation, prisoners themselves recognize this as being only half the battle. Anonymous Prisoner 17 held in Drumheller Institution described this imbalance, echoed by other prisoners who wrote to us, with the following:

> I believe that there needs to be a balance between programs to help one become an emotionally balanced person and educational opportunities to become employable. Over the years, CSC's focus seems to be to fix the individual (i.e. their emotional or addictions issues) to the detriment of training for work that will allow them to survive upon release.

To him and other prisoners "this makes no sense" because, in his words, "I can control my emotions, but if I cannot put food on the table, I am put in a position where I may need to turn back to crime to put food on the table, but I will be polite about it!" There seemed to be a particular emphasis placed upon the fact that there is a "*lack of educational upgrade opportunities beyond high school equivalence*" and prisoners were looking for more meaningful engagement (Anonymous Prisoner 20 held in Mission Institution). While prisoners who wrote to us were aware of the financial pressures and fears of public perception which led to the elimination of the post-secondary education program in 1993, some described even their "attempts at self-education through prisoner paid for correspondence courses are met with extreme administrative red tape and an all-around lack of support" (P.R. held in Mission Institution).

Very much related to prisoner's access to education and vocational training is their access to technology, and in particular computers. Prisoners frequently described the limited avenues available to them to better themselves in this domain. A.C.C.L. held in Beaver Creek Institution who is serving a life sentence reminds us that "Computers are a big part of the outside world and people like myself who have been in since the 1990s do not have the experience with email, texts and so on. Computers are used in all places for everything and not knowing anything about them puts us Lifers at a great disadvantage". He, along with several other prisoners, recommend that CSC revisit their policies around access to technology so that they might better prepare themselves for life in the community.

Given the current state of affairs, many prisoners liken their time in the penitentiary to being warehoused. Without opportunities to better themselves, many prisoners feel as though their being incarcerated is an expensive waste of time. Anonymous at Beaver Creek Institution makes this point noting, "there is such a wasted opportunity for educational training, including post-secondary trades. If offered in a more expansive way, it would make all the difference in the world". To make this difference, some prisoners suggested that penitentiaries be supplanted with "holistic rehabilitation centres, rather than penitentiaries. These centres would revolve around addiction (i.e., alcohol, drugs, psychological, etc.) and preparing prisoners through education and vocational training to reintegrate into society" (1417 held in Riverbend Institution).

Case Management / CSC Staff Culture
As noted earlier in this paper, CSC made sweeping changes to its case management policy framework (CSC, 2014). These changes, along with a general trend towards a culture of harsh punitiveness found throughout the entire system, have necessarily resulted in a climate where the authority granted to parole officers and other decision-makers in the system has effectively become a form of extra-judicial punishment. One prisoner described his experience with case management as one where they "outright lie, exaggerate, and tailor documents to reflect the narrowest scope and most damning impressions of the prisoner. They have become very skilled in creative writing and delaying tactics – 'sluffing us off'" (Mark Simpson held in Kent Institution). Many authors, in fact, described a poor relationship with their case management team which is not surprising when, as Trevor Bell held in Mission Institution observes:

> I have had as many as four different parole officers within a twelve-month period. How is a prisoner supposed to build a working relationship, address their dynamic risk factors and move forward within the system when they are seeing a new face every other week?

Some prisoners also had concerns about "inaccurate information" being placed on one's file. This could affect important correctional decisions such as one's security classification or whether one is listed as being a member of a security threat group. Given the fact that many prisoners reported an inability to access legal services, challenging inaccurate information on one's file can sometimes be an impossibility as prisoners described the internal grievance system as being broken.

Prisoners also described to us a pattern of "risk averse... decision-making" on the part of Institutional Parole Officers and other decision makers in the system (Anonymous Prisoner 8 held in Beaver Creek Institution). A group of Anonymous Prisoners held in Mission Institution described to us an experience of having "little case management outside of timelines" and being in receipt of correctional plans that "lack any reality and teeth in that they act more as a record of ineffective programs", rather than a plan to "move forward into a more productive lifestyle as a contributing member of society, which requires updated programs with accurate facts". Their experience of case-management was depicted as one with "few opportunities to apply goal setting or model the behaviours using the very skills taught in our Integrated Correctional Program Model (ICPM) programs".

Not only have prisoners become especially attuned to the implications of such changes to the CSC Case Management Policy Framework and how this may affect decision-making, but they have become acutely aware of the way that 'law and order' attitudes have become commonplace throughout the entire system. 1417 held in Riverbend Institution captures this with the following statement: "It is not only the confinement, it is the treatment. Guards have a master-slave view of their position. As such their own psyche can make for adversarial conditions". Joe Convict held in Mountain Institution describes this change in attitude as a product of "reverting back to a system of punitive measures, rather than actually encouraging meaningful rehabilitation". He tells us that "One product is that many staff express views on a daily basis that are either demeaning or completely dismissive of pain and suffering" and calls for "significant independent oversight", possibly through the "appointment of a true ombudsman only answerable directly to Parliament and not to the government of the day via the Minister of Public Safety".

Moving forward, prisoners' expectations from their captors are not unrealistic – they simply ask what the system is asking of them, which is to be held accountable for their actions. As Ronald Small held in Mission

Institution reminds us: "these people signed *the Declaration* agreeing to undertake and maintain, in the course of their employment, the standards of professionalism and integrity that are therein set forth". Prisoners' calls for professionalism and integrity in corrections are fair requests.

Parole and Conditional Release Conditions

Parole was a common issue identified by prisoners. The two main changes that prisoners mentioned in their letters were the removal of the accelerated parole review by the Harper government and the extension of the amount of time that Lifers have to wait after being denied parole before applying again, which is now five years.

Anonymous Prisoner 1 held in Grand Valley Institution argues that Accelerated Parole Review (APR) was "a very important law and policy that must be in place to allow certain first-time federal prisoners to re-enter society at one-sixth of their sentences so that they can avoid the damage of incarceration, which undermines community safety". In reference to the change in the eligibility period which an individual must wait before re-applying for parole, Alan Beaulieu of Stony Mountain Institution recognises that this policy shift importunately affects those serving longer sentences and more particularly, Lifers. Under the previous policy, upon reaching their eligibility date for a parole review, if a prisoner was denied, they could re-apply in two years, yet as he describes, under the current policy "you can be warehoused for years. The institutional parole officers often fail to review and update Lifer files for parole review".

Effectively, for many prisoners the above-noted changes in policy have become a *de facto* lengthening of the portion of their sentences they serve behind bars. These punitive measures also coincided with other changes that restricted prisoners' access to the community in a timely fashion, such as those placed upon access to Unescorted Temporary Absences and Escorted Temporary Absences. For many prisoners, these passes typically serve as stepping stones towards release and offer them an opportunity to experience life in the community, while also building credibility with their case management teams in advance of their parole hearings. Many prisoners who wrote to us now described being caught in a sort of "catch-22" (Anonymous Prisoner 12 held in Beaver Creek Institution). A.C.C.L of Beaver Creek Institution speaks to this dilemma: "I am essentially being barred opportunities to prepare myself for release and the way the system is setup for Lifers, it seems that many of us that can safely re-enter the community will be incarcerated beyond their full parole eligibility dates".

In terms of how prisoners are experiencing these changes to parole, they have noticed that they are often persuaded to postpone their parole hearings to a later date by their parole officers. J.D. held in Mission Institution observes:

> I have found that in my case, and in most of the prisoners that talk to me about their case, we are being persuaded and pushed to waive our right to apply for parole when we are eligible. I have been told things by IPOs such as "I will not support you for parole unless you wait it out", "I am 99.9% sure that you will not get parole if you do not waive or postpone your application for parole", and "why are you in such a rush to get out of prison?", at which point I had been in prison for over half of my sentence.

With regards to parole conditions, many prisoners have stated in their contributions that they are often set up to fail with restrictive conditions that are not always related to the offences that they originally committed. For example, William Allan Beaulieu held in Stony Mountain Institution explains: "The various minor parole breaches could be for drinking a bottle of beer, being late for curfew or talking to anyone with some type of conviction or accusation. This social behavior is the norm in a free and democratic society".

Among the solutions to address the issues noted above was to reinstate APR for first-time, non-violent prisoners, which would also ease penitentiary crowding. It was also recommended that "one's [parole] conditions can only include restrictions that are directly related to the offense. For example, if alcohol was not attributed as a cause of an offence then why put a restriction on a parolee that they cannot consume alcohol?" (1417, Riverbend Institution). While others suggested that there should be "alternatives to imprisonment for parole violations when the law is not broken" (Rachel Fayter and Sherry Payne held in Grand Valley Institution). It is argued by prisoners that a more liberal approach towards conditional release and restraint in the use of incarceration as a remedy to minor violations of parole would "facilitate rehabilitation by reducing time spent incarcerated and cutting down on the more than $100,000 per year that it takes to house each one of us".

Pardons

With sweeping changes made to the eligibility and wait times for which a person in conflict with the law can receive a pardon (see Doob and Webster, 2016), several responses from prisoners indicated the need to reverse reforms enacted under the previous government. Under the old law, individuals seeking to apply for pardon were required to wait three years following warrant expiry of their conviction and sentence for a summary offence and five years following their conviction for an indictable offence (ibid). While in power, the Conservatives nearly doubled these wait times and made certain categories of the criminalized un-pardonable, while at the same time imposing heavy handed user fees of $631 that make even submitting an application for a pardon unfeasible for some (ibid).

Hyper A'Hern, who is completed an undergraduate degree and was accepted into medical school prior to his offence, notes the impact of not being able to apply for a pardon:

> It was originally intended to allow people to not be defined by a single action and provide them with an incentive to work towards making amends by becoming a law-abiding citizen who contributes to society. Today's system is a mockery of those once proud ideals as the Harper government continually tore it apart so that it is nearly impossible to obtain. Many of the criminalized are no longer even potential candidates for a pardon and even if they are, the amount of time it takes to obtain a formal pardon would usually put one well into their golden years. In my situation, I would like to reiterate that not only did I once have grand dreams, but I am not a candidate for pardon. I have a schedule 1 offence with violence and so I am immediately precluded from a candidate position to obtain a pardon. This means that for the rest of my life, the best I can hope to achieve is mediocrity. Where is my incentive to contribute to society? Where is my incentive to not commit an offence again? Do we want a society where an individual is defined by a single action and their only deterrence for not committing harm is prison?

It was also recognised by some prisoners that with changes in technology, accessing information about an individual's past is often only a click away. 1417 held in Riverbend Institution recognised that "in today's world any criminal record against someone will live on forever. There is no 'pulling up stakes and restarting' somewhere else as you could have in the pre-internet age". He advocates "that on a first offence that does not include violence and is punished with a sentence of less than five years that no record can be accessed by the media once the warrant has been completed".

Overall, the changes to pardon laws in Canada, described by Hyper A'Hern as "spiteful in nature" and contrary to the "ideals of the Canadian Values", require reform. The path forward that he offers is that the federal government and Canadians "to believe in the redemption of your fellow citizens, and support their efforts to change and become a productive member of their communities". Undertaking a serious examination of the changes brought about by the last government and adjusting the current policy in a manner that is supportive of such efforts seems to be a sensible course of action to take.

CONCLUSION

At the outset of this *Response*, we expressed optimism that perhaps Prime Minister Trudeau's professed commitment to "sunny ways" and mandated review of the penal system could lead to meaningful change – change that is desperately needed to calm the storm that has been raging in CSC facilities during the past decade. Recognizing that any attempt at meaningful change behind the walls ought to involve the voices of prisoners who have been weathering this storm and experienced recent penal reforms first hand, we are optimistic that the courageous and eloquent contributions will be received by the federal government as a reasonable forecast for change.

Yet our optimism, like the prisoners who wrote to us, is cautious. Many prisoners, in their letters to us, indicated that they had previously received many letters similar to ours asking for input and saying that their feedback could lead to change. There seemed to be a feeling of despair, as their previous interventions did not lead to the positive changes that they had wished to see. As stated by Daniel W. Threinen, who is chairman of a seniors group at Dorchester Penitentiary:

> What really perturbs me about initiatives such as this collection is that a lot is said, but very little seems to come of it. You can publish in whatever journal you wish, but politicians do not read journals. I personally have been in this penitentiary system for 40 plus years without release and have engaged in

several "studies" of various types concerning incarceration. I have yet to see
any of them bare any fruit. But having said that and being the optimist that I
am, I must go by the adage, "nothing ventured, nothing gained".

Forging beyond his pessimism, he nonetheless took the time and risk to submit
a contribution to this endeavour. It was not lost to us or the prisoners who
wrote to us that despite their *Charter* protected right to freedom of thought,
belief, opinion and expression, participating in this exercise could result
in retaliation. In fact, many of the prisoners who wrote to us, both opened
and closed their letters with expressions that reveal the resiliency of their
spirits and a certain optimism in spite of the challenges that they have faced
and will continue to face if the government does not act now to address the
issues they raised. A.C.C.L. from Beaver Creek Institution captured this with
his statement that: "I believe people can change. I believe in rehabilitation
and that people are genuinely good. Even as I am surrounded by negativity,
constantly pounded, and put down by CSC, I have to believe in what people
on the outside and parolees tell me when they say to hang in there, that when
I am out things will be different and people are good".

In reflecting upon this project, it should also be recognized that many
of the prisoners who wrote to us also began their letters with expressions
of accountability for the harms which have brought them to prison in the
first place, often putting the burden of responsibility squarely on their own
shoulders without reference to the structural factors that have invariably
impacted their lives. One prisoner opened his letter to us with the inculpatory
statement "To be very clear, my story is not about me decrying the fact I am in
prison. I am very guilty and justifiably sentenced as a 'dangerous offender'".

On the whole, the responses that we received from prisoners comprise
a comprehensive account of the impacts of the punishment agenda of
2006-2015, including a pragmatic forecast for change moving forward.
As facilitators of this collection, we do not claim or endorse every
recommendation for change as our own, nor unreflexively accept that every
account of penitentiary life found within the margins of these pages can be
taken as the impermeable testimony of life behind the wall, as is the case of
all accounts of penality, whether produced by captives, captors, academics,
the media or anyone else. With this said, that certain issues were repeatedly
identified by federal prisoners housed in penitentiaries in all of CSC's five
operational regions should speak to the credibility of their words. The voice

of one person raising an issue can be easily dismissed, but when several people are bringing forward similar concerns engaging in denial ought to be viewed as disingenuous.

It is our hope that our readers, and in particular Prime Minister Justin Trudeau and his Minister of Justice and Attorney General of Canada Jody Wilson-Raybould who was mandated to review criminal justice laws, policies, and practices enacted during the 2006-2015 period under the previous government, will take seriously the voices of prisoners. It is vital that they seriously consider and act upon reasonable calls for change moving forward in numerous areas.

Moreover, it is our hope that the all too often marginalized voices of women, Indigenous, Black, LGBTQ, and elderly prisoners will also be heard, and that their concerns will be meaningfully addressed. It is our belief that despite the fact that many of the challenges which prisoners face in the Canadian carceral state transcend the Harper-era, repealing the laws, policies, and practices introduced from 2006 to 2015 would be a "sunny way" to start the work needed to diminish this country's reliance on incarceration and working towards justice that heals wounds, instead of creating new ones.

REFERENCES

Arbel, Efrat (2015) "Contesting Unmodulated Deprivation: Sauvé v Canada and the Normative Limits of Punishment", *Canadian Journal of Human Rights*, 4(1): 121-141.

Comack, Elizabeth, Cara Fabre, and Shanise Burgher (2015) *The Impact of the Harper Government's "Tough on Crime" Strategy: Hearing from Frontline Workers*, Winnipeg: Canadian Center for Policy Alternatives.

Cook, Alana N. and Ronald Roesch (2012) "'Tough on Crime' Reforms: What Psychology Has to Say About the Recent and Proposed Justice Policy in Canada", *Canadian Psychology*, 53(3): 217-219.

Correctional Service Canada (2016) *Report on Plans and Priorities 2015-2016*, Ottawa.

Correctional Service Canada (2015) *Report on Plans and Priorities 2014-2015*, Ottawa.

Correctional Service Canada (2014) *Report on Plans and Priorities 2013-2014*, Ottawa.

Correctional Service Canada (2013) *Report on Plans and Priorities 2012-2013*, Ottawa.

Correctional Service Canada (2012) *Report on Plans and Priorities 2011-2012*, Ottawa.

Chricton, Hayley and Rose Ricciardelli (2016) "Shifting Grounds: Experiences of Canadian Correctional Officers", *Criminal Justice Review*, 4(1): 427-445.

Doob, Anthony N. and Cheryl M. Webster (2016) "Weathering the Storm? Testing Long-Standing Canadian Sentencing in the Twenty-First Century", *Crime and Justice*, 45(1): 359-418.

Doob Anthony N. and Cheryl M. Webster (2006) "Countering Punitiveness: Understanding Stability in Canada's Imprisonment Rate", *Law & Society Review*, 40(2): 325-368.

Elliot, Kari G. and Kyle Coady (2016) *Mandatory Minimum Penalties in Canada: Analysis and Annotated Bibliography*, Ottawa: Department of Justice.

Fine, Sean (2015) "Prisoner Launches Class-Action Suit Over Use of Solitary Confinement", *Globe and Mail* – July 17.

Fournier-Ruggles, Lynn (2011) "The Cost of Getting Tough on Crime: Isn't Prevention the Policy Answer?", *The Journal of Public Policy, Administration and Law*, 2(1): 9-28.

Harris, Kathleen (2016) "Prison Watchdog Sees Sharp Decline in Use of Solitary Confinement", *CBC News* – March 14.

Jackson, Michael. (2015) "Reflections on 40 Years of Advocacy to End the Isolation of Canadian Prisoners", *Canadian Journal of Human Rights*, 4(1): 57-87.

Jackson, Michael (1983) *Prisoners of Isolation: Solitary Confinement in Canada*, Toronto: University of Toronto Press.

Jackson, Michael and Graham Stewart (2009) *A Flawed Compass: A Human Rights Analysis of the Roadmap to Strengthening Public Safety.*

Kerr, Lisa C. (2015) "The Origins of Unlawful Prison Policies", *Canadian Journal of Human Rights*, 4(1): 89-119.

Martel, Joane, Renée Brassard and Mylène Jacoud (2011) "When Two Worlds Collide: Aboriginal Risk Management in Canadian Corrections", *British Journal of Criminology*, 51(2): 235-255.

McElligott, Greg (2009) "The Political Economy of Corrections: Is Canada Ready for Penal Mass Production?", *81st Annual Conference of the Canadian Political Science Association, May.*

Monchalin, Lisa (2016) *The Colonial Problem: An Indigenous Perspective on Crime and Injustice in Canada*, Toronto: University of Toronto Press.

Monaghan, Jeffrey (2014) "Security Traps and Discourses of Radicalization: Mapping the Surveillance of Muslims in Canada", *Surveillance and Society*, 12(4): 485-501.

O'Connor, Joe (2015) "'Sunny ways my friends, sunny ways': Lessons of Wilfrid Laurier Not Lost on Trudeau, 120 years later", *National Post* – October 20.

Office of the Correctional Investigator (2015) *Administrative Segregation in Federal Corrections: 10 year trends*, Ottawa.

Office of the Correctional Investigator (2016) *Annual Report of the Office of the Correctional Investigator 2015-2016*, Ottawa.

Office of the Correctional Investigator (2015) *Annual Report of the Office of the Correctional Investigator 2014-2015*, Ottawa.

Office of the Correctional Investigator (2014) *Annual Report of the Office of the Correctional Investigator 2013-2014*, Ottawa.

Office of the Correctional Investigator. (2013) *Annual Report of the Office of the Correctional Investigator 2012-2013*, Ottawa.

Office of the Correctional Investigator. (2012) *Annual Report of the Office of the Correctional Investigator 2011-2012*, Ottawa.

Paquin-Marseille, Lysiane, Brian A. Grant and Steven Michel (2012) *Review of the Prison Crowding and Double-Bunking Literature*, Ottawa: Correctional Service Canada.

Parkes, Debra (2015) "Ending the Isolation: An Introduction to the Special Volume on Human Rights and Solitary Confinement", *Canadian Journal of Human Rights*, 4(1): vii-xiii.

Parkes, Debra (2014) "The Punishment Agenda in the Courts", *Supreme Court Review*, 67(2d): 589-615.

Piché, Justin (2015) "Playing the "Treasury Card" to Contest Prison Expansion: Lessons from a Public Criminology Campaign", *Social Justice*, 41(3): 145-167.

Piché, Justin and Karine Major (2015) "Prisoner Writing in/on Solitary Confinement: Contributions from the Journal of Prisoners on Prisons, 1988-2013", *Canadian Journal of Human Rights*, 4(1): 1-33.

Reitano, Julie (2016) *Admissions to Adult Correctional Services in Canada, 2015-2016*, Ottawa: Statistics Canada.

Ricciardelli, Rose, Hayley Chricton and Lisa Adams (2014) "Stuck: Conditions of Canadian Confinement", *Punishment and Incarceration: A Global Perspective*, 19: 95-120.

Sampson, Robert, Serge Glascon, Ian Glen, Clarence Louis, and Sharon Rosenfeldt (2007) *A Roadmap to Strengthening Public Safety*, Ottawa: Minister of Public Works and Government Services.

Shook, Jarrod (2015) "Incentive to Scrutinise", *Journal of Prisoners on Prisons*, 24(1): 52-54.

Shook, Jarrod (2013) "Debunking Double Bunking in the Correctional Service of Canada: A Critical Qualitative Account", *Journal of Prisoners on Prisons*, 22(1): 64-67.

Syles, Gresham M. (2007[1958]) *The Society of Captives: A Study of a Maximum Security Prison*, Princeton: Princeton University Press.

Tonry, Michael (2013) ""Nothing" Works: Sentencing "Reform" in Canada and the United States", *Canadian Journal of Criminology and Criminal Justice*, 55(4): 465-479.

Trudeau, Justin (2015) *Minister of Justice and Attorney General of Canada Mandate Letter*, Ottawa: Office of the Prime Minister of Canada.

Union of Canadian Correctional Officers (2011) *A Critical Review of the Practice of Double Bunking Within Corrections: The Implications on Staff, Inmates, Correctional Facilities and the Public*.

Webster, Cheryl M. and Anthony N. Doob (2015) "US Punitiveness 'Canadian Style'? Cultural Values and Canadian Punishment Policy", *Punishment & Society*, 17(3): 299-321.

Zinger, Ivan (2016) "Human Rights and Federal Corrections: A Commentary on a Decade of Tough on Crime Policies in Canada", *Canadian Journal of Criminology and Criminal Justice*, 58(4): 609-627.

Journal of Prisoners on Prisons
c/o Justin Piché, PhD
Department of Criminology
University of Ottawa
Ottawa, Ontario, Canada
K1N 6N5

1 March 2017

RE: Call for input and/or submissions

Dear Inmate Committee Chairman:

Upon being elected, Prime Minister Justin Trudeau mandated his Minister of Justice and Attorney General of Canada Jody Wilson-Raybould to review criminal justice laws, policies, and practices enacted during the 2006-2015 period under the previous government. We believe that part of this process should involve prisoners who have experienced recent penal reforms first-hand to assess what have been their impact on the criminalized and what changes are needed going forward.

To this end, we are writing you to request your observations on what has changed in the prisons where you have served time during the last decade as part of the Harper government's "punishment agenda". We would like to know not just what you think about those changes and how they have impacted your lives, but also what you would like to see moving forward in terms of your main priorities for change and the types of social action those outside of prison walls could engage in to help address the challenges that presently characterize life in a federal penitentiary. It would be appreciated if you could provide via correspondence a list of the top 10 issues that you see as being priorities. For those in "multi-level" prisons, we would also welcome responses from individuals in settings like segregation or other areas of the prison where prisoners may not have the opportunity for "normal association". We understand that an individual's experience of incarceration may differ based upon their location within the prison.

This project is being led by Dr. Justin Piché (a criminologist at the University of Ottawa), Jarrod Shook (a former federal prisoner and now student studying criminology) and Bridget McInnis (a social work and criminology student about to enter law school). Together we would like to compile your responses and publish them in an upcoming issue of the *Journal of Prisoners on Prisons* (www.jpp.org), an academic peer-reviewed journal that privileges the voices of those with lived experience relating to being criminalized and punished. Our goal is to offer you a platform to inform debates about Canadian penal policies and practices.

We sincerely believe that what you know to be true about federal prison life has value and we would like to see your knowledge reflected in the government's review of the criminal justice system. Please respond back to us by 30 March 2017 or shortly thereafter so that we may begin incorporating your experiences into our analysis. If you need any resources that may assist in this process or have any questions regarding the project or the *Journal of Prisoners on Prisons*, please do not hesitate to get in touch with us. We stand together with you in solidarity.

Sincerely,

Justin Piché, PhD
Bridget McInnis
Jarrod Shook

PRISONERS' STRUGGLES

Prisoners' Legal Services on Segregation
Simon Cheung

There is an abundance of horror stories about the practice of solitary confinement, and plenty of voices calling for its end as a cruel and counter-rehabilitative practice. However, there have also been scant few full-scale proposals detailing exactly how solitary confinement could be eliminated in Canada. In an effort to change this, on 28 November 2016 Prisoners' Legal Services (PLS) released *Solitary: A Case for Abolition* – a 112-page report that offers a variety of solutions supported by historical research, academic articles and precedents from other jurisdictions – to address the issues currently responded to using solitary confinement.

The primary purpose of the report is to initiate discussions aimed at finally ending solitary confinement, also known as segregation and separate confinement in the Canadian federal and British Columbian prison systems respectively. The scale and complexity of such a process is not lost on PLS. We understand the process will likely take years of reform. However, *Solitary: A Case for Abolition* contains a comprehensive collection of current research and recommendations that, if implemented, could form a firm foundation for future dialogue in working committees or meetings between correctional organizations and stakeholders like PLS.

PLS is a legal clinic located in Burnaby, British Columbia that started off as a branch office of the BC Legal Services Society (BC legal aid) in 1980 and continued as a Legal Services Society-funded non-profit in 2002. Executive Director Jennifer Metcalfe oversees a small team of legal advocates and administrative staff who strive to further the organization's mandate of protecting British Columbian prisoners' liberty rights as enshrined under section seven of the *Canadian Charter of Rights and Freedoms*. Under this section, individuals in Canada are protected from government-imposed deprivation of their right to life, liberty and security of the person except in accordance with the principles of fundamental justice.

Complaints regarding solitary confinement – defined by the United Nations as "the confinement of prisoners for 22 hours or more a day without meaningful human contact" – from prisoners in both federal and provincial institutions across BC are commonly raised at PLS. On a day-to-day basis, PLS provides a range of support for clients in such circumstances: summary advice over one of our six phone lines; written advocacy; and in-person representation by advocates and lawyers. However, *Solitary: A Case for Abolition* represents a longer-term ambition of our organization. It is intended to be, in essence, a blueprint for the abolition of solitary confinement.

The United Nations considers the use of solitary confinement on prisoners with mental disabilities or for anyone for more than 15 days to constitute torture or cruel treatment. For this reason, the *United Nations Standard Minimum Rules for the Treatment of Prisoners* (the *Mandela Rules*) prohibit the use of solitary confinement for those with mental or physical disabilities that would be exacerbated by its use, and limits its use for other prisoners to 15 days.[1]

In order to facilitate the abolition of solitary confinement, *Solitary: A Case for Abolition* proposes a multi-faceted alternative system focused on addressing the therapeutic needs of prisoners via the implementation of a trauma-informed approach, dynamic security techniques and de-escalation practices. Correctional organizations are encouraged, for example, to establish specialized mental health units in greater numbers than currently exist, as both the federal and BC status quo are not adequate to the task of providing psychological treatment to prisoners who require it. These resources would, the report argues, largely prevent the problematic behaviours that solitary confinement not only fails to address, but in many cases aggravates and escalates.

On this point, *Solitary: A Case for Abolition* references a 2010 report by Dr. Margo Rivera concerning the Correctional Service Canada's treatment of prisoners deemed to be mentally ill. In it, she found that dismissive or confrontational responses from staff to prisoners' negative behaviour or complaints only serve to foster contentious relationships between captors and captives, which often leads to an escalation in conflict.[2] Dr. Rivera recommended that segregation staff selection, training, supervision and evaluation be reviewed and enhanced, and encouraged the staffing of a stable, high calibre team in segregation units trained in conflict-diffusion skills and the use of professional, respectful, encouraging, and empowering communication with prisoners.[3]

The report also draws on research such as the work done by Niki Miller and Lisa Najavits, who argued that a trauma-informed approach – where correctional staff are familiar with and sensitive to trauma and its symptoms, and are thus better prepared to compassionately handle its common responses and reactions from prisoners – combined with interventions designed to address trauma symptoms, would reduce both harm to prisoners and staff, as well as decrease correctional security costs.[4] It seems clear that such a system would also result in less reliance on solitary confinement in response to behavioural issues.

As well, *Solitary: A Case for Abolition* canvasses case studies from Canada, the United States and the United Kingdom to not only identify common problems, but find success stories where jurisdictions have drastically reduced their use of solitary confinement and initiated innovative mental health programs for prisoners.

The State of Colorado and its Department of Corrections, for instance, have been lauded for their progressive legislation and policy that places strict limits on their use of solitary confinement, as well as specifically directing resources to prison mental health services and requiring regular, public reporting of data from their solitary confinement practices. Notably, the state not only banned the use of solitary confinement for those with serious mental illnesses, but expanded the definition of "serious mental illness" to include, regardless of diagnosis, any prisoner indicating a high level of mental health needs demonstrating significant functional impairment within the correctional environment. The combined effect of these measures reduced Colorado's segregated prison population from 1,500 in August 2011 to 177 in September 2015.

Even with such preventative measures, however, PLS recognizes that there may be occasions when prisoners require immediate separation from the open prison population. *Solitary: A Case for Abolition* advocates for limiting cell lock up to a few hours within one day, while ensuring that prisoners who are separated from other prisoners are provided sufficient daily meaningful human contact to ensure that their mental health is not impacted by isolation. This would also require greater external oversight of correctional institutions' use of population management practices and mental health supports in general. For guiding principles behind such oversight, the report looks to the 1996 Arbour Report, the 1997 Task Force on Administrative segregation, various reports of the Correctional Investigator of Canada, the 2016 Ombudsman of Ontario report *Segregation: Not an Isolated Problem*, to the Ontario Ministry of Community Safety and Correctional Services' review of segregation policies, and the 2015 *Mandela Rules*.

Solitary: A Case for Abolition draws on testimonies from prisoners who have experienced derelict conditions in solitary confinement to reinforce the importance of strictly limiting its use. Prisoners regularly contact PLS reporting segregation cells spackled with biohazards like urine, feces and blood. They describe excessive uses of force by segregation staff and guards who shut off water, lights and power to cells as punishment to prisoners. This is in addition to the cruel practice of isolating prisoners in a cell for 23 hours or more with little to no human interaction.

Canada has already felt the consequences of insufficient action to curb such inhumane treatment. On 19 October 12007, Ashley Smith died from self-strangulation while correctional officers watched after being segregated for 11 months despite her severe mental illness. Her death was later ruled a homicide by an Ontario coroner. Since then, prisoners like Edward Snowshoe, Christopher Roy, Terry Baker and others all tragically ended their own lives after segregation and their resulting compromised mental health.

Solitary: A Case for Abolition contains 39 total recommendations aimed at a more evidence-based, treatment-oriented and security-conscious correctional system. The most ambitious involve the complete prohibition of solitary confinement in Canada. PLS recommends the following legislative changes:

- The prohibition of solitary confinement in legislation requiring that, if it is absolutely necessary, solitary confinement (or short-term cell lockup) only be used for as short a period of time as necessary within one day, and requiring sufficient meaningful human contact each day; and
- The complete prohibition of solitary confinement on prisoners with mental disabilities and youth under the age of 21.

If the practice of solitary confinement continues, PLS recommends the following legislative changes:

- Enforcement of prisoners' statutory right to procedural fairness, including the right to an oral hearing of the evidence, legal representation of the prisoner's choice, and binding independent adjudication of segregation or separate confinement placements;
- Authority given to independent adjudicators to remove prisoners from segregation or separate confinement, order access to programs

or privileges, and recommend investigations and disciplinary proceedings against correctional staff who have violated law and policy;

- Time limits of 15 days' continuous placement, with an annual limit of 30 days; and
- External oversight of solitary placements to ensure that prisoners are not isolated, are provided opportunities to keep their minds productively occupied and have adequate levels of meaningful human contact each day.

PLS recommends the following general practices for housing prisoners in solitary confinement:

- Segregated prisoners should have as much human contact as possible with people from outside the institution, as well as with programming, religious and medical staff;
- Small groups of prisoners should be allowed to socialize if there are no serious safety concerns, such as for religious ceremonies, programs or in the yard;
- Access should be provided to counselling and behavioural therapy, programs, school, work and religious or community support;
- Psychological services should be offered to prisoners in segregation or separate confinement in a private area, rather than only through the cell door;
- All segregated prisoners should have access to television and personal effects within one day;
- A complete prohibition on double-bunking in segregation;
- The discipline and removal from vulnerable prisoners of any staff who behave inappropriately in relation to segregated prisoners or who fail to provide segregated prisoners with daily access to showers, telephones, cleaning supplies and a separate hour of daily exercise; and
- The provision of de-escalation training and conflict-diffusion skills as a central part of all correctional officer training, with refresher courses required every three years.

As well, since mental health issues are so commonly linked to institutional decisions to segregated prisoners, PLS recommends the following practices:

- Funding to designate at least half of the beds in each prison as therapeutic living units on an ongoing basis, adequately staffed by appropriate mental health professionals;
- Legislation specifying that the number of specialized therapeutic beds available must be sufficient to meet the mental health needs of a broad and inclusive class of prisoners with mental health needs (including prisoners who, regardless of diagnosis, demonstrate significant functional impairment within the correctional environment);
- That specialized mental health units no longer be considered transitional units, but that prisoners be permitted to stay in these units as long as they are benefiting from a therapeutic environment;
- The provision of additional mental health supports for any prisoners in voluntary segregation or separate confinement due to mental health problems, and offers for placement in units specifically designed for prisoners who have difficulty interacting socially with others, staffed by correctional officers and mental health professionals skilled at encouraging positive social interaction; and
- Guidelines stipulating that health care professionals who work in prisons must not play any role in approving prisoners for solitary confinement, must report to the warden if they consider a prisoner's physical or mental health is at risk by continued solitary confinement, and must report the use of solitary confinement on prisoners with mental disabilities or solitary confinement of more than 15 days to the applicable regulatory College of Physicians, the federal Correctional Investigator or provincial Investigation and Standards Office, and the federal or provincial Minister of Justice.

These and the other recommendations in *Solitary: A Case for Abolition* aim to protect prisoners and correctional staff alike. The adversarial culture that often manifests in Canadian corrections has resulted in preventable harm and, at times, deaths. As well, prisoners are often released who are more familiar with the blunt end of institutional security measures than rehabilitative counseling, and feel embittered against the correctional system – and thus, society as a whole – as a result. PLS proposes a system with the belief that we can do better and implores Canadian corrections start a dialogue toward making these ideals a reality.

ENDNOTES

1. UN General Assembly, United Nations Standard Minimum Rules for the Treatment of Prisoners (the Mandela Rules): note / by the Secretariat, 29 September 2015, A/C.3/70/L.3, [The Mandela Rules]. Online: http:// www.refworld.org/docid/56209cd14.html.
2. Rivera, Margo (2010) *Segregation Is Our Prison Within The Prison: Operational Examination of Long-Term Segregation and Segregation Placements of Inmates with Mental Health Concerns*, Ottawa: Correctional Service Canada, page 65.
3. *Ibid* at pages 65 and 83.
4. Miller, Niki A. and Lisa M. Najavits (2012) "Creating Trauma-informed Correctional Care: A Balance of Goals and Environment", *European Journal of Psychotraumatology*, 3: 10.

CONTACT INFORMATION

Simon Cheung
Legal Advocate
Prisoners' Legal Services
302-7818 6th Street
Burnaby, British Columbia, Canada
V3N 4N8
Telephone: (604) 636-0470
Fax: (604) 636-0480
Email: scheung@pls-bc.ca

Call for Artwork
50ᵗʰ Anniversary of the Department of Criminology at the University of Ottawa

The Department of Criminology at the University of Ottawa was founded in 1968 and has since developed a reputation for interdisciplinary and critical criminological scholarship that advances alternative ways of seeing and responding to criminalized acts and other social harms. This orientation characterizes much of the department's work today despite the growth of managerial and administrative criminologies elsewhere, along with the rise of explicitly exclusionary and punitive state policies and practices with respect to 'crime' and 'security'.

uOttawa
Département de criminologie
Department of Criminology

As part of the 50ᵗʰ anniversary of the Department of Criminology at the University of Ottawa, we invite artists who have experienced imprisonment and others forms of state repression to submit one or more pieces of artwork that make visible the realities of criminalization and other forms of social exclusion. Twenty (20) submissions will then be selected for, and sold at, an art exhibition at the University of Ottawa with all proceeds going to the artists. Non-selected artwork will be returned to the artists by mail.

SUBMISSION GUIDELINES

Please send a short biographical statement, as well as a title for and brief description of your artwork, along with your submissions to the address below. Also include a return address where we can direct all correspondence and send funds from the sale of your artwork (if applicable).

* Artwork: "Breaking the Chains" by Ronnie Goodman (2012) at www.ronniegoodman.com

KEY DATES

1 May 2018 - deadline to submit artwork
1 June 2018 – selection of artwork announced / non-selected artwork returned to artists
10-13 September 2018 – art expo and silent auction at the University of Ottawa
13 September 2018 – art purchasers announced at 50ᵗʰ anniversary conference
1 October 2018 – proceeds from art expo and silent auction sent to authors

FOR MORE INFORMATION PLEASE CONTACT
justin.piche@uottawa.ca (English) and
Sylvie.frigon@uottawa.ca (French)

PLEASE MAIL YOUR SUBMISSIONS TO
CRM Art Expo and Silent Auction
c/o Department of Criminology
University of Ottawa
120 University Private, Room 14002
Ottawa, Ontario, Canada
K1N 6N5

Oeuvres d'art recherchées
50ᵉ anniversaire du département de criminologie de l'Université d'Ottawa

Le Département de criminologie de l'Université d'Ottawa a été créé en 1968 et s'est depuis démarqué par son interdisciplinarité et sa recherche en criminologie critique qui propose des façons alternatives de conceptualiser les activités criminalisées et autres torts sociaux et d'y répondre. Cette perspective oriente aujourd'hui le travail du département malgré la croissance généralisée de courants criminologiques administratifs et gestionnaires, ainsi que la montée de pratiques et politiques publiques explicitement punitives sur les questions de « crime » et de « sécurité ».

u Ottawa

Département de criminologie
Department of Criminology

Dans le cadre du 50ᵉ anniversaire du Département de criminologie de l'Université d'Ottawa, nous invitons les artistes qui ont vécu l'incarcération et autres formes de répression étatique de soumettre une œuvre d'art ou plus afin de rendre compte des réalités de la criminalisation et autres formes d'exclusions sociales. Vingt (20) œuvres seront donc choisies et vendues lors d'une exposition à l'Université d'Ottawa. Tous les profits iront aux artistes. Les œuvres non-choisies seront retournées aux artistes, par la poste.

DIRECTIVES DES SOUMISSIONS

Une courte biographie ainsi que le titre et une brève description de l'œuvre devraient accompagner l'œuvre soumise à l'adresse indiquée au bas. Ajouter une adresse où toute correspondance et les profits de la vente pourront être acheminés (le cas échéant).

* Oeuvre d'art: "Breaking the Chains" par Ronnie Goodman (2012)
www.ronniegoodman.com

DATES À RETENIR

1ᵉʳ mai 2018 – date limite pour soumettre une œuvre
1ᵉʳ juin 2018 – annonce de la sélection des œuvres/œuvres non-choisies retournées aux artistes
10-13 septembre 2018 – exposition et encan silencieux à l'Université d'Ottawa
13 septembre 2018 – Acheteurs des œuvres annoncés à la conférence du 50ᵉ anniversaire
1ᵉʳ octobre 2018 – profits de l'encan silencieux transmis aux artistes

POUR DE PLUS AMPLES RENSEIGNEMENTS CONTACTER :

justin.piche@uottawa.ca (anglais) and
sylvie.frigon@uottawa.ca (français)

VEUILLEZ TRANSMETTRE VOTRE SOUMISSION ARTISTIQUE À

CRM exposition d'art et encan silencieux
c/o Département de criminologie
Université d'Ottawa
120 rue Université, pièce 14002
Ottawa, Ontario, Canada
K1N 6N5

COVER ART

Peter Collins was a writer, artist, musician, cartoonist, activist, fi lmmaker, organizer and prisoners' rights advocate. Peter was a social critic who off ered thoughtful insights about the structures of violence inherent in the world around us. His tireless commitment to social justice from inside prison made him a target of harassment by Correctional Service Canada (CSC), which ultimately prevented his release. Peter passed away on 13 August 2015 of bladder cancer after having served 32 years on a Life-25 prison sentence. He was 10 years past his parole eligibility dates. A collection of his comics, art and written work, entitled *Free Inside: The Life and Art of Peter Collins*, will soon be published by Ad Astra Comix (see www.adastracomix.com).

Front Cover: "Maple Leaf"
                 Peter Collins

Back Cover: "If You Build It…"
                 Peter Collins

www.ingramcontent.com/pod-product-compliance
Lightning Source LLC
Chambersburg PA
CBHW050504270326
41927CB00009B/1901